Jan 26, 1991

Sparks

REPORT FROM BLACK AMERICA

by Peter Goldman

SIMON AND SCHUSTER · NEW YORK

FIRST PRINTING

SBN 671–20609–5
LIBRARY OF CONGRESS CATALOG CARD NUMBER: 77–130194
DESIGNED BY IRVING PERKINS
MANUFACTURED IN THE UNITED STATES OF AMERICA
PRINTED BY MURRAY PRINTING COMPANY
BOUND BY AMERICAN BOOK–STRATFORD PRESS, INC.

For my parents

Contents

Foreword

THIS IS A BOOK about a poll—the third in a unique series of black opinion surveys begun by *Newsweek* in 1963. Until then, no in-depth national poll of Negro Americans existed; a good many people, black and white, would announce at intervals What The Negro Wants, but nobody really asked him except at election times, and elections have never been fine-grained registers of public opinion. There have been other polls of black people since that first *Newsweek* report; the riots inspired some excellent ones, including single-city studies in Watts and Detroit and a fifteen-ghetto survey conducted by the University of Michigan for the President's riot commission. But the *Newsweek* polls taken together remain the only continuing profile of Negro opinion as it changed and crystallized and changed again through a tumultuous decade of revolt.

The first poll was conducted in the summer of 1963, just after the great symbolic triumph of Martin Luther King's nonviolent legions in Birmingham and just before the assembly of a quarter of a million Marchers on Washington at the foot of the Lincoln Memorial. There were storm signals even then, both in the poll and in the daily spill of events. But the times were romantic and the returns in the poll* euphoric;

* The results of the first *Newsweek* Poll were published in *Newsweek*, July 29, 1963, and in William Brink and Louis Harris, *The Negro Revolution in America*, Simon and Schuster, New York, 1964. The results of the second appeared in *Newsweek*, August 22, 1966, and in Brink and

black people, who were still called Negroes then, were singing
"We Shall Overcome" precisely because they believed that
they would.

Events had begun to challenge that faith when the second
poll was conducted three summers later. Selma, the last of the
great arena theaters of nonviolence, had produced the Voting
Rights Act of 1965. But soon thereafter Watts burned, and by
the time the poll interviewers moved out across the nation, a
turned-off child of the revolution named Stokely Carmichael
was yelling about something new and vaguely menacing called
black power. It was an inflamed and a turbulent period. Yet
the single, central fact of the poll once again was the moderation—and the hardy optimism—of the great majority of black
Americans.

Could that spirit endure? Currents of change quite obviously were running when The Gallup Organization, Inc.,
conducting its first poll for *Newsweek*, fielded its interviewers
in the last three weeks of May 1969. Martin Luther King was
dead: what were the consequences for the Negro rights movement? Newark's ghetto, and Detroit's, and scores of others had
burst into flames; had the black revolt then moved into a
period of chronic kamikaze violence? Militants in the streets
and on the campuses were spinning out new ideologies of
blackness which involved guns or separatism or both: how
deep did the vein of alienation run—and how much farther
distant now was the dream of reconciliation of the races? The
questions pressed at the nation's consciousness at a time when
the races seemed more estranged than they had ever been—
when those white Americans still disposed to speak to the
Negroes were no longer even certain what to call them.

The 1969 questionnaire was drawn in an attempt to sound
the depth of the new currents. Many questions were held over
from the 1963 and 1966 polls to test whether the attitudes of

---

Harris, *Black and White: A Study of U.S. Racial Attitudes Today*, Simon
and Schuster, New York, 1967.

the masses of black people actually were changing as radically as the headlines and the rhetoric of revolt suggested. Other questions, reflecting new developments, were framed by the editors of *Newsweek* and by The Gallup Organization. The entire questionnaire was reviewed separately by a group of black *Newsweek* staff members; some questions were rewritten and others added at their suggestion. Gallup fashioned a national cross-sectional sample of Negroes (*see* Appendix A) and, beginning on May 10, its poll takers—themselves all Negroes—interviewed 977 black men and women in cities, suburbs, small towns, and rural backwaters scattered from Boston to Oakland, from Detroit to Tacoma, from Harlem to St. Matthews, South Carolina, and Lisbon, Louisiana, and Estelline, Texas.

Once again the dominant strains were moderation as to ends and means—and optimism as to the outcome. The results reported in this book will not greatly please those militants who have sought to portray the blacks, and particularly the black poor, as an angry, embittered and sullen mass of colonials with no other intent as a people but to do violence to whites or to separate from them. Black Americans are not *that* angry in the main; their aspirations are the common ones of minorities in our society—a rightful place in the American commonwealth—and their choice of weapons runs to politics, diplomacy and nonviolent action. Yet the returns will equally displease those who believe that Negroes are not really as discontented as they have been represented as being and that they would quiet down if some few outside agitators could be locked up or shut up. For dissatisfaction remains the norm in the black community; its impatience is deepening; and large and growing minorities, as we shall see, are in fact estranged to a point where violence has more credibility than petition or prayer and where secession has more appeal than integration.

And so, when we read a poll, we must not expect it to tell us too much. A poll is an extremely valuable guide to what people want, how far they are prepared to go to get it and what they will settle for; it describes the psychic milieu in which leaders seek constituencies and vice versa, in which slogans and movements arise and flourish and die, in which events happen. But it does not always define probabilities, because events do not always conform to polls. Martin Luther King's nonviolent marches in Birmingham and Selma were the works of a minority of a community; so were the firestorms in Watts and Detroit; so, for that matter, was the Boston Tea Party, which no doubt was perceived by a majority of His Majesty's subjects in America as a riot. The point is that history, with certain occasional exceptions in democratic societies, does not proceed by referendum; it is often the creation of an activist minority, sometimes a relatively small one, and one must therefore watch the dissonances of the minority as closely as one attends the will of the majority. And one must equally bear in mind that numbers in a poll are terribly absolute and so are death to nuance. The reader will discover in these pages, for example, that only a fraction of the blacks admired Malcolm X and that considerably more thought ill of him. To read this too literally is to miss the possibility that there is a little of Malcolm in every black man; King, who believed (as Malcolm did not) in the possibilities of nonviolence and Christian love, was nevertheless once moved to confess to a friend that, yes, he too felt a little twinge of empathic hatred when he would see Malcolm excoriating white people on television.

This book accordingly moves, like its predecessor volumes, well beyond the poll itself and attempts to set the social and political context in which that abstract entity called "public opinion" actually operates. A considerable body of reporting was amassed for *Newsweek*'s June 30, 1969, cover story on the poll, and more was undertaken exclusively for this book. The discussion of the poll data is supplemented with this material and with other previously published and unpublished reporting in *Newsweek*'s files. And between the chapters are a series of reports on conversations with black people who are in varying ways influential in today's reconstituted Movement. (One hesitates to call them "Negro leaders," since not all of them have personal followings and since the term has in any event been badly abused by various commentators, black and white, over the years.) They are not a scientific sampling of the black leadership community; they are not even necessarily representative of the most important minority currents in Negro thought, let alone the will of the majority. They are included because each is in a position to affect events at given times and places and because, even if this were not so, their voices deserve our attention.

The author's thanks are due The Gallup Organization, and particularly Paul Perry and Irving Crespi, for the basic raw material in this book. The data is theirs; any errors in analyzing it are my own. Neither should the judgments herein expressed be attributed to the editors or the staff of *Newsweek*. This book is the product of group journalism, a craft at which *Newsweek* particularly excels, but the opinions in the end are my own; I can only hope that those colleagues who have contributed so much to the project will not feel badly served by the result. I am particularly indebted to *Newsweek*'s editor-in-chief, Osborn Elliott, who initiated these polls before anything like them existed or was even thought necessary and who assigned me to put this one into book form; to National Affairs editor Edward Kosner, who headed the task force that produced the 1969 cover report; to at least a score of staff correspondents, past and present, whose reporting enriches these pages, especially to Tom Mathews, Nicholas Proffitt, Richard Stout, Joseph Cumming, Jr., Henry Leifermann, Donald Johnson, Gerald Lubenow, Johnathan Rodgers, Ruth Ross, Frank Morgan, Edward Cumberbatch, James Jones, Robert Stokes and John Dotson; and most of all to chief National Affairs researcher Lucille Beachy, who pursued, found, digested, collated, organized, verified and endured the mass of information distilled into this report. Helen Dudar, a lady of surpassing sensibility, suffered the work in stages and encouraged the author to believe that it could be committed to print.

New York City
February, 1970

. . . That night I dreamed [my grandfather] told me to open my briefcase and read what was inside and I did, finding an official envelope stamped with the state seal; and inside the envelope I found another and another, endlessly, and I thought I would fall of weariness. "Them's years," he said. "Now open that one." And I did and in it I found an engraved document containing a short message in letters of gold. "Read it," my grandfather said. "Out loud!"

"To Whom It May Concern," I intoned. "Keep This Nigger-Boy Running."

—RALPH ELLISON, *Invisible Man*

. . . And yet it hangs there, this Veil, between Then and Now, between Pale and Colored and Black and White—between You and Me. Surely it is a thought-thing, tenuous, intangible; yet just as surely is it true and terrible and not in our little day may you and I lift it. . . . The Doer never sees the Deed and the Victim knows not the Victor and Each hates All in wild and bitter ignorance. Listen, O Isles, to these Voices from within the Veil. . . .

—W. E. B. DU BOIS, *Darkwater*

PROLOGUE:

Black America
in the 1960's

FOR THE BLACK NINTH of the nation, the 1960's were a time of revolution—a decade of triumph as sweet and defeat as bitter as any in the Negro's long and tragic passage in white America. There was a glow of innocence about its beginnings, in the sit-ins and the Freedom Rides and the choruses of black children and white singing "We Shall Overcome" as if they believed they really might. But a taste of ashes soured the waning days of the decade. America had been seared in the fires of Watts and Newark and Detroit; it had witnessed the arrival of a new generation of Negro militants who preached separation and armed for war; it had been examined by a Presidential commission, mostly white and moderate to a fault, and advised that we are after all a racist society. And suddenly the Second Reconstruction of relations between the races in America seemed in imminent peril of ending as the First had, with the exhaustion of the white man's will even to carry on the attempt. The two Americas were separate and alien when the decade of the 1960's began. They were farther apart still when it ended.

Black America did not will it so, as the *Newsweek* Poll reported in these pages once again amply demonstrates. One of the enduring burdens of Negroes in America is to have whites forever ask what *they* want *now*—but rarely to ask it of

17

them. The answer, for all the babel of voices claiming with
more or less justice to speak for the Negroes, can hardly be
considered mysterious any longer. All the buffets of a decade—
the false starts, the mixed counsel, the hopes raised and
cheated—have left Negro Americans a trace sadder, a bit
wiser, several shades blacker and more impatient now than
they have ever been. But their central claim on the nation has
not changed. Their intent is not to burn America down or to
secede from it, though an angry minority stands ready to do
either. What Negroes want now is what they have wanted all
along: an equal place in America's life and an equal share in
her plenty.

Yet, as The Gallup Organization's pollers and *Newsweek's*
correspondents moved into the field in the late spring of 1969,
the evidence was that the message had not yet got across. The
protests, the petitions, the demonstrations, even the chaotic
fury of the riots, were each in their way an effort to force the
white man's attention to the black man's problems. "When
things blow in the city," an Oakland youth worker named
Mark Comfort told the U.S. Civil Rights Commission at the
eve of the riotous summer of 1967, "people want to know
why, and all the time we're telling you why." But by spring
1969, things had been blowing in the cities for five successive
summers, and a sixth riot season had begun before the first
thaw. "If you apply the standards of insurgency we use in
underdeveloped countries," said one expert who served as a
consultant to President Johnson's riot commission, "we have a
state of insurgency." The trouble was that even a state of
insurgency had come to seem a normal condition of urban life,
and now, when cities blew, no one asked why any more.

Or needed to. The orthodoxy of the enlightened was that
the riots were a rude, desperate form of protest and that they
flowed with chilling logic out of the black man's 250 years in
slavery and 100 of separate inequality. "What white Americans have never fully understood—but what the Negro can

never forget—is that white society is deeply implicated in the ghetto," the riot commission wrote after its seven-month study. "White institutions created it, white institutions maintain it, and white society condones it. . . . White racism is essentially responsible for the explosive mixture which has been accumulating in our cities since the end of World War II." The commission proposed a fat and costly bundle of remedies, aimed ultimately at dispersing the ghettos and integrating blacks at last into the life of mainstream America. But there was scanty evidence that the white majority really accepted either the diagnosis or the cure. The far more common folk view among whites was that the riots were criminal or Communist or both, not spontaneous acts of protest, and that the answer accordingly was not to "reward" the rioters but to contain them.

And even those whites still disposed to listen found it more difficult than ever to sort out the bewildering cacophony of voices from the ghetto. One of the enduring myths of race is that a single man or group of men can speak authoritatively for Negroes generally, and The Movement of the early 1960's—its private differences more or less submerged in the common effort to bring down Jim Crow in the South—did much to keep the notion, and the search, alive. "They're looking for a latter-day Booker T. Washington," Warner Saunders, a Chicago poverty worker, guessed dourly, "but he just ain't there any more."

He never was. Martin Luther King, Jr., more than any single man, commanded the universal admiration of Negro Americans—even those who could not accept his faith in nonviolence, love and the conscience of the white man. But King's Dixie-bred style did not travel well in his first gingerly efforts to export the revolution northward. And his death by an assassin's bullet in Memphis in April 1968 left a kaleidoscopic jumble of leaders who materialized, burned brightly for a season and flamed out almost as quickly as they had appeared.

Malcolm X, a prophet dishonored during his lifetime, was rediscovered and beatified only in death. Stokely Carmichael preached the gospel of black power to electrifying effect for two years, then went off into tense and footloose exile in Guinea. Rap Brown, his successor for one incendiary summer, wound up silenced and under virtual house arrest in New York. CORE, mostly white and militantly integrationist when the decade began, turned all-black and separatist before it ended. SNCC disappeared underground—all but old warrior James Forman, who, with mixed success, mounted a drive to exact three billion dollars from the nation's churches as "reparations" due the Negroes for 350 tragic years. The Black Panther Party exploded out of the Oakland, California, ghetto, all guns, berets and black looks, and made a national name as the baddest militants yet—until the law put founder Huey P. Newton in prison for killing a cop, drove laureate Eldridge Cleaver into flight to Cuba and Algeria and reduced the party's second-line leadership very nearly to ruins. And the ghettos cast up a whole new wave of block and neighborhood and community leaders, tough, abrasive and wised-up in combat in the boondocks of the South and the slum streets of the North.

Not only the faces but the vocabulary of the revolution seemed to change. Whites became "honkies," Negroes "black men," riots "rebellions," integration an irrelevant abstraction, at least for now—and perhaps forever. "The black man realizes he'll never be accepted in this country," said William Clay, a new-breed St. Louis congressman whose credentials include a stretch in jail for demonstrating for Negro rights— and out of that single widely shared premise flowed a whole new politics of protest in the late 1960's. Violence, among the despairing, took on a certain legitimacy—"as American," Rap Brown proclaimed, "as cherry pie." And separatism, once the marginal fancy of the Black Muslims and a few kindred spirits, achieved a currency it hadn't enjoyed since Marcus

Garvey's back-to-Africa crusades of the 1920's. CORE's new leadership quite seriously imagined the black ghettos seceding from the U. S. and forming an Indonesia-style "island republic." Black students struck campuses from Northwestern to Vassar, demanding—among other concessions—separate-but-equal dormitories for Negroes. And even old-line integrationists took up the cry for a sort of black power—a new and meaningful voice for Negroes in decisions affecting their common destiny. "Community control," said the Urban League's Whitney Young, "is the most crucial issue now. Institutions have failed because control isn't in the hands of the people who live in the communities. We ought to have the same right to fail as anyone else."

White America seemed baffled and angered and not a little frightened by it all: the riots, the inflamed rhetoric, the loudly advertised break with the old strategy of nonviolence and the old goal of integration. And white America's response was not promising. Once, Martin Luther King had stood on the steps of the Lincoln Memorial and dreamed aloud of a day when righteousness would flow like a mighty river—and on that blazing August afternoon in 1963, so recent and yet so distant now in memory, he made it all sound possible. But before the decade was out, even the most liberal whites were afflicted by a spreading despair at the dimensions of the problem and the depth of the resistance to dealing seriously with it.

For the sad fact was that three major civil-rights bills, a declaration of war on poverty and all the bounteous good works of the Great Society had not substantially altered the conditions of life in the ghetto—or reduced its potential for explosion. Inflation and war pinched the nation's resources; the intractable complexity of race sapped its will to press on. "We face an almost universal sense of impotence," said one Washington social engineer in the discouraged late days of the Johnson Administration. In so melancholy a climate, it became respectable and even fashionable once again for whites to speculate openly whether blacks were inherently inferior in intelligence—and whether "equality" was therefore an illusory goal. "Look at the ones who have succeeded," said an MIT professor. "They're almost all light-colored."

Just such judgments within the intellectual establishment signaled the collapse of the First Reconstruction nearly a century ago—and signs that the Second might now too be ending were everywhere at hand. The nation suddenly remembered "The Forgotten American"—Richard Nixon's name for the silent white middle-class majority—and discovered the frightening depth of his discontent over all the attention that had been paid the Negroes for a decade. There were rumblings of a counterrevolution that did not quite materialize; George Wallace, the banty-rooster Alabama segregationist, marshaled no more than 14 per cent of the 1968 Presidential vote with his third-party war against anarchists, bureaucrats, pointy-heads and other integrationists, and open white-backlash candidates lost at least as many state and local elections as they won. But The Forgotten American did assert his presence and the power of his numbers in ways that could decisively influence American politics for a generation. "You better watch out," warned longshoreman-philosopher Eric Hoffer. "The common man is standing up and someday he's going to elect a policeman President of the United States." He wasn't ready for anything that drastic—not yet. But in 1968 he did elect Richard Nixon.

And Nixon's accession to the White House marked an unmistakable step back after eight years of active and particular concern for the nation's Negro minority. That special relationship had had its bumpy places during the Democratic years just past; Watts and Newark and Detroit brought Lyndon Johnson down from the euphoric high of spring 1965, when he twice cried, *We shall overcome!* in a memorable speech to Congress, to the bruised and gloomy low of 1968, when he received and shelved the report of his own riot commission without so much as a word of praise. And Nixon, for his part, did not really propose to abandon the blacks to their fate and their own fragile resources. He chose instead to tackle the American dilemma as though it were a problem of class, not color—an economic strategy concentrated on broadening job opportunities for Negroes, particularly in the high-wage building trades, and reforming the whole dismal welfare system from the ground up.

But the high cost of war and a burgeoning defense establishment meant short rations for programs already on the books, let alone the sort of vast and visionary agenda proposed by the riot commission. Nixon, moreover, came to office with substantial political debts to the South—and, as his advisers were frank to say, none at all to the blacks. The most moderate Negro leaders found their lines of communication to the White House abruptly cut. Judicial conservatives were posted to vacancies on the Supreme Court. Pressure on the South to integrate its schools relented—a slowdown that finally exhausted the Court's patience, sixteen school years after Brown vs. Board of Education, and moved it to order an end to segregation "at once." And suddenly the certain friendship of the President—a constant of the freedom struggle through the Kennedy-Johnson years—seemed to many blacks to evanesce. "He really don't care for Negroes," a young black shoe salesman in Pittsburgh told a Gallup interviewer—and in much of black America the feeling was palpably mutual.

The riot commission, in the spring of 1968, had taken a bleak and chilling glimpse into the American future: "Our nation is moving toward two societies, one black, one white— separate and unequal." The drift, as the commissioners described it, was not so much a consequence of choice as of the absence of choice—a willy-nilly slide toward a garrison America divided between tindery black cities and frightened white suburbs. The nation, said the report, could check the trend

only by adopting a master strategy combining massive aid to
the ghettos with meaningful efforts to break them up—not by
pursuing the patchwork policy improvisations of the recent
past. But there was little in the spring of 1969, or in the
months that followed, to suggest that America was ready to
undertake any such course of action. Quite to the contrary, a
joint follow-up study by The Urban Coalition and Urban
America, Inc., catalogued all that had and hadn't been done
in the year since the commission's report and concluded:
"Poverty remains a pervasive fact of life . . . Ghetto schools
continue to fail . . . There are no programs that seriously
threaten the continued existence of the slums." And: "A year
later, we are a year closer to being two societies, black and
white, increasingly separate and scarcely less unequal."

And so an edge of pessimism tinged the councils of Negro
leadership in the waning 1960's—a suspicion that white
America might once again retreat from its commitment to
Negro equality with the labor only barely begun. So low did
morale sink during the riotous summer of 1967 that several of
the nation's best-known Negro leaders, King among them,
entertained (but finally rejected) a plan to announce jointly
that they would quit their civil-rights command posts in six
months unless something was done. As whites turned away,
the new-breed Negro leaders turned inward, to celebrate their
blackness, to declare their psychic independence of The Man
and to work at what the new lexicon of the revolution came to
call "nation-building." The campus coffeehouses and the
Movement storefronts buzzed with prophecies of black terror
and white repression. ("The concentration camps," writer
C. Sumner Stone guessed wryly, "will be air-conditioned.") The
optimism of the great hallelujah days of the early 1960's ebbed
low. "I honestly don't think we're gonna get free on this go-
round," Booker T. Bonner, a campaign-wise civil-rights veteran from Houston, ventured sadly. "Oh, we're better off than

the 1860 go-round. But not enough people realize this may be our last chance."

Perhaps. But 350 years of history have instructed Negro Americans well in the arts of survival, and Negro America passed through all the trials and all the traumata with its resilience—and its determination—very much intact. "It is a beautiful and an ugly thing through which we are going," Bayard Rustin said during that anxious spring—ugly in its potential for confrontation and war and yet beautiful in what it revealed about the stubborn vitality of the black community.

There are storm signals in this third *Newsweek* Poll—in the sizable and growing minorities who so despair of America that they favor abandoning her for a separate black nation or taking up arms against her. There is evidence as well of an increasing radicalization of the young and the middle class in the urban ghettos of the North. Yet against all this—against all the portents of defeat and the prophecies of war—stands the enduring moderation of the majority. "We can't lose," Walter Bremond, a community worker in riot-charred Watts, told a reporter. "Our cause is just, our cause is moral. We just can't lose."

Black Americans, in the spring of 1969, quite agreed. They understood that the struggle of the 1960's would continue into the 1970's and that it was full of the gravest peril. But they believed, on the most mixed evidence, that they were winning.

DIRECTIONS:

Harry Edwards

Harry Edwards is big, black and bad as they come—a great furious giant who stands 6-feet-8 in his track shoes, scowls down at the world from behind inky-black glasses and lives in a permanent state of revolutionary rage. He burst on white America's consciousness as the organizer of the 1968 Olympic boycott movement—the black athletes' rebellion that wound up with two brilliant U.S. sprinters, Tommie Smith and John Carlos, ascending the victors' pedestal in Mexico City and standing through "The Star-Spangled Banner" with heads bowed and fists raised high. Edwards was on leave from the front lines, studying for a doctorate in sociology at Cornell, when Newsweek's Tom Mathews dropped by his bachelor apartment in leafy little Dryden, New York. The day was placid; the sun glowed in the dandelions outside; Miles Davis and John Coltrane cooled the room. But Harry Edwards, jackknifed into a ridiculously small chair under a photo poster of Malcolm X, was still an explosion waiting for a spark. "He is not," Mathews wrote later, "a blood to mess with."

Anger is his thing. "The black man," he said, jabbing the air with a long finger, "is in worse shape than ever. Here we are living in the twentieth century, dumping wheat into Lake Michigan, paying off farmers with millions not to farm. And people are starving in Harlem! Well, man, we're just saying enough of this bullshit. And let me tell you, the generation coming up behind me—those kids kicking ass in the junior

27

high schools right now—are going to make Rap, Stokely, Eldridge and Harry Edwards look like stone Toms. They are determined that this is where the bullshit ends."

He stroked his lower lip with the stem of his pipe. "Integration? Integration means, 'All you niggers get like white people, 'cause you sure shit now.' Well, The Movement's going into a new phase that's different from the old, where nonviolence was the sole tactic and integration was the sole goal.

"Where's Wilkins? Where's Young? Where's Randolph and Rustin? They are irrelevant, man, The Movement has left them behind. The Movement's in a new phase and those not willing to keep up are being left behind. Or they have become traitors to their race. In the old days, all the way back to Booker T. Washington, the white man told the patient nigger, 'We gone treat you right—you just be an Uncle Tom.' Then they told Randolph and Wilkins, 'We gone treat you right— you just go through the courts.' Then they told Martin Luther King, 'We gone treat you right—you just appeal to our consciences.' Well, man, we're tired of that bullshit too."

He stared out the sliding glass doors for a moment, across the grass and the dandelions to the low forested hills beyond. When he turned back, the black glasses hid what was in his eyes. "What are we supposed to do these days?" he snorted. "Go sit in in a jail? Go sit in in a squad car? Malcolm, Stokely and Rap told us, and we're beginning to understand—why the hell should we go sit in to get open housing in Long Island when most black people will never get out of Harlem? In the old Movement, we'd go out there and get our skulls crushed. Black women would be washed down the streets like rubber balls by firehoses. And when you got the open housing, who would move in but a bunch of bourgeois midde-class knee-grows" —he drew the word out scornfully—"who could afford $30,000 a year for an apartment?"

So Edwards saw little use for the old-line leaders ("Those bootlickers aren't even working at all") and none whatever for conventional politics. "I say blow that shit, man," he exploded. "The only justification I can see for black people to trade in politics is to heighten the contradictions in the country. Before Nixon moved in there, we had four pigs in the White House—a whole family of them. Now it's just the same trough and different pigs."

The only answer, in so despairing a view, is to turn away from the world outside. "Most whites say that segregation and separatism are the same thing," said Edwards. "Well, that's an out-and-out fallacy. In segregation, the dominant majority pushes the minority into a corner—exploits, brutalizes and colonizes them. Like in Harlem—the blacks have separate schools, rat- and roach-filled housing and no jobs. But in black separatism we're talking about people moving out on their own to gain their destiny. The idea runs very deep now. It runs as deep as the old idea of integration.

"From World War II to now, the goal of integration was the panacea. The Negro wanted to get up, get a job and move out where the white folks lived. What we have now is a matter of controlling and building up the black community so that the community is inhabitable." He paused. "Take a small example. George Washington was a first-class racist, slave owner and rapist. But if you go into a school in Harlem today, there's his picture up on the wall." He left no question whatever that if it were his wall, Washington would come down. "The goal," he said, "is for black people to have as much control over the schools in their community as whites have in theirs."

Edwards wonders why whites find the idea so upsetting. "Look," he said, uncoiling out of the chair, hauling a fat sociology text down from a shelf and riffling through the index to "Negro." The subheads ran from "illiteracy" to "race riots." Edward's lip curled. "Where's the heading for 'mobility'?" he asked. " 'Community structure'? 'Culture'? 'Values'? Oh, man, let me tell you, this is a racist country. I almost have a Ph.D. and I know more about white culture than black. We've always

been separated physically from whites, and now, in their Ne-
anderthal way, whites may see this is what they have wanted
all along. The only reason I can see for the whites to be
against separatism is that some cracker is going to be hurt in
his pocketbook. He knows the days of white dominance are
over. And when you talk about the end of white dominance,
man, you find a lot more white knees shaking than George
Wallace's."

But Harry Edwards, big, black and bad, is an optimist of a
sort; perhaps all revolutionaries are. "I see a strong future
for black people," he said, a grin spreading across his dark
features. "Since I believe in the higher law that people—especially white folks—will do anything to survive, I'm optimistic
about the future. Because if there isn't a future for black
people in this country, there isn't going to be a future for
anybody."

CHAPTER 1

The Unfinished Agenda

ONCE UPON A TIME, in some hardscrabble Southern town whose name everyone has long since forgotten, Martin Luther King and his little band of disciples materialized with their Bibles, their go-to-jail denims and their nonviolent war on the way things had been for a hundred years. The siege followed the changeless pattern—nightly prayer meetings, daily mass marches, hourly shifts in the bill of demands—until finally a white townsman who ought to have known better asked King's deputy, Ralph David Abernathy, "What do you *want?*" Abernathy gazed at him for a moment with heavy-lidded melancholy, then rumbled, "What have you *got?*"

The parable sums up a decade of revolution: the great majority of black Americans wanted then, and still want now, a fair share of what white Americans have already got. The pilgrimage down Freedom Road has taken many detours, and a large and growing fraction of the Negro community— perhaps 10 or 15 or even 20 per cent by varying measures—is so bitterly alienated today that no foreseeable gesture by the larger society is likely to win back all of the disaffected. Yet Cleveland's talented black mayor, Carl Stokes, once ventured, "I don't know any Negro who doesn't really want the American dream. . . . You get some of the most militant Negroes in the United States, give them the things middle-class America enjoys, and they'll barely listen to anybody yelling '*uhuru!*'" And there is considerable evidence that he was right.

At the end of a decade's struggle, moreover, most Negroes—far from despairing—believed they were in fact moving toward that place in the American sun. The sense of personal progress recorded by the *Newsweek* Poll, particularly on economic issues, was striking—and the expectation of more to come pervasive. Two Negroes out of three reported drawing higher pay than they had five years ago. Three out of five felt better off in their work, in their chances for getting their children decently educated and in having the right to live in any neighborhood they could afford. The returns were ambivalent only about housing; slightly more than half the Negroes said they were living in better homes or apartments than five years ago, but nearly as many said they were not. And even then, a buoyant two-thirds expected to be doing better still five years hence on all these fronts, housing included—a level of expectancy even higher than in *Newsweek*'s 1966 poll and every bit as high as it was at the romantic peak of the civil-rights movement in 1963.

The optimism was neither euphoric nor universal. All of the economic indicators of the 1960's pointed to a sharp and widening cleavage in black America between those Negroes who are making it and those who are not, and the poll results made the psychic impact of the gap poignantly clear. Robust majorities of Negroes above the $3,000-a-year poverty line said they had made progress in the years just past on the bread-and-butter problems of jobs, pay and housing. But fully half of those below the poverty level felt their lives and fortunes actually had stood still or got worse—at precisely a time when the rest of America was battening on the longest, richest economic boom in the nation's history.

Nor was the view quite so sanguine from the souring Harlems and Houghs of the North as it was from the Catfish Rows and the Buttermilk Bottoms of the South. The 1960's had seen the climactic assault on the whole legal structure of segregation in Dixie, and if a good many of the victories were more token than real, there were enough of them to charge Southern blacks with an enormous sense of progress struggled for and won. Had things got better for Negroes generally in the past five years? A rousing 80 per cent in the South voted yes. So did 60 per cent in the North. But the glow there was shadowed by the fact that 31 per cent—nearly a third of the teeming and volatile ghetto population—believed that the lot of Negroes had stagnated or got worse. "I mean, outside of this district, time marches on," a Gary, Indiana, ghetto housewife once put it at a U.S. Civil Rights Commission hearing. "They build better and they have better. But you come down here and you see the same thing year after year after year. People struggling, people wanting, people needing, and nobody to give anyone help. . . . It's one big nothing. I mean you can live here for millions and millions of years and you will see the same place, same time and same situation. It's just like time stops here."

Yet the soaring expectations of black America for the future are shared by the ghetto North as well as the South, the very poorest blacks as well as the working and the middle class—and there is both hope and peril in their optimism. "Man, black people are beautiful," a Watts community worker told *Newsweek*'s Nicholas Proffitt. "We just fell into a funky bag four hundred years ago, that's all. But we're going to pull out of it. There's no way we can come out of this a loser." He spoke for more blacks than a troubled America might have imagined in that tense season. But all around him Watts still bore the scars of the last time that spiraling hopes and hard realities came into explosive collision.

Were the black man's great expectations misplaced?

The struggles of a decade, and of the entire century since Emancipation, had borne rich fruit. A Congress long dominated by the grandees of the Old South produced three major civil-rights acts in five years—an effort which, if it did not precisely legislate an end to the color problem, at least committed the nation to the attempt. Lyndon Johnson, in an even shorter space of time, persuaded Capitol Hill to enact a portfolio of social and economic legislation unexampled since the New Deal, and most of it disproportionately benefited the blacks because the blacks are disproportionately among the poor. The flush times of the 1960's, even more than the initiatives of government and the business community, lifted tens of thousands of Negro families out of poverty and into fragile participation in the richest economy the world has ever known. And the very fact of the struggle—its defeats as well as its victories—had worked powerful and liberating changes on black America's psyche.

Yet it was not easy to read the balance sheet as it stood at the beginning of the 1970's and to see in it the happy endings that so many Negro Americans believed were coming so soon.

The South was indeed in the process of profound change. The courts, the Congress and a generation of mostly anonymous black protestants had brought down the legal underpinnings, if not the reality, of Jim Crow in the schools, buses, trains, hotels, restaurants, parks and public facilities. The Voting Rights Act of 1965, won by Negro and white demonstrators at great cost in Mississippi and Alabama, doubled Dixie's black registration in five years (from 1.5 to 3.2 million) and installed more than 500 Negroes in elective office—a measure of black power unmatched since the collapse of Reconstruction. And all the clamorous days and insomniac nights of the civil-rights movement had left an infrastructure of Negro protest organization across the Old Confederacy. "At times," *Newsweek*'s Atlanta bureau chief, Joseph B. Cumming, himself a native Southerner, reported after a journey through Dixie in mid-1969, "I was taken with a dreamlike sense that nothing had happened—that all those encounters with The Movement, with blacks becoming men lit with dignity, had all been a fantasy. . . . But despite all the sly

alignments that have worked to keep the Negro poor, dependent, uneducated and politically powerless, a deep and subtle
change of climate has taken place that will not be undone.
The Second Reconstruction will work if the Federal government does not lose its nerve. Wherever Negro voter registration is large, demagogy is muted; wherever local blacks have
something going that they can call a movement, the power
structure tends to call them 'Mr.' or 'Mrs.'; and wherever
schools are significantly integrated, future generations will be
less susceptible to the fearful myths. . . ."

Yet the fearful myths and the sly alignments of color and
caste still ruled much of the life of the South. Even free access
to public accommodations—a right written into Federal law
after the sit-ins, the Freedom Rides and the harrowing Battle
of Birmingham—proved to be more theoretical than real in
the small-town and rural South. Restaurants, swimming pools,
even drive-in barbecue stands turned into "private clubs"
with memberships approximately equal to a town's white population. Some filling stations took down the WHITE MEN,
WHITE WOMEN and COLORED signs from the toilet doors—but
since a customer still had to ask the manager for the key, the
effect was precisely the same. Courthouse-square restaurants
still refused to serve Negroes—except carry-out orders poked
through a back window. ("Seems like to me it's for dogs to get
fed out the back," a Black Belt Negro told Cumming. "So I
don't go there.") In Greenville, Alabama, a new black
preacher lately arrived in town let on that he was going to sit
downstairs one Sunday night at the Ritz Theater—a breach in
the ancient protocol that consigns Negroes to the balcony.
Town authorities got wind of his plan and, rather than try to
stop him, put out word to the boys in the chili cafes: Stay
away, it's only a test, it won't come to anything. The preacher
sat downstairs at the Ritz that Sunday night; on Monday, the
blacks were all in the balcony again. "Course," said one town
official amiably, "they *can* sit downstairs but seems like they

just *rather* go in that side door and on upstairs." Such tales abound outside the big cities. "Everything has happened," sighed one old civil-rights hand. "Nothing has changed."

And the sudden let-up in pressure to desegregate Dixie's public schools once Richard Nixon took office suggested that the Federal government's nerve could not in fact be taken for granted any longer. An integrated education had theoretically become the inalienable right of every Southern black child fifteen years earlier, when the Supreme Court, in Brown vs. Board of Education, held that separate schools for Negroes could never be truly equal. But the Court, as it was later to discover to its own chagrin, made two bad tactical mistakes: It delayed enforcement of its decision for a year, thus giving the resistance a chance to organize, and then laid down only the vague mandate that the schools desegregate "with all deliberate speed." The first ten school years produced precious little speed; a great deal of deliberation, much of it concentrated on how to avoid integration; a series of nasty white insurrections from Little Rock 1957 to Ole Miss 1962—and, in the Black Belt South, practically no integration at all. By the fall of 1964, after ten years of concerted pressure by Washington and the civil-rights movement, roughly one Negro child in forty across the Old Confederacy—and not even one in a hundred in the deepest South—was going to school with whites.

But Congress, in the Civil Rights Act of 1964, voted the government a powerful new club: the authority to cut off Federal funds to any district that wouldn't desegregate. The South, which had over the years developed a certain genius for beating systems, quickly discovered a way to minimize the impact of this one: by adopting "freedom-of-choice" desegregation plans, which on paper gave Negro parents the right to send their children to white schools if they wanted to but in practice laid them open to threats and reprisals if they did. ("White folks told some colored to tell us that if the child went, he wouldn't come back alive or wouldn't come back like he went," a backwater Mississippi Negro couple told Federal investigators. They sent the child to the white school anyway, and their home was shot into by night riders.) Even at that, integration bounded ahead until, in the 1968–69 school year, 20.3 per cent of the South's black students were attending integrated schools—an eightfold increase in four years. And when the Supreme Court at last ruled out "freedom-of-choice" plans unless they produced real results, the stage seemed set for the last critical push beyond tokenism to true desegregation—fourteen years after Brown vs. Board. Washington, in the last year of the Johnson Administration, laid down a 1969–70 deadline for an end to dual school systems throughout the South. Whether the directive could have been enforced to the letter was quite another matter, but, as Johnson's Attorney General, Ramsey Clark, noted later, appearances counted. "We always felt," said Clark, "that we could never indicate even the slightest lack of determination."

Enter Nixon & Co., however, and the show of determination melted away into a display of confusion, irresolution and retreat—a performance that fairly begged critics to believe that the Administration was trying to appease old friends and win new ones in the white South. Washington's new management first indicated in a wondrously cloudy policy directive that the autumn 1969 deadline might not really apply to everybody—and then actually went to Federal court to plead for a reprieve for thirty-three Mississippi school districts just as they were about to desegregate. To the vast amusement of the attorneys for the segregated school districts, this move brought on an unprecedented falling-out between the government and NAACP Legal Defense Fund lawyers, one of whom finally snapped in exasperation, "The U.S. government for the first time has demonstrated that it no longer seeks to represent the rights of Negro children." But the President himself answered the rising wave of criticism with the extraordinary judgment

that those who demanded "instant integration" sixteen au-
tumns after Brown were being just as unreasonable as those
who said "segregation forever"—and that his duty as President
was to ply a middle course between those two "extreme
groups."

The "extremists," as soon became evident, included Nixon's
own Chief Justice Warren E. Burger and a unanimous Supreme Court, which icily declared in the Mississippi case that
the time for "all deliberate speed" was at an end and that it
was now mandatory on "every school district . . . to termi-
nate dual school systems at once." A lower court shortly
reassembled the Mississippi school authorities and served notice on them that, as a Georgia-born Federal judge put it, they
could "complain and feel bad but there's nothing you can do
about it." What judges could not compel, however, was the
resolve of the Federal government to enforce their rulings
vigorously. Nor could they stem the rush to the "segregation
academies," an overnight growth of private schools which by
the fall of 1969 had already siphoned off 300,000 of the South's
7.4 million white students, and was still booming. The number of Southern Negro children attending classes with whites
jumped from one in five to one in three that autumn, mostly
on the momentum of the Johnson years. But an end to Jim
Crow schooling in Dixie was nowhere yet in sight.

There were signs nevertheless that a decade's revolt against
the old order had set new and hopeful psychic currents
running in the black South—a resurgence of spirit too hardy
to be dimmed by the day-to-day vicissitudes of the struggle or
even by the bleak economic reality of the Negro's situation in
Dixie. The hard truth was that new crops and the new farm
technology were fast making the old Negro field hand obsoles-
cent—and his audacity in demanding his rights, particularly
the right to vote, seemed only to hasten the process. "Them
white folks got a lot more interested in machinery after the
civil-rights bill was passed," one dispossessed Black Belt Negro

observed. And a Greene County, Alabama, planter, in the midst of switching from cotton to soybeans and from black to white field labor, quite agreed. "The niggers," he said, "is got to go. We used to think if we lost our niggers the world would come to an end. Now, we don't want 'em all to leave—we just want to thin 'em out so's we can live with 'em."

Yet, in the era of the ghetto riot, the old myth of a promised land Up North appeared at last to be yielding to a sense of brightening possibilities in the South. The great northward diaspora slowed in the late 1960's to 80,000 a year—little more than half what it had been in the 1940's and 1950's. There were the first fragile signs of a countertrend—a trickle of returning exiles, particularly among the activist young, who had chosen to make their fight back home. "We been hearin' from our folks to come on back," said one of them, lounging outside the courthouse in Yazoo City, Mississippi, while a Movement pal was standing trial inside. "Things are happening." And some never went away. "All the hell I raised, I never said I wanted to leave," said Fannie Lou Hamer, the queen mother of the Mississippi movement, sitting huge and impassive on her front porch in Ruleville. "I saw my mother he'p clean up this land with an ax that a man does now with a bulldozer. I'm part of this land. Mississippi is home. I love it."

Myths, of course, die hard. Anything looks better to Negroes who live in unpainted tenant shacks papered over inside to keep the wind out, who sleep three, four or five to a pallet made of fertilizer sacks stuffed with raw cotton, who sustain themselves and their children on a diet of grits and beans and rice. Many of them still imagine that the rainbow ends in Memphis or Chicago or Newark; it is not the welfare statistics who write home. "The boys hear all this talk about Up North," said a farm youth in Alabama's Lowndes County. "All the money is Up North. There just ain't no money here."

And so the trek goes on to what the great Negro sociologist

E. Franklin Frazier predicted long ago would prove to be "the city of destruction"—a ghetto deeply mired in the culture of poverty and the pervasive climate of failure. A decade of unbroken boom times, coupled with the proliferating public and private aid programs sparked up by the ghetto rioting, was in fact helping to create a large and growing Negro middle class. Perhaps three million blacks crossed the line out of poverty in ten years, and by the end of the decade more than a fourth of all Negro families were earning $8,000 or more a year. Yet a third were left behind in poverty, and the gulf between them and the emergent middle class was widening dangerously.

Even by conventional measures, unemployment among Negroes was frozen at recession levels—and a 1966 Department of Labor study of ten big-city ghettos concluded that the conventional measures were "irrelevant" against the real dimensions of the problem. The survey totted up not just unemployed blacks who were looking for work but those who had given up trying, or who were working for less than bare living wages, or who were working part-time when they needed full-time jobs. The bleak conclusion: "The situation . . . is that more than a third are unable to earn a living, and between 10 to 20 per cent of those who ought to be working aren't working at all. No conceivable increase in the gross national product would stir these backwaters. . . . Unemployment in these areas is primarily a story of inferior education, no skills, police and garnishment records, discrimination, fatherless children, dope addiction, hopelessness."

The government did make some inroads with its manpower-training and anti-poverty programs, and the fledgling National Alliance of Businessmen—prodded together by Lyndon Johnson and Henry Ford II in the frightening aftermath of the 1967 Detroit riot—hired a reported 269,000 of the hard-core jobless, black, brown and white, in less than two years. But the Federal programs labored under a chronic shortage of funds. And critics of the NAB operation complained that its definition of "hard-core" was too broad, that many of the openings were for dead-end jobs as porters, maids and the like, and that half of NAB's recruits soon disappeared—well above the normal turnover rate for industry. Some of the complaints were no doubt unkind as against the heartening fact that corporate America had at last involved itself in the problem, sometimes with great energy and ingenuity. Even so, the sum of the entire public-private effort fell far short of the target proposed by the riot commission—two million new jobs in three years—to clear the tinder from the ghetto streets.

Education has been the classic exit for America's under-classes. But the ghetto's schools remain a tragic failure, so demoralized that it often matters little whether a student quits (as more than 40 per cent do) or sticks through to graduation. The notion that they could be "enriched" by heavy investments of money and talent came under serious challenge in the late 1960's before a growing body of evidence that enrichment doesn't really work—that only integrated schooling makes a significant difference to the children of the city of destruction. But a 1967 Civil Rights Commission study revealed that three-fourths of the nation's black elementary school pupils, North and South, were in all-Negro or mostly Negro schools—and that de facto segregation, far from diminishing, was spreading as whites deserted to private or suburban schools. Big-city public education in America thus increasingly meant black education (the public-school systems of seven of the nation's ten biggest cities now have Negro majorities) and, with a few exceptions in small and middle-sized cities, serious efforts to integrate collapsed under furious white opposition.

Black militants in turn took up the new orthodoxy that Negroes didn't really want integration anyway and that the real answer was to give the ghetto control of its own schools. But one of the few real experiments in community control, in

Brooklyn's Ocean Hill–Brownsville slum, provoked a bitter
teachers' strike, opened a Pandora's box of racial animosities
and was threatened with extinction before the returns were in.
And so the schools hobbled on as they always had, bucking
Negro youngsters along from year to year—regardless of performance—until they dropped out or graduated. "Our average
applicant," the director of an employment center in Boston's
Roxbury ghetto reported, "has an eleventh-grade education
and a third-grade reading level." The riot commission, in
1968, recommended massive spending on the ghetto schools
coupled with a carrot-and-stick campaign to get the North to
desegregate. Neither course materialized, and, a year later,
some perfectly responsible experts on education were dolefully
wondering aloud whether it might not be a good idea to give
up on the public schools and contract some or all of their
functions to competing private systems.

The schools, of course, were nothing more or less than the
ghettos in microcosm—so many mostly black or all-black preserves which, as the Negro psychologist Kenneth Clark once
observed, make it brutally plain to the black man how little
his society values him. His housing is old, crumbling and so
desperately overcrowded that—at the density rate of parts of
Harlem—the entire U.S. population could be squeezed into
three of New York City's five boroughs. Two-thirds of urban
black America lives in neighborhoods where at least part of
the housing is deteriorating or dilapidated beyond repair.
Garbage festers uncollected on the sidewalks; building codes
go unenforced; rats breed and fatten and run free. ("The
kids," said a housewife in Cleveland's Hough ghetto, "they
play with rats like a child would play with a dog or something.") Disease rates run high; one Harlem block is so TB-
ridden that residents call it "Lung Street."

And the ghettos are growing. The black population explosion in the central cities began leveling off in the late 1960's,
but the white flight to suburbia trebled suddenly to 500,000 a

year. Congress, to its own great surprise, was moved by the assassination of Martin Luther King to pass an open-housing bill which would in time apply—at least on paper—to 80 per cent of the nation's housing sales and rentals, and the Supreme Court shortly thereafter resurrected a forgotten Reconstruction-era law with even broader sweep. But the record of state and local open-housing laws, ordinances and understandings was not promising. Martin Luther King won a fair-housing agreement from Chicago's white establishment with a long, provocative mass-marching campaign in 1966; three years later, the city was still turning black at the rate of three blocks a week. Chicago will have a Negro majority by 1985, according to current estimates. So will Cleveland and St. Louis and Detroit and Baltimore and Oakland and Jacksonville, Florida. Washington and Newark already do. The ghettos today, says Ralph Bunche, "are like the native reserves in South Africa. They symbolize the Negro as unacceptable, inferior and therefore kept apart." Tomorrow, in many key metropolitan areas, the ghetto will *be* the city, and the inheritance the blacks will be coming into is not a happy one.

Too often, in so barren and so powerless a world, everything crumbles. A bottle of muscatel becomes an anesthetic, narcotics a refuge, transient sexuality and casual violence the twin proofs of manhood for Negroes who cannot furnish the customary evidence: the ability to provide for a wife and children. Families break up. Illegitimacy becomes a norm. A fourth of all black babies—and half in some big-city ghettos—are born out of wedlock. Welfare dependency grows. Northern ghetto blacks, in the *Newsweek* Poll, considered the dole more harm than help to Negroes—but six Negro children in ten subsist on it for at least part of their lives. Failure becomes a self-fulfilling prophecy. Men wander aimlessly from one dead-end low-wage job to another, quitting on the flimsiest real or imagined provocation since they expect to be fired anyway. Crime proliferates, most of it directed at other Negroes. Arrest records are cheaply accumulated and dearly lived down. Families who do struggle out of poverty into the working class live constantly haunted by the fear that the streets will swallow up their children. "Well," a mother in Cleveland's Hough ghetto told Civil Rights Commission investigators, "Sam see a pimp with a $125 suit and a big car and he feel that he won't have to go to school because he can get the same thing. . . . And he may want to leave school for this easy life."

For the life of the street corner always beckons, and the street corner is only a way station on the journey to the end of the line. Gary Robinson, a bright thirtyish poverty warrior in Boston, kept tabs on nineteen boyhood pals from his old block in Harlem and, after fifteen years, totted up the score. One had beaten his child to death and was executed. Others had died of narcotic poisoning, or gone to prison on charges ranging from mugging to murder, or simply vanished. Only four besides Robinson were still in society: two cops, a doorman and a hustler. And Robinson himself nearly didn't make it; he did 28 days in the Tombs on a pot charge when he was 23, and the experience left him with a certain patient fatalism about failure. One of his wards—a man for whom Robinson had lined up a job in a hothouse—shuffled across his path one morning, generously nursing a toothache on muscatel wine and offering amiably, "Sure, I'll be workin' tomorrow. . . . A man's got a right to do a little hurtin', ain't he?" Robinson has not forgotten the Tombs, and so he swallowed his disappointment and agreed, "A black man's got a right to hurt."

Today, for all the certainty of the majority that the tide is running their way, black men in white America still hurt— and their sense of grievance over the ancient disabilities of color is if anything higher than ever. In a fifteen-city survey conducted for the riot commission in early 1968, three-fourths of the ghetto blacks were convinced that at least some Negroes miss out on jobs and decent housing because of discrimination—a gloomy consensus that no amount of fair-hiring and fair-housing legislation has been able to dispel. And the *Newsweek* Poll showed growing majorities of Negroes believed that blacks are paid less than whites for equal work; that they are charged steeper rents than whites for comparable housing; that their youngsters have less chance than whites to go to college, and that even those who go and graduate won't get jobs as good as white college men will.

By the spring of 1969, moreover, Negroes had come to regard Vietnam as their own particular incubus—a war that depletes their young manhood and saps the resources available for dealing with the ills of the ghetto. Negroes, for all their travail in America, have always been invincibly patriotic ("The only thing that kept black people out of the John Birch Society is their color," said Los Angeles radio newsman Booker Griffin); and in 1966, when the war was young, they supported it. But three years later, the tide had dramatically turned. The view that blacks ought to oppose the war because they have less freedom in this country—a 35 per cent minority opinion in 1966—had become the verdict of a 56-to-31 per cent majority.

The reasons for the turnabout were plain. Negroes actually made up about 10 per cent of the military personnel in Southeast Asia and 13 per cent of the war dead—roughly equivalent to their proportion of the population. Yet black Americans were persuaded by a two-to-one majority that their young were doing a disproportionate share of the fighting—and by seven-to-one that Vietnam was a very real drain on the home-front war against poverty. There were emotional tugs in the opposite direction; a solid and rising majority in this age of unabashed black pride, for example, saw the war as evidence that Negroes make better combat soldiers than whites. But the anti-war tide was nonetheless powerful. It helped, in the space of three years, to reverse the old prevailing black view that the military gives black youth a better break than they can get in civilian life; Southern Negroes still cling to that notion but Northerners now reject it by nearly two to one. And Vietnam further soured the Negro's already curdled view of Richard Nixon's new Administration. "He said he would end the war and then he goes to Florida all the time to rest," said a 21-year-old shipping clerk in Thomasville, North Carolina. "And I got a draft notice yesterday . . ."

Yet not even the shadow of Vietnam materially altered the Negro's continuing bill of demands on America. What are the most urgent problems confronting black people today? The answers, in the *Newsweek* Poll, ran the whole sad range of grievance from the anomie of the ghetto streets ("The crime rate amongst our people—it's awful") to the deep, brooding suspicion of the cops ("White police should keep their hands off Negroes") to the fading of the old-time religion ("I think one thing, they need to pray, get acquainted with God, and all these other things will be made right"). There were traces of an accommodationism as old as Uncle Tom: "Our colored race," a 63-year-old Pittsburgh housewife thought, "are doing better than they ever done in their lives. God ain't promised us nothin' but a livin' and a killin'. Just wait on God—just trust Him." And there was a vein of anger as new as Malcolm and Stokely and Rap. The Negro's No. 1 problem? "White people," snapped a 24-year-old Harlem man.

But the unfinished agenda that emerged from it all was only too painfully familiar:

· *Jobs and pay*—mentioned by 60 per cent of the poll sample—remain far and away the first order of business for black Americans today. "On my job," a 40-year-old Atlanta workman said, "they hire whites off the street and give them a better job than Negroes who have been there five or ten years." Such complaints remain the common currency of the ghetto, and, if all the public and private programs have had a meaningful impact, it is not yet apparent to great numbers of Negroes. "You can't see what they're *doing* with all that money," a young woman clerk in Kansas City said. "And it's supposed to be helping us."

• *Schools* were cited by 38 per cent, No. 2 on the list. A 55-to-30 majority of Northern blacks, curiously enough, is satisfied that its children are getting as good an education as whites—a rather rosy view that bears little obvious relationship to the objective record. (Southerners, whose youngsters were still overwhelmingly consigned to Jim Crow schools, are considerably less sure. "The high school," said a 35-year-old Lisbon, Louisiana, housewife, "don't teach no trade. So our children can't get a job 'cause they don't know how to do nothin'.") The improvements most frequently volunteered by ordinary black people, moreover, have interestingly little to do with either integration *or* community control; they center instead on the nitty-gritty matters of cash, facilities and teaching talent.

• *Housing*—mentioned by 33 per cent of the interviewees—ran a close third. Some specifically wanted measures against overt discrimination by whites in housing rentals and sales. "White people," a Pittsburgh housewife said, "must open up homes all over the city to us. We like nice houses in good neighborhoods, too." But far more protested the subtler discriminations that assign the oldest, ricketiest housing to Negroes, whether because they are black or because they are poor or both. "People that rent need a better place to live," a middle-aged Thomasville, North Carolina, woman said dolefully. "We don't have no closets, no cabinets, no bath, no shower, no hot water . . ." The dreary catalogue plainly might have gone on forever; it simply trailed off there.

So Negro America's demands had not changed in a decade—perhaps not even in a century. What was changing was the black man's quickening impatience for results. And by 1969, that impatience had reached its highest pitch yet—higher even than when his revolution first spilled into the streets in the early 1960's.

In each of *Newsweek*'s three polls, blacks were asked whether they considered the pace of progress in the struggle for Negro rights too fast, too slow or about right. The results chart the ebb and flow of a militant impulse that surged high in the days of Birmingham and the March on Washington, sagged a bit during the anxious riot summers of the middle '60's—and rose to a new crest in 1969 even as a mood of reaction was plainly spreading among whites. The fever chart:

BLACK IMPATIENCE

	1963	1966	1969
THE PACE IS:			
About right	31	35	22
Too fast	3	4	7
Too slow	51	43	59

The impatient majority has been a majority all along in the ghetto North. The real upsurge came in the South, where the focus of the struggle was only just moving beyond the old WHITE ONLY signs to the incredible complexities of poverty and race—and where the number of blacks chafing for faster results had swollen in the process from a 31 per cent minority in 1966 to a 56 per cent majority in 1969. And the youngest Negroes in both regions—the under-30 generation who do most of the picketing, sitting in, mass-marching and, if it comes to that, rioting—are by far the most impatient of all. A simmering 65 per cent of them are dissatisfied with the tempo of the struggle today.

"There's only one problem and it's simple enough," says one of those restive young men, a 29-year-old electrical worker in Rockford, Illinois. "Just make sure the Negro has all that any other American has." The question, of course, was whether the nation could very soon deliver on that dream even if the will was there—and the will had fallen very much into question since those days in mid-decade when Lyndon

Johnson still talked about helping the Negro move beyond equal *rights* to equal *results*. Just such uncashed IOU's as that have helped to excite black expectations to heady new highs—and to stir black discontent when the delivery turned out to be no more than a trickle. The mix is full of danger—and of hope. "All we want," Detroit's young new-breed Negro Congressman John Conyers once said, "is for America to be what it says it is"—and the fact that black men were still willing to fight on for that dream was perhaps the most telling measure yet of the hardihood of their confidence, their courage and their faith.

DIRECTIONS:
Charles Evers

Years ago, when Medgar and Charles Evers were kids in Mississippi, Theodore Bilbo came campaigning in their home town, spied them sitting in the crowd on the courthouse steps and hollered, "Y'all see them two niggers down there? If you don't keep them in their place, someday they'll be up here where I am." The Everses never forgot that. An assassin cut Medgar down from ambush in 1963 before a black man could yet dare imagine standing where Bilbo had stood. So Charles Evers, a large sad-eyed man who had been making it in Chicago, came home to Mississippi. He picked out tiny Fayette precisely because it was home to some of the meanest, Ku Kluxingest whites in the state; he opened a shopping center and a freedom movement; he nagged, prodded, agitated, mass-marched and registered the town's 70 per cent black majority until they elected him mayor. When Newsweek's Henry Leifermann visited Evers's little city hall office in the autumn of 1969, he had been running Fayette for nearly three months and was eager to talk about it—about all of it except the Kluxer who had just been caught stalking him with a carload of guns. There are blacks in Fayette who would have whipped or even killed the man at a nod from Evers, but Evers saw to it that he was given a hearing and freed on bond instead. "Thing about it is," shrugged the mayor, "he didn't kill me."

What Evers wanted to talk about was Fayette and the stake that its blacks and whites alike had in throwing off the burden of their past. "You know," he said, his voice soft and slurred, "this community, this whole area, is dead and no one cares. Because the whites who were in office before just didn't care. They weren't concerned about the poor whites or the poor blacks, and ninety per cent of the people here are poor. They were only concerned with that ten per cent that had a little something. And most whites know this. No one has cared. Now that's my main object and my main concern, is to get poor blacks and poor whites to learn to respect each other and work together for a common cause. And that's to get off the ground, you know, and get up. Because they're both down there wallowing in dirt together, and they're the masses. They know that. We are the masses, and if we can get together and join hands and start voting together, and spend our money together, and working together, we can overthrow the kind of denial we have lived."

That dream has been dreamed before, and Evers had no illusions that it will be easy to bridge the far distance between the races. "You know how you white folks are—you're all hard-headed and can't tell y'all nothin'," Evers told Leifermann; he smiled when he said it but Mississippi blacks know it is true. That will not stop him from trying. "What people don't understand," he said, "is the white people, particularly the poor whites, are the most forgotten people in the world. They're the only somebody that doesn't have a voice. You stop and think—who speaks for the poor white fella? Nobody. Nobody. Course, we blacks got fellas like Charles Evers screamin' every day, and we got Stokely screamin' every day, and we have others screamin' every day. Mexicans got any number of 'em screamin' every day; the Indians, now they're beginnin' to scream. But no one's screamin' for the poor white man, and that's why we got to somehow bring 'em along, because most of our problems is between the black and the poor white. If we can get a relationship going with them, our problem's going to be on its way to being solved.

"You know," he went on, "let's face it, the guy that's out in the pasture, twelve o'clock at night, with a sheet over his head, with a shotgun, a bomb, is not no enemy—is not no man that's worth ten or fifteen or twenty thousand dollars or a hundred thousand dollars. He's just some guy who doesn't have ten cents and he's mad and all he knows to do is to destroy. So he's been told by the white power structure and the white middle class, upper class, that you're better than a nigger, and all you got to do is keep that nigger down and you will at least be over somebody. And he believes that. But if we can ever get him—if we can get enough of them—with the kind of income that's gonna put them also in the upper- or middle-income bracket, they won't have time to talk about hatin' niggers or goin' around out there with a sheet over his head, twelve o'clock at night. He's too busy tryin' to make more money, and get better jobs and better business and better education and better automobiles and better homes, and that's where his mind will be."

The years pursuing that end for black people have developed in Evers a keen sense of the realities of power, and the tactics of his revolution have altered accordingly. "There used to be a time you'd be cussing and raising hell and picketing and boycotting and going on, but that was necessary then. That was to get the door open, you know. We were fighting about we couldn't register. We were fighting about we couldn't go in the restaurant. We were fighting about we couldn't go in the motel, fighting about we couldn't go to school. But that's over. We can go now. Now our job is to get inside and become a part of that operation. For instance, we got to start owning restaurants, got to own them grocery stores. We got to start now competing rather than trying to get into. And we got to become the lawmakers in the community, at least a part of it. And you can't get it keep marching and picketing. They'll let you march till your soles get thin as a dime now. Nobody'll even look at you. You got to march to the polls; you got to march to the

registration books; you got to teach people about economics—
how to become economically independent." It did not even
dismay him that the town school had not yet moved beyond
token integration. "We're not goin' to worry about that," he
said softly. "We're not gonna picket 'em. We're not gonna
boycott 'em. We not gonna do nothing—just wait till next
year. 'Cause the school board is elected too."

Fayette is not just a constituency for Evers; he sees it as part
of an unending series of tests for the Negro, and, that warm
October afternoon, he seemed to feel the heavy weight on him
to make it work. "The local white man—they just don't know
us," he said. "And my job is to get them to know us, and I can't
get them to know us by being as lambastious and dodging them
the way they dodged us. That's why I go out of the way to see
them. I meet them on the street. I talk to them. See, what you
got to understand is that white people have been taught all
their lives that we're different—in the first place, that black
people are all dirty; next thing, they all steal; next thing, they're
all ignorant—and most white people, the majority that don't
know blacks, believe this. And they just don't believe that a
black man can run a government. They don't believe it, that a
black can be mayor. They didn't even believe a black man
could run a football or catch a baseball till we proved it. And
it's one of those things. It's bad—I hate to use the word 'prove'
—but we got to prove it." Yes, he could have had the man
who came hunting him killed. "But we got to prove to the
white folks that we're bigger than they are and stronger than
they are—that we know an eye for an eye just won't solve
the problem. We're being tested and we're being tried. But
we'll pass our tests."

Evers believed that whites were beginning—just beginning—
to get the message. "There's a slight awareness of the fact that
black folks—that folks—are gonna really become a part of this
country," he said. "And there's no point in them trying to keep
us out. And I think that whites are gradually beginning to ac-

cept the fact that they gotta do something—maybe not much but something. And I think that if we blacks just get together and don't lose our heads, we're gonna be able to get all the things which Medgar and Bobby and the rest of them died for." Fayette is Charles Evers's monument to Medgar and Bobby and the rest of them—Medgar most of all. "Some people say, 'Well, we haven't accomplished anything,' " he said, the eyes soft and sad and not at all ironic. "Oh, yes, we have accomplished something. I mean the mere fact that I've been mayor for two and a half months and ain't been shot—that is a hell of an accomplishment."

CHAPTER 2

Who Speaks for the Negro Now?

SEVEN MONTHS BEFORE, on an April afternoon gone from gold to pewter gray, they had borne Martin Luther King through Atlanta to his grave and stood in numb silence while Ralph Abernathy, his ebony face streaked with tears, made their goodbyes for them: "The cemetery is too small for his spirit, but we commit his body to the ground. . . ." And now it was November, and a ragged, tense first summer without King had left the heirs to his Southern Christian Leadership Conference more painfully aware than ever of the depth of their dependence on him. So fifteen of them booked Room 301 at Paschal's Motor Hotel in Atlanta, locked themselves in with a psychiatrist and a psychologist, sat on the floor on a circle of cushions, told the operator "no calls"—and tried in two raging twelve-hour days of group therapy to exorcise the ghost among them. "We've never buried Dr. King," said one of them, going in, "and we won't be able to do anything until we do."

SCLC's problem, in important measure, was black America's: to bury Dr. King. Through the twelve years from his stewardship of the Montgomery bus boycott to his assassination on a Memphis motel balcony, King more than any single man had been the voice and the embodiment of the Negro revolution—even after the revolution ran beyond him and set a hundred ghettos ablaze. His faith in nonviolence and re-

55

demptive love as a strategy for social change may well have
run its useful course before he died; it rested heavily on
pageantry, and by the late 1960's, too many Americans—angry
blacks and frightened whites alike—were plainly tiring of
parades. So Resurrection City, the encampment of the poor at
the foot of the Lincoln Memorial in the late spring and early
summer of 1968, might have failed if King had lived. Without
him it never had a chance. It ended an ill-planned, ill-
understood shambles, and SCLC came away from the wreckage
edgy, disorganized, short of cash, shorter on ideas and brutally
conscious of the loss it, and Negro Americans generally, had
sustained. "We've got to understand he's not with us any
more," said one of the inheritors in Room 301 at Paschal's. "He
can't save us when things go wrong."

Much of what passed in that room centered on SCLC's
internal problems—the inevitable tensions, jealousies and ego
collisions of a group of talented and individualistic men
operating under constant pressure. King had always kept them
more or less together, mainly by sheer force of personality. But
with his death, the strains had begun showing, and the sessions
at Paschal's brought them out in the open. One, two or three at
a time, staffers were thrust to the center of the circle, to be
ragged, baited, cursed, called names, thrown jaw to jaw with
antagonists. No anxiety over race or sex or personal inade-
quacy, no dark corner of ego was too private. "Y'all just stood
there like a bunch of *fools*," one staffer blurted, free-associat-
ing about a tense moment in some past campaign. "Why did
you use the word 'fools'?" the psychiatrist demanded, and the
staffer disclosed, to the circle and to himself, that he felt
intellectually superior to the rest of them. A young black
confronted a white colleague who had more book learning
than he and harried him into confessing that it was only
because, as a white, he had been favored with more opportunity. Andy Young, SCLC's strongest administrative hand,
found himself admitting that he was trying to carry too big a

workload—partly because he couldn't bring himself to give any of it up. Abernathy, who had never got beyond a master's degree in sociology, let slip the pangs he felt when King would be invited to Harvard to pick up another honorary doctorate. Not even King escaped unscathed; he had been a distant and even a forbidding man, as prophets are, and some of the disciples discovered now that they had resented it. Said one: "Everybody was always afraid of him—afraid to say anything to him."

Beyond SCLC's internal agonies, however, lay questions of great moment for black America generally—not the least of them the matter of the succession to King's mantle. Room 301 thus became a critical testing ground for Ralph David Abernathy. He had come out of Montgomery and the bus boycott with King and stayed at his side to the end, a dark round gnome who introduced King at rallies ("the Moses of our people . . . the moral leader of the universe . . ."), who marched and prayed and went to jail with him and who, more than any man, could lay claim to his friendship and his confidence. SCLC's senior hands turned to Abernathy almost reflexively after King's death, partly because the two had been so close—and partly because his comfy down-home presence seemed a way to prevent, or at least to defer, an intramural struggle for a chance to be the next Dr. King. Abernathy, in his first summer, proved something less than that. He had none of King's soaring majesty; he was earthy where King was ethereal, sweaty when King seemed always air-cooled; SCLC people still chuckle over the memory of him nodding off at staff meetings in the days before he had to run them. His command debut in Resurrection City was not exactly a triumph—a fact which probably had more to do with hard historic realities than with his management but which diminished his reputation nevertheless. By the time he and the staff met at Paschal's the common gossip of The Movement was that the real rising star in SCLC was the Reverend Jesse Jackson,

who headed its most successful continuing enterprise, a boycott program called Operation Breadbasket (and who missed
the Atlanta sessions because of illness).

So Abernathy had to endure some painful moments in the
circle at Paschal's; staffers faulted him for being egotistical and
bluntly questioned whether he had the intellect to run SCLC.
But endure he did. He shouted as loudly as anyone; he got it
straight with his colleagues that he did not pretend to be Dr.
King, that he recognized that he had only begun his journey. "I
know," he told them, "that I will have to go by way of Samaria
to get to Jerusalem"—just as Christ, in John 4:4, had to pass
through Samaria and convert the doubters there in accord with
"the will of Him that sent me" before He reached Jerusalem.
And when they had finished, Abernathy was, by general agreement, more solidly in charge than he had yet been. "He was
really beautiful," one comrade said. "He came out of it a man.
When that session was over, there was no question that Abernathy was our leader."

What was very much in question was whether Abernathy
could begin to fill the void left by King's passing. It was easy to
forget, among the confusions and the disappointments of
King's last years, just how much he had meant to black
America. He had, by the spring of 1968, unquestionably passed
the apogee of his extraordinary career. But he had, in his day,
transformed the face of Negro protest with the 381-day boycott
of Montgomery's buses—a show of massive black resistance so
marvelously successful that hardly anyone remembers today that
a court order, not the boycott, finally put the victors in the
front of the bus. He led a black children's crusade in Birmingham until it became a national crisis of conscience and forced
John F. Kennedy to propose the broadest civil-rights legislation
in the nation's history. He waged the nonviolent war in Selma
that moved Lyndon Johnson to cry, "We shall overcome"—and
Congress to pass the voting-rights law that gave hundreds of
thousands of Southern blacks the ballot for the first time since

Reconstruction. He stitched Christ, Gandhi, Thoreau, Hegel, Marx and King into a blurry but ennobling new social gospel—a fighting faith that gave all the tumult of the Negro revolt a coherence it probably never really had. He seemed at times to fill the stage so completely that people thought he *was* the civil-rights movement. He wasn't. But The Movement might never have gone so far so fast without him.

And it is for those days that black America honors him still. King was first a Southerner and a preacher, and his great contributions were uniquely Southern and Christian. He turned numberless sweltering clapboard churches with names like Shiloh and Mount Zion into outposts of revolution, and, from their pulpits, his rolling, cadenced sermons called up courage and hope and dignity out of the despair of blackness in the Jim Crow South. By any pragmatic measure, he lost more campaigns than he won. But no black who marched with him, in body or in spirit, was likely ever to be the same again. "We are marching to freedom!" he told a column of followers one day in some Southern backwater. "Hell," an NAACP sophisticate scoffed from the sidelines, "they're not marching to freedom—they're marching to jail." The judgment was literally accurate—and yet utterly wrong.

For King persuaded a generation of Southern Negroes that they could in fact march to freedom—and that they could get there without violence. Nonviolence, a holy order for King, was never more than a tactic for some of his militant followers, and it fell out of intellectual fashion well before King died. But those black activists who understood nonviolence to mean submissiveness—and those whites who thought it promised comfort—both mistook the message. King and his men were consciously provocateurs; their object in a town was precisely to make its life intolerable. "Nonviolent direct action," King wrote in a celebrated letter from Birmingham jail, "seeks to create such a crisis and foster such a tension that a community which has constantly refused to negotiate is forced to confront the issue. It seeks so to dramatize the issue that it can no longer be ignored." King's marchers bedeviled Birmingham until Bull Connor loosed his dogs and fire hoses on them; they goaded Selma so mercilessly that Sheriff Jim Clark and his posse broke up an attempted pilgrimage to Montgomery by raw billy-swinging force. The strategy was always exemplary—not to reform a single town but to shame an entire nation to action. And, in Birmingham and Selma, it worked.

Yet King was pre-eminently a figure of what his old friend Bayard Rustin called the "dignity period" of The Movement— the days when the bull's-eye issue was Southern Jim Crow and when civil-rights leaders still spoke a common language. Even then, some of King's peers to the right and the left within The Movement envied his celebrity, mistrusted his visionary cast of mind, doubted (with considerable justice) his talents as a day-to-day tactician; they tended often to see him less as a leader than as a powerful icon to be borne along and displayed at the head of a procession. And as the "dignity" issues gave way to the subtler, more stubborn questions of poverty and caste, events seemed to tumble past him. Harlem and Watts and Detroit burned—partly out of expectations King himself had helped to quicken. Young radicals exploited his drawing power on the 1966 Meredith March through Mississippi and made it a showcase for the angry heresy of "black power." King's first Northern venture in Chicago fizzled. He got increasingly into the peace movement—a necessity of conscience for him, a bootless digression in the eyes of The Movement's moderate elders. He began organizing the Poor People's Campaign, knowing full well that it would be a critical test of whether nonviolent protest was even possible, let alone useful, in a climate as explosive as America's in 1968.

He stopped first in Memphis to mount a series of mass marches in support of a strike by the city's mostly black garbage collectors. But some harum-scarum teen-aged militants ran away with one of them and turned it into a little spree of window smashing. King retired briefly to Atlanta, deeply depressed and thinking of death. Yet he could not, in the end, stay away. "Nonviolence," he told friends, "is on trial in Memphis." So, on April 3, he went back, and that night he stood at the altar of Mason Street Temple, under a blazing yellow neon cross lettered SUNSHINE BAND, to preach what was to be his last public sermon.

"It is no longer a question of violence or nonviolence in this day and age," he intoned. "It is nonviolence or nonexistence." Near the end, with a hard rain drumming on the vaulted metal roof high above him, he spoke of the latest threats against his life. "Well," he said heavily, "I don't know what will happen now. We've got some difficult days ahead. But it really doesn't matter with me now. Because I've been to the mountaintop, and I don't mind." The "amens" and the "yes sirs" were coming thicker now, and he said, "Like anybody, I would like to live a long life; longevity has its place. But I'm not concerned about that now. I just want to do God's will. And He's allowed me to go up to the mountain. And I've looked over, and I've seen the promised land."

The promised land in fact had rarely seemed farther distant to King than it did the next afternoon when he and a very few of his inner circle met in his brother A.D.'s room at the Lorraine Motel and talked about the future of nonviolence. King was a small man—people who did not know him were forever surprised at how small he seemed as against their imaginings— and he was trying to shake a cold; that afternoon, he looked particularly liquid-eyed and vulnerable. The mini-riot in Memphis had reawakened an ugly anxiety that had been haunting him since Watts in 1965—the notion that some failure of his was to blame for the violent turn the Negro revolution had taken. He was nervous about the prospects for keeping the Poor People's Campaign peaceful; he half suspected that it would fail even if he did. He was thinking, he said that afternoon, of stepping back from the struggle for all of 1969 and perhaps

much of 1970 as well, to go into retreat and get the message of
nonviolence down on paper in terms so clear and so compelling
that it could not help but carry the day.

But Memphis, and Washington, had to be confronted first,
and, that afternoon, King drew on some inner resource of faith
to buck up his staff for the hard way ahead. Doubts had lately
been rising among them. Two of the low-echelon office help
had started abstractly arguing the legitimacy of violence as a
tactic for liberation; King had heard and forced their resigna-
tions because, he told staffers, nonviolence was at so critical a
pass that SCLC would have to be clearer of vision and purer of
heart than it had ever been to keep the faith alive. Yet still,
among the little group at the Lorraine, the talk was gloomy.
"The question," Andy Young recalled later, "was whether or
not we could turn the tide of the country and show once again
that the same kind of success could come out of nonviolence
that had come out of Birmingham and Selma. And, frankly, we
doubted that." So King, as he had often in the past, preached
them a sermon, and toward the end of it he came again to the
subject of death. When you come to grips with the question of
your own death, he said, *when you know that you're willing to
die for what you believe,* then the little problems of nonviolence fall into place; you no longer have to ask yourself every
moment, What am I going to do this time, what am I going to
do the next time? King looked around the little circle and told
them softly: "I have conquered the fear of death."

On his way out to dinner that evening, King dawdled for a
moment on the open-air walkway outside his own room at the
Lorraine and chatted with Jesse Jackson and a musician friend,
Ben Branch, who were standing in the lot below. In that
moment, an assassin hidden in a squalid rooming-house bath-
room precisely 205 feet away fixed him in the cross-hairs of a
telescopic sight and fired a single shot. King said, "Oh!"—nothing more—and then he was dying on the concrete floor. That
night, and in the nights that followed, the ghettos of 172

American cities erupted in rioting—an explosion whose fury would have appalled King, as so many spectators noted, but whose terrible inevitability he most certainly would have understood. And King was gone, his body drawn through Atlanta by two spavined mules at the head of a last sad procession, 150,000 strong; and seven months later, the stricken young men who had seen him to his grave broke at last from Room 301 at Paschal's, wounds bound and spirits high, and ambled arm in arm to a black night club called The Birdcage for drinks. "I think," said one of them, "that most of us have buried Dr. King."

Black America, in the spring of 1969, had not buried him—not just yet. In life, King had always towered over the field in polls of the Negro community, *Newsweek's* and everybody else's. Now, in death, 83 per cent of *Newsweek's* national black sample rated his work "excellent" and a near-unanimous 95 per cent gave him positive marks—figures so high, and so far ahead of the pack, that one Gallup analyst called them almost meaningless. So they are, if one reads too much into the benign glow of the majority and expects events to conform to it; to do so is to forget that angry black youngsters—some of whom no doubt admired King in the abstract—shouted him down in the flesh on a disastrous 1965 peace-making visit to Watts, and reduced that last demonstration in Memphis to a violent shambles. Yet the majority is overwhelmingly there, and all the militants who propose to speak for the black masses today still operate in its shadow. The faithful—those who rated King's ministry excellent—were nearly as numerous in the chill ghetto North (80 per cent) as in his native South (85 per cent). His enormous pull swept in most of the old and the poor, who tend to be the most conservative elements in Negro America, and most of the young and the relatively well off, who tend to be the most militant. Even among the switched-off Northern ghetto young —by far the angriest blacks of all—a diminished but still

healthy majority of 71 per cent graded King excellent, and 94
per cent gave him positive ratings. They might or might not
have followed him in the crunch. But *their* Martin Luther King
clearly bore little resemblance to King as the militants imagined
him to be—that swollen-headed, shuffle-gaited and totally fictitious accommodationist they mockingly called "De Lawd."

King, indeed, was far too important to black Americans for
them to credit the official theory that his assassination was the
work of a single man and not some sinister racist conspiracy. All
the evidence pointed to James Earl Ray, a stir-wise fugitive
convict who left an incredible olio of clues at the scene and was
finally captured trying to disappear via Lisbon, London and
Brussels into some mercenary army in Africa. But had Ray
acted alone? Everyone close to the case—the FBI, the Department of Justice, the Memphis authorities, Ray's authorized
biographer, even the defense lawyer who finally got him to
plead guilty—wound up believing he was the lone or at least the
principal assassin. Yet Ray himself let on that a mysterious
Latin (or French Canadian) stranger named "Raoul" had hired
him into a King assassination plot, and he stuck to the tale even
after entering the studiedly ambiguous plea ("Yes, *legally*
guilty, unh-hunh") by which he beat the electric chair and took
99 years in prison instead. And black America, which by then
had lost not only King but Malcolm X, Medgar Evers, two
brothers named Kennedy and any number of lesser-known
martyrs, was disposed to believe him. Fully 82 per cent in the
Newsweek Poll were persuaded that a conspiracy was involved,
and 67 per cent doubted that white America had yet put the
case to full and honest investigation.

And many had the uneasy sense that an era was ending—that
the ideal of nonviolent protest had been sorely if not mortally
damaged by the death of its most eloquent spokesman. "What
did nonviolence do for *him?*" an 18-year-old Andrews, Texas,
girl asked bitterly. King, of course, would have argued that that
was not the question; he always understood that he might

someday die for his faith. But, a year after his passing, a clear majority of Negro America thought that his ideas about nonviolence had in fact been losing ground since his death. And the suspicion became a three-to-one certainty among the Northern middle-class Negroes who have everything to do with setting the climate of black opinion. "Dr. Martin Luther King," said Floyd McKissick of CORE, shaken and red-eyed after King's death, "was the last prince of nonviolence. Nonviolence is a dead philosophy, and it was not the black people that killed it."

So the blacks expected troubled times, and they were anything but certain who in King's absence would guide them through. The idea that one man—King or Walter White or Booker T. Washington—could speak for all of black America has always been a white man's fantasy. And, as the *Newsweek* Poll clearly suggests, it has never been farther from the truth than it is today. What the figures reveal is a state of flux in the competition for the allegiance of black Americans—and particularly the black young. They show the moderates still in command of the center and the militants still consigned to the margins with the enthusiastic backing of no more than 5 to 15 per cent. But the landscape was shifting and, though its new contours were not yet clear, it was apparent that the trend was not on the side of moderation.

Gallup pollers read the interviewees a list of Negro organizations and leaders, living and recently dead, and asked them to rate each one excellent, pretty good, only fair or poor. The list was not comprehensive (the obvious omissions run a wide range from Roy Wilkins to Rap Brown) nor was it designed to be. The intent was not a popularity contest among particular personalities, who tend more and more to be transient, but a reading of what styles of leadership and what sorts of personality can be expected to appeal to Negro Americans as they move into the 1970's. The following table shows, first, the overall balance of sentiment in the Negro community from year to year—the percentage of blacks who rated each leader or group approvingly ("excellent" or "pretty good") and the percentage who were disapproving ("only fair" or "poor"). Those figures do not necessarily tell who will follow whom but they do offer a rough guide to Negro America's shifting mood through the turbulent 1960's—a mood that still heavily favors those leaders who profess moderation, integration and nonviolence but was beginning to blacken a bit by the decade's end. The last column—the percentage of Negroes who rate each entry *excellent*—is a far more certain measure of the real constituencies from which any given leader or group could actually expect to draw active support.

THIRTEEN LEADERS: 1963–1969*

	1963		1966		1969		
	+	−	+	−	+	−	*Excellent*
Martin Luther King	88	4	88	3	95	3	83
NAACP	91	3	81	7	76	17	37
Ralph Abernathy	x	x	x	x	64	24	26
Whitney Young	x	x	33	8	42	16	19
CORE	59	8	60	11	46	21	16
Urban League	54	10	50	9	46	23	15
Stokely Carmichael	x	x	19	13	31	46	12
Malcolm X	x	x	x	x	27	35	13
SNCC	18	4	44	14	32	20	11
Elijah Muhammad	15	35	12	43	22	40	9
Black Panther Party	x	x	x	x	15	32	5
Black Muslims	11	44	9	49	13	48	4
Bayard Rustin	x	x	22	10	15	11	3

* The list also included Mayors Carl Stokes of Cleveland and Richard Hatcher of Gary, Indiana, and Julian Bond, the young Georgia state representative. Since they are, strictly speaking, political rather than race leaders, the findings are reported in Chapter 3 in a discussion of the new black politics.

The table amounts to the box score of an undecided contest. But some trends can be read in the figures:

· *The old-line moderates—the NAACP and the Urban League—still commanded the loyalties of black America's own great silent majority, but cracks were beginning to show.*

A poignant irony of the Negro revolt in the late 1960's was the progressive isolation of men like the NAACP's Roy Wilkins, the Urban League's Whitney Young and senior Movement theoretician Bayard Rustin—men who clearly embodied the will of the overwhelming majority of black people to work within The System but who found it ever more difficult to persuade The System to deliver. In the low-ebb days of 1967, with Detroit and Newark still smoking and Washington in a mood of reaction, Young put out feelers to the Johnson Administration to see if two or three of them couldn't go before Congress to plead for black America just as General William Westmoreland had recently spoken in support of the war in Vietnam. "We might be able to head off the backlash, the economy wave, the reprisals," he argued. But nothing came of it then, and, with the entrance of Richard Nixon a year and a half later, the old-liners had trouble getting audiences with anyone at all in high-level Washington. Even the term "moderate" began to gall them in those days when, as Young put it, "no one is for gradualism, no one counsels patience, no one thinks in terms of compromise." But their inside-Jericho approach could not compete forever with the incendiary anger of the militants unless they could produce visible, meaningful victories with it. And as victories of any sort got scarcer in the late 1960's, their credibility—and their followings—showed the first telltale signs of erosion.

The moderates still spoke the language of most Negro Americans. The NAACP, with its 76 per cent favorable rating, remained by far the best-known and best-liked entry still in the field after King's passing, and the Urban League—though it plays to a smaller audience—got a two-to-one positive vote from those who knew its work. Their critical problem was less a depletion in numbers than a diminution of confidence—a long-term shrinkage of the constituency of true believers who rate them excellent and hence presumably would be most likely to follow their leadership. The figures:

THE INSIDERS: DANGER SIGNS

	"Excellent" ratings in		
	1963	1966	1969
NAACP	75	58	37
Urban League	27	25	15
Whitney Young	x	16	19
Bayard Rustin	x	10	3

Only Young among them bucked the tide, possibly because—
as the youngest and trendiest of the name moderates—he had
moved stylistically with it. ("He even has Jim Linen saying
'black power,'" grinned one Urban Leaguer—meaning James
Alexander Linen III, the Time, Inc., hierarch who is president
of the League.) Yet neither Young's personal appeal nor his
thoroughly modern "ghetto-power" programming for the
League could keep its stock from dropping 10 points in three
years. And the figures bore sadder tidings still for the NAACP
after 60 years' leadership in the struggle for Negro rights. Its
corps of enthusiasts tumbled by half in six years, and *its* stock
by 1969 was three times as high among Southern Negroes of 50
or older as it was among the young in the ghetto North—a
perilous generation gap for the biggest, longest-running civil-
rights organization of them all.

· *Ralph Abernathy came into an important base of support
as Martin Luther King's official heir-designate—but his grits-
and-gravy Southern style may sharply limit his impact as a
national figure.*

Abernathy got A grades from 26 per cent of the sample and B
or better from 64 per cent—higher than anyone now in the field
except the NAACP. But his following amounts to only a fraction of King's nationally. Particularly telling is the fact that his
popularity ran twice as high in the rural and small-town South
(where 38 per cent of the Negroes rated him excellent) as in
the inner-city North (where only 18 per cent were all that
enthusiastic). And coolest of all were the Northern young—the

volatile kids who were so often beyond even King's substantial powers of persuasion. The clear message: Abernathy's strongest appeal, and hence his best chances to be effective, lay back home in Dixie. And Dixie, sure enough, was where instinct led him once Resurrection City folded. Abernathy found his Samaria in palmetto-fringed Charleston, South Carolina, where he and SCLC adopted a black hospital workers' strike and helped win it with a pulpit-thumping, hymn-singing, mass-marching freedom campaign straight out of the old glory days.

· *Malcolm X and his progeny—CORE, SNCC and Stokely Carmichael—won significant beachheads for black radicalism, particularly among the Negro young, but they remained minority voices distinctly outside the Negro mainstream.*

Malcolm X during his lifetime—particularly that part of it he spent in the service of Elijah Muhammad and the Black Muslims—was never quite respectable for most Negroes, and his polls showed it; only 1 per cent in a 1964 survey picked him from a short list of Negro leaders as the one who had done most for the blacks. (The winner, with 88 per cent: Martin Luther King.) But after Malcolm's break with Muhammad that year, his assassination in 1965 and the publication of his extraordinary autobiography shortly thereafter, a process of rediscovery and redemption began—a spreading belief that Malcolm had not been a mere hatemonger after all but a prophet who had terrible truths to tell about the oppression of black people in white America. "Black folks were saying the same things for years before Malcolm," a Chicago youth worker said, "only they were saying them in back alleys. Malcolm freed them and a whole lot of other people to come out of the alley and say, 'Now, Whitey, this is the way it is . . .'" He remained, in 1969, a taste that much of Negro America had not acquired; nearly twice as many rated him poor as excellent. But he was becoming an authentic folk hero in the Northern ghetto and particularly among the restive young: 52 per cent of them liked him (to 26 per cent who didn't) and 27 per cent thought him excellent—second only to Martin Luther King on their list. "To me," said one of them, a Brandeis coed, "Malcolm X has never died."

Dead prophets, of course, are easier to love than live ones; Malcolm's first-generation heirs—the angry young blacks who let the black-power genie out of the bottle in 1966 and in the process altered the entire language and style of the Negro revolt—have had rather mixed fortunes since. SNCC and CORE had stored up considerable capital in the nonviolent war against Southern segregation in the early '60's and so both still had more friends than foes in the Negro community in 1969. But their loyalist followings shrank every bit as precipitously as the moderates' after they embraced black power—SNCC's from 23 to 11 per cent of all Negroes, and CORE's from 34 to 16 per cent. And Stokely Carmichael, the first and most talented of that initial wave of black Jacobins, tended mostly to polarize Negroes. He could, by 1969, count perhaps a tenth of all black Americans (and a fifth of the ghetto young) as his real fans and possibly a third as at least somewhat sympathetic—very likely as large a following as any militant could then have mustered. But the bearers of bad news always pay a price; very nearly half of black America stood (or leaned) against Carmichael—a no vote rivaled only by Muhammad and the Muslims.

Malcolm and his children had an impact far greater than their numbers on black America's psyche—particularly to the extent that they wakened the surge of black consciousness and black pride that quickened through the late 1960's. But they remained outsiders, and, by 1969, they were in disarray. SNCC, spiritually exhausted after one year chaired by Stokely and another by Rap Brown, dropped virtually out of sight. CORE, under the new management of a bright, bearded and very stagecrafty nationalist named Roy Innis, took a straight-out separatist stance and so moved even deeper into isolation from the Negro mainstream. And Stokely Carmichael was in residence in Guinea, far distant from the struggle he had so transformed. *Newsweek*'s Richard Z. Chesnoff encountered him that summer, holding court on a sun-washed hotel balcony in Algiers in a dove-gray African bush suit and dark shades. He was ready as ever with revolutionary aphorisms for Negro Americans ("Armed struggle . . . means that you have a gun and you use it to struggle for what you believe in"), but *his* struggle of the moment was the restoration of his fellow exile, the Redeemer Kwame Nkrumah, to the presidency of Ghana.

And far behind, in the dust if not yet the dustbin of history, were the Black Muslims. The world had changed since those simpler days when the Messenger of Allah, Elijah Muhammad, and his little Lost-Found Nation of Islam in the Wilderness of North America seemed so menacing to so many whites. History had revealed them to be after all a rather conservative lot— persuaded, to be sure, that the white man is the devil but content for now to keep to themselves, live clean Muslim lives and wait for Allah to deal with the devil for them. Yet their press, from the moment America discovered them in the late 1950's, was wretched, and they have never lived it down. Muhammad's personal popularity roughly doubled in the 1960's, but his doomsday brand of separatism ("Join onto your own kind, the time of this world is at hand!") packed considerably more appeal for the oldest and poorest Southern Negroes than for the militant young in the North. And the Muslims, with a 4 per cent excellent rating, remained frozen where they had been throughout the decade—at the outermost margin of Negro American life.

· *The Black Panther Party, best-known of the new black revolutionaries who materialized and flourished in Stokely's train, were looked on unkindly by most Negroes who knew of them at all—except the cooled-off generation coming of age in the ghetto North.*

The Panthers—the brainchildren of a bright, charismatic Oakland street prophet named Huey P. Newton and some ghetto coffeehouse pals—were like some white nightmare of the

Black Revenge come chillingly to life: an armed, angry revolutionary cadre uniformed in berets and black leather and bristling with guns. They spent their first years flashing their irons and their hostilities everywhere; they put the word "pig," for policeman, into the radical vocabulary; once they even marched their rifles and their hard looks into the corridors of California's state capitol while the legislature was debating a gun-control law they opposed. The design of it all was to establish their credentials for *badness* in that black underground where bad means tough and male and therefore good. It worked; Newton's kaffee klatsch grew in three years into a nationwide black resistance with 2,600 members in 70 chapters. And most prized of all the recruits was Eldridge Cleaver, a brilliantly talented ex-convict who had excited radical whites with his Folsom Prison memoir, *Soul on Ice,* and who brought their affection and their cash to the Panthers with him.

To be bad in black America, however, is to flirt constantly with doom, and the Panthers shortly found themselves in a running blood-feud with the law. "The cop on the beat," one Chicago detective said, "he figures it's like Red China—one day he's gonna have to take these guys on and he'd rather do it while they're still weak." It was a war with provocations on both sides but only one possible loser: the Panthers. Newton was convicted of killing a cop in an Oakland street shoot-out and sentenced to fifteen years in prison. Co-founder Bobby Seale and seven radical whites were charged with fomenting the 1968 Democratic Convention disorders in Chicago; he behaved so noisily at trial that he was briefly gagged and chained, then sentenced to four years for contempt. Cleaver was caught in a police siege in which another Panther was shot dead; his parole was revoked and he fled the country rather than go back to Folsom. Twenty-two Panthers were indicted for allegedly plotting to dynamite five New York department stores, fourteen more—including Seale—charged with murdering a suspected informer in that case. Dozens of others across the country were arrested for high crimes ranging from jaywalking to sniping. At least a dozen more were killed by police in situations invariably described by the authorities as "gun battles" and by the Panthers as murder.

The attrition moved the Panthers to try to broaden their ties with white radicals and to soften their image with a miscellany of good works including, notably, free breakfasts for the ghetto's poorest children. ("How," asked a chary California policeman, "can anyone be against feeding kids?") But their reputation at the time of the *Newsweek* Poll was still bad, and opinion divided accordingly. Most Negroes either had not heard of them or had no opinion about them. But those who had an opinion rated them negatively by 32 to 15 in the leadership poll, 23 to 14 on a separate question ("On the whole, do you approve or disapprove . . . ?"). What does the Panther stand for? "Means trouble to me," a 65-year-old Philadelphia janitor told a Gallup interviewer. "Intimidation," said a Denver truck driver of 51. "Black supremacy," said a 64-year-old Houston schoolteacher.

But the ghetto young who had formed opinions came down, by a 25-to-20 plurality, on the Panthers' side. "They feel the white man is the oppressor and we are the oppressed," said a 25-year-old Harlem housewife who had got the message and approved it. And a Pittsburgh college freshman, 18 years old, got it too. "Only through force is it likely that America will understand the black man," he said. "If we can't gain our freedom and equality any other way, there is always the gun."

Talk of guns was common currency among the young ghetto leaders of the generation liberated from the alleys by Malcolm, Stokely and Rap. "It's like the Tartar Creed," said one of them in Chicago. " 'A hand that can't hold the sword can't hold the scepter'—that's the feeling in the ghetto today." The bookshelf of the black revolution passed from Camus, Gandhi and King to Malcolm, Che Guevara and Frantz Fanon—the last a black psychiatrist who, during the Algerian terror, had discovered a therapeutic value in violence visited by the oppressed native upon the white oppressors. The most incendiary rhetoric flourished, all of it pro-black and much of it explicitly anti-white. A guerrilla psychology swept up some of the young—a style of mind that, at its most strung-out, proceeded from fantasy to the stockpiling of real guns and the scheming (if rarely the execution) of real acts of terror. Others retreated into the ancient dream of separation—a vision that had languished largely in the custody of the Muslims since Marcus Garvey's heyday but which now flowered again. The Republic of New Africa established itself temporarily in Detroit (it hoped ultimately to take over Mississippi, Louisiana, Georgia, Alabama and South Carolina) and called fugitive black revolutionist Robert Williams home out of eight years' exile in Cuba, Africa and China to be its president-in-waiting. And CORE dreamed its dream of a nation of black "islands" stretching from Harlem to Watts. Impractical? "Hell," snorted Roy Innis, a man with a gift for making the outrageous sound credible, "I can get to the West Coast and rap with [Watts nationalist Ron] Karenga quicker today than Alexander Hamilton could get from New York to Philly in 1770."

It was mostly the excesses and the confusions of the new black mood that got onto television and into the headlines—a babel that tended to blur the depth and the subtleties of a profound shifting of tides within The Movement. The brightest of the inheritors of the revolution tended, after all the Tom-calling, to recognize and to acknowledge their historic debt to King. "He's the one," says Dr. Alvin Poussaint, a young black Harvard psychiatrist, "who most mobilized the black community—who made the civil-rights movement a movement of the grass roots and not the middle class." But the mission of those days, as they saw it, has been accomplished; the old movement had brought down the legal pinnings of segregation in the U. S.—and discovered how little real difference those victories had made in the day-to-day lives of the black poor. So today, said new-breed leader Herbert Carter, the director of the Los Angeles County Human Relations Committee, "there's no more holding hands, no more community sings, no more Overcoming—those days are gone forever. In the early days of the civil-rights movement, people were trying to change certain *conditions* of life. Now they're trying to change an entire *way* of life, and *this* Movement is much more complex."

It is much more diffuse as well—a condition that strikes many whites as mere confusion of strategy and purpose but which blacks insist upon as a reality and even a virtue. A good many white Americans missed Martin Luther King almost as grievously as the Negro community did; he was someone they could talk to in the reasonable assurance that, if he was not the single voice of all the blacks, he at least spoke for more of them than anybody else. That luxury is gone now, and some of the younger leaders think Negroes will be better for it. "There is nothing wrong with the black leadership in this country today," said Warner Saunders, head of Chicago's Better Boys Foundation, "except that white America can't call up one black man and get a quick fix on what the black community feels." What King's death revealed to whites was a diversity that actually had existed through all those years when they were asking one another who speaks for the Negro—and imagining that a single answer existed.

The new wave has, to be sure, produced its own national figures—men who endured after the Stokelys and the Raps flamed out. Ralph Abernathy, for all the provincial antique in him, kept SCLC's spark alive—and so did Jesse Jackson, whose turtle-necked, bell-bottomed, Afro-thatched good looks gave the old style a touch of mod and an edge of militance. Charles Evers and Julian Bond came out of The Movement into a new Southern politics and attracted followings far beyond their little Dixie constituencies. Harry Edwards, the guru of the Olympic boycott campaign, established himself as a militant of enormous

dash and considerable promise. And none more typified the
new style at its savviest and sharpest-edged than George Wiley,
a great natural-coifed bear of a man with a gentle manner, a wry
smile that makes him look as if he has just bitten into a particularly sour lemon—and a following of 70,000 mostly black and
unanimously angry welfare mothers.

Wiley is a sometime professor of organic chemistry who came
up through CORE in the early 1960's, departed during one of
its intermittent internal upheavals and, in 1966, began organizing what was to become the National Welfare Rights Organization—a network of local groups dedicated to the single purpose
of making life on the dole supportable and quite prepared to be
as unpleasant as necessary about it. Monomania, indeed, was
NWRO's genius, and Wiley's; they have, for example, stayed
out of the whole debilitating quarrel over whether whites ought
to be allowed in The Movement and in fact recruited and
prominently displayed enough of them to remind the nation
that, in Wiley's words, "you're not just talking about black
people when you talk about welfare." All Wiley and his moms
really wanted to talk about, and demonstrate against, was the
fact that the average U.S. welfare family, black or white, was
drawing $2,000 a year—and probably needed $5,000 or $6,000
to get by. "Our struggle," said Wiley, "is having a political
impact now known as the 'welfare crisis' "—his face creased
into the lemony smile—"which is causing people to re-evaluate
the whole welfare system. But our contention is that the system
has been in crisis for the recipients since it began—it's been
inadequate, it's been cumbersome, it's been bureaucratic, it's
been unresponsive to their needs, it's invaded their privacy and
destroyed their dignity." NWRO people were not certain that
it would be necessary to break the existing system to reform it
but they thought it might. "The present system," said Wiley,
"wasn't really designed to benefit poor people. We're trying to
make it do something it really wasn't designed to do."

What made NWRO so apt a metaphor of its time, however,

was not its national management but its local orientation. The guiding genius of The Movement had passed from the New York–Washington–Atlanta orbit of the old Big Five (or Big Six or Big Ten, depending on who was counting and when) to a ghetto-bred generation with reputations no larger than a single city or neighborhood or even a particular block. The fact that they were so many and so various troubled them not at all. "In many ways," Julian Bond thought, "it's beneficial fragmentation. Where you used to have the predominance of one or two organizations and one or two directions in a town, a city or a state, now you have fifty or sixty. And I think on the whole that's good—it means that if you're an integrationist and you have a program, then you feel free to work on it, a separatist has *his* program to work on, and so on. And on very crucial and key issues, there's a great deal of unanimity." To which Elma Lewis, the director of a Boston black cultural center, added dryly: "In the white community, that would be called diversification. In the black community, it's called chaos. But it's not."

The variety, indeed, concealed a certain community of outlook and of purpose that overrode many of the intramural frictions that had so plagued The Movement in the past. "All the groups," said Watts community worker Walter Bremond, "have to do their own thing—the NAACP, the Panthers, CORE, SNCC, SCLC. It all helps get us a little further down the road. But if you look real close, you see an orchestra that's in harmony. You have your snare drums and you have your violins. But you still hear that four-four beat—which is black."

And black was a style of thought as pervasive among the younger front-liners, if not yet the masses of Negro Americans, as the old ideology of nonviolence and integration had been for the generation just before. The new tongue often sounded violent and separatist—more so than many and perhaps most of its practitioners really intended. The death and destruction visited lopsidedly on the ghetto through a half-dozen summers of rioting took a good deal of the romantic *guerrillero* appeal out of street fighting; even the Panthers' Bobby Seale was in the field in the spring of 1969 warning slum blacks against making the summer "a hellhole of spontaneous disruption."

And much of what sounded like separatist talk in fact came down to a declaration that integration was an irrelevant abstraction for most Negroes now ("You white folks," said Wiley, "won't let it happen") and that, as long as they are stuck indefinitely in the ghetto anyway, they ought to move for control of its political and economic life. *Community control,* in the nearly universal phrase, was where it was at in the late 1960's; no other term so defined the new leadership or dominated the new vocabulary of The Movement. It was on one hand an umbrella for rowdy and sometimes violent demonstrations against institutional authority of every sort. But it was even more a spur to a heightened feeling of community ("a sense of nation-building," author Chuck Stone called it) and a proliferating number of self-help projects, some of them government- or foundation-financed, others too black and too proud to take white help, all of them filled with a heady new independence. "We all grew up," said Dr. Price Cobbs, the San Francisco psychiatrist and co-author of *Black Rage,* "with the feeling that somehow Mr. Charley was going to save us—with a 'rescue fantasy,' in psychoanalytic terms. Well, we're not going to be saved by anyone but ourselves."

The new tone was often abrasive, sometimes inflammatory. But it bore the sad edge of disenchantment as well. Hosea Williams is a top hand in SCLC, a stocky man with a brambly beard, an engaging warmth and a flair for showboating. He soldiered with Martin Luther King for integration in Birmingham and Selma and Chicago; he was one of the group who tried, through those two ragged days at Paschal's Motor Hotel, to lay King's ghost to rest. Now it was a year later, and Williams was a year older, and integration was no longer what he was fighting for or even talking about. "I don't think," he said, "that there will ever be a separate black state here in America.

But I must admit that at this time black people must regroup. Before we can gain meaningful integration in this country, there must be a period of meaningful segregation." He paused and tugged at his beard. "I used to tell my black brothers that if they want to buy a decent home, buy it in the white neighborhood. But now I realize that I was actually saying that the white neighborhood is decent and the black neighborhood is indecent. Well, black neighborhoods *are* indecent—not because black people live there but because powerless people live there.

"So now I'm at the position where Booker T. Washington was about sixty or seventy years ago. I say to my brothers, 'Cast down your buckets where you are.' We must turn these run-down slums and ghettos into havens of beauty—that's what I mean by meaningful segregation. We must control these communities—politically, economically and socially."

It was a far leap from King to Williams, from integration to segregation, "meaningful" or otherwise—a leap that black America, from the evidence of the *Newsweek* Poll, was not prepared to make just now. Yet it was equally clear that the issue of who speaks for the Negro was, if anything, less settled at the end of the tumultuous 1960's than when the decade began. Would more and more Negroes opt out into militancy? Or drop out in despair?

Or would the moderates finally prevail? To the extent that they needed victories to show for their labors, events in the ebbing years of the decade did not favor their cause—and neither did the deep subsurface currents of black public opinion. The field still belonged to them when the '60's ended. But how securely they could hold it, and for how long a time, was a suddenly and dangerously open question.

DIRECTIONS:

Beulah Sanders

She sat dark as mahogany and large as a mountain in her fly-specked walk-up office in Harlem, waging war for the revolutionary proposition that people who are forced to live on welfare ought to be paid enough welfare to live on. Mrs. Beulah Sanders's credentials were the three children she was raising on the dole and a certain combative genius for survival; her troops, eight or ten thousand welfare mothers as formidable and as angry as she; her command post, the headquarters of the New York City Wide Coordinating Committee of Welfare Groups, which she chairs. When Newsweek's Tom Mathews found her there, her mood was fine and mellow as the autumn afternoon. But all about her lay the paraphernalia of Beulah Sanders's war: a mimeograph machine, a telephone, stacks of posters ("Thanks," one said, "for Nothing") and leaflets, and a rumpled hand-lettered placard that told it all—A HEAP SEES BUT FEW KNOWS THEY ARE MURDERING US.

Mrs. Sanders was just back from Washington and an especially abrasive confrontation with the House Ways and Means Committee—a body of fiscally prudent white people who by then knew her well but who still treated her rather as though she were Madame Defarge come to announce the Terror. The session had not gone particularly well. "You're doggone right we want more money," Mrs. Sanders had hold the committee, and she was quite matter-of-fact about how she and the welfare-rights movement meant to get it if all else failed—by disrupt-

80

ing the capital, the state and the nation until they had no choice but to help the poor. But nothing had happened. The conservative management of the committee was unmoved, and one of its liberals, James A. Burke, a Democrat from Massachusetts, told Mrs. Sanders numbly, "Many of us have spent twenty, twenty-five years fighting for the things you are fighting for . . . I agree that it's taken too long. But you make my crusade very difficult when you come in here and make threats."

Beulah Sanders had long since lost patience with crusades that take twenty or twenty-five years and still deliver so little. "I didn't want to hear all that crap," she told Mathews; the real power in Ways and Means, as she was quite keenly aware, lay not with the James Burkes but with Chairman Wilbur Mills of Arkansas, a welfare-watchdogging conservative whose dour face appears on a WANTED poster on her office wall. "Those wealthy white Southerners in Congress—those cats don't want to give us nothing," she said. "And then they turn around and go allocate ten million dollars for beauty parlors in Congress so all those Congressmen's chicks can look pretty. I tell you, I pissed a natural boogie when I heard that. I thought that was just the livin' end, and there wasn't no hassle over it at all."

Her third-floor cubicle is in the heart of Central Harlem; her neighbors include a police station, a treatment center for junkies and the teeming housing projects. Beulah Sanders knew those streets and their life; she dreamed of something better; and when she did, she became, for a fleeting and revealing moment, not a hard-talking revolutionary but a hard-pressed mother fighting for air. "Poverty," she said softly, "is like cold weather—it don't wait for nothin'. Take when I shop—I watch for the Sunday papers to see what's on sale. If I had enough money, I wouldn't have to read the Sunday paper always—I'd just go downtown to the market and shop. And that's one of the things I want." The dream was not a very grand one, but Beulah Sanders discovered some years ago that she would have to fight to get it, or even a piece of it. "They were tearing down the houses on my block for an urban renewal project," she said. "In 1962, a lot of people got scared and run. I just stayed there. I must have stayed a month in a house on West Ninetieth Street just by myself. Everyone else just ran away."

She lost that battle, of course—the building simply went to seed around her—but she had discovered a will to do battle for herself and her kids, and it had not deserted her since. She was left with no awe at all for the great; she dismissed Nelson Rockefeller, with his favored tax position, as "the biggest welfare recipient in this nation"; and, while she confessed some affection for John Lindsay, New York's liberal mayor, she thought he would need some "whumping in the head" to keep him righteous. She had not given up on conventional politics —not yet. "A lot of poor folks don't think votes count," she said. "We know they count—every vote in this country counts." But she was not so sure of most of its practitioners. "Elected officials aren't listening to us," she rumbled; her fist thumped down on her desk and an ashtray, with a half-eaten dill pickle in it, jumped perceptibly. "That forces us to demonstrate and disrupt. When you do that, everybody wants to hear you. We disrupt them suckers all right—if we have to."

That was all she had wanted to tell the committee; but all they had wanted to ask her about, so it seemed to her in retrospect, was illegitimacy and birth control, and Beulah Sanders had heard that song before. "Look at the middle class—hell, they right in there," she said with a seismic chuckle. "You see them standing up all the time saying, 'This here is a love child.' Look at Mia Farrow and André Previn—hon, that man's not talkin' about marriage. They rich. They got the money to provide for their kids. Poor folks don't. That's the difference between them. Period."

Yet committees are difficult to communicate with. In the end, Mrs. Sanders left it with the House Committee on Ways and Means that America would have hell on its hands if it messed with the poor; then she returned to Harlem and her war. She had, in a sense, never left that house on West 90th Street; she was still making her stand and daring the authorities to budge her. But this time she was not alone. "We're beginning to have enough power and strength to have great impact," she said. "We cuss and yell at each other, and then we get our shit together and go out to fight that system." And would it always have to be a fight? "Honey," said Beulah Sanders, "if you ain't got nothing, you can't get nothing. That's what I try to explain to people. But people just don't want to hear that."

CHAPTER 3

A Choice of Weapons

THE TIME WAS SPRING 1968; the place a luckless little pocket of poverty named Marks, Mississippi; the cast a few dozen men and women who had packed up their belongings—those who had any to pack—in cartons and shopping bags and cardboard suitcases and now stood waiting with that deep impassive patience of the Southern black poor. "I was talkin' to the Lord about five-thirty this mornin'," cried the SCLC's Reverend James Bevel, an elfin doe-eyed young man to whom the experience was quite apparently both real and familiar, "and He told me to tell y'all He wasn't goin' to deliver y'all. . . . We got to deliver *ourselves!*" And then they plodded off through the dust to the highway and north toward Washington, to occupy a tiny squatters' city called Resurrection amid the monuments and the cherry trees—and to wait some more until the President and the Congress promulgated their deliverance.

It never came. That first column from Marks, and eight others from big-city slums and backwater hamlets across the nation, did move into their homemade shantytown beside the Lincoln Memorial's reflecting pool and hung on there, up to 2,500 strong, into a steamy capital summer. But in the end they failed, just as Martin King feared they might, and their failure was instructive for what it told about the possibilities of moving America any longer with the sort of grand morality plays he used to stage so well. SCLC was partly to blame; it designed (or, rather, improvised) Resurrection City as a sort of scale-model slum and succeeded disastrously well, down to such true-to-life details as winos, junkies, thieves, bopping gangs, hunger, paranoia, chronic boredom and separate, segregated ghettos for the black, white, Latin and Indian poor. But the camp-in failed even more because neither the capital nor the nation was of any mind, at that divided hour, to let it succeed.

Washington is unfailingly nervous about visitations of any large groups of citizens not wearing convention badges or Boy Scout uniforms, and this visitation, mostly black and very angry, happened to come close behind a particularly ugly riot over King's assassination. So, with a few notable exceptions in each branch, the Administration and the Congress looked on the pilgrims with all the warm regard Rome must have felt for Attila the Hun; even Lyndon Johnson, who once had identified himself with the Negro's cause more closely than any other President, was said to regard them as potentially explosive and to wish they hadn't come. The poor people ultimately were forced to settle for the only victory possible under the circumstances: they endured for the duration of their six-week permit and only then let the government run them out, to its manifest relief and their own. "The nation cannot hide from poor people as long as they are here," Ralph Abernathy said toward the end, far more wishfully than hopefully. But hide it did, and when Resurrection City finally closed down, few doubted that the era of the big parades had ended with it.

That era was predicated on the view that America has a collective conscience and that Negroes could catch it, so just was their cause, if only they petitioned peaceably enough and in large enough numbers. Parading as a mode of protest reached its high style in the decade between the Montgomery bus boycott of 1955–56 and the Selma-to-Montgomery voting-rights pilgrimage of 1965; its finest hour was the August 1963 March on Washington, an invasion the capital dreaded as much as Resurrection City (the Kennedys saw to it that the city's bars were closed for the day) but which proved to be an event of

irresistibly moving effect. Yet spectacles of the sort depended
on the audience seeing the Negro as victim, not as aggressor—
an act of imagination which has never been easy for many
whites and which became more difficult still with the ghettos
exploding and the new-wave militants preaching war. The
devastating Watts riot of 1965 was very probably the turning
point; the old innocence, or whatever was left of it, was no
longer supportable thereafter for blacks or whites. The Movement attempted one more grand pageant the following summer, the Meredith March against Fear in Mississippi—and
came away so traumatized by the black-power schism that
neither moderates nor militants were eager for a reprise soon
again. The civil-rights establishment accordingly was less than
delighted when it heard of King's plans to march the poor to
Washington in the spring of 1968. The climate seemed to them
clearly wrong; the riot commission's fifteen-city poll that season
showed that more than a fourth of the whites were against even
orderly civil-rights marches and fully a third could see no
difference between nonviolent protest and rioting.

Abernathy's improbable little commune, in the event, was
never so menacing as all that, though—like any slum—it did
have its subculture of hoods, j.d.'s and street-corner revolutionaries and its nightly log of brawling and petty crime. Everything
seemed to conspire against its success. SCLC, which had always
run its enterprises with a spontaneity verging on whimsy, threw
this one together too quickly after King's death, out of a
stricken sense that they owed it to him to go on. "The Lord will
provide," staffers said and shrugged whenever the logistics got
sticky. But the Lord's terrestrial agents couldn't get the encampment of A-frame huts ready in time. Ditches for temporary
water and sewer lines were only half dug when the first settlers
arrived, and a record May rainy season shortly left them ankle-
deep in muck. The ethnic minorities fell to squabbling: The
Mexicans, who wanted to push some land claims, and the
Indians, who were interested mainly in fishing rights, were
irritated because, as one of them complained, SCLC's blacks

kept harping on "jobs, jobs, jobs." The goals of the march meandered dizzyingly over 49 pages. "What can we do for you?" one Congressional staff man nervously asked a visiting deputation of the poor. "That's the question," a black high school dropout from Buffalo shot back. "What can you do for us?"

Washington, as it developed, was not really disposed to do anything, especially anything that might cost money. Resurrection City, for all its internal dissonances, had its moments, and none more affecting than a one-day outpouring of 50,000 marchers at the foot of Abraham Lincoln's Memorial. There, Coretta King stood in the deepening dusk, eyes flashing, and read the peroration of her husband's great "I Have a Dream" speech of five years before; and Ralph Abernathy, bobbing and rocking behind the lectern, promised again to plague the pharaohs until the poor were delivered from bondage. But the pharaohs seemed not so much inspired as relieved that Washington was still standing when the 50,000 day-trippers left town—and hopeful that Resurrection City would soon follow them out. So—WHAT NOW? the tabloid Washington *Daily News* headlined the next day. Resurrection City, sad to say, had no idea; it just stayed there, its days increasingly aimless and its nights increasingly violent, until its permit ran out. Then, on a drizzly, sauna-hot June morning, Abernathy lined up 250 surviving settlers—some with squalling babies in their arms, others lugging whatever gear they could carry—and led them out of the compound on one last maundering march to Capitol Hill and then to jail. They left 124 others staying stubbornly on in Resurrection City, some protesting the end of the affair, some dug in because Resurrection City—as woebegone as it seemed to strangers—still beat any place they had ever lived. ("I ain't worried about *ever* leavin'," one old black told an SCLC man. "I never owned my own home before.") But helmeted police moved in and herded them off to jail, too, and the next morning wrecking crews hammered Resurrection City flat in a matter of hours.

The moment was full of poignant symbolism for black Americans—a suggestion that a watershed passage in their history was indeed drawing to a close. What the era of parades had provided for countless thousands of Negroes was an opportunity, rare in history, to become the movers and not just the objects of history—and, rarer still, to move history nonviolently. The common effort swept up enormous numbers of them. As they told it to the *Newsweek* Poll, one in four had boycotted a store in the cause; one in five had joined a protest march; one in ten had sat in or picketed; one in twenty-five—perhaps the most extraordinary figure of all—claimed to have gone to jail for Negro rights. It does not matter if the vagaries of memory or of ego led some blacks to say they had involved themselves in action when they had not; the point was that so many felt impelled to say that they had—to assert, in effect, a place in the history of their time. And a far larger number looked back on the protest style of the 1950's and 1960's and found it good. Seven out of ten believed that all the picketing, the sitting in, the selective buying and the treadmill trips to jail had helped the black man's cause.

Yet the glow was beginning to rub off; *Newsweek*'s Poll showed the first telling signs of disaffection from the activist tactics that had worked so well in the Jim Crow South. The number who thought those tactics had helped in the past was as stubbornly high as ever. But the number who declared themselves ready to join in in the future took a sudden and revealing dip:

THE ACTIVISTS: READY OR NOT

	1963	1966	1969
WOULD YOU:			
Sit in	49	52	40
March	51	54	44
Picket	46	49	41
Boycott a store	62	69	57
Go to jail	47	45	33

The figures show an enormous ready reserve still prepared for action—a pool that is, predictably, largest of all among the young and the middle class, North and South, who have always provided the revolution with most of its foot soldiers. But the tail-off nevertheless commands attention. The number available to march or sit in—a majority of black America in the middle '60's—was suddenly a minority. And only a third even claimed to be prepared to go to jail for Negro equality; it cost nothing to *say* yes, but the old glory had plainly diminished since King, CORE and SNCC were filling jailhouses to the bursting point in the backwater South.

Why the slide? The poll strongly suggests that it owed neither to contentment nor to resignation among Negroes but to precisely those doubts that so shadowed King's last days: the suspicion that no one could any longer guarantee that black protest would stay nonviolent. The defections from the pool of activists were by far largest in the ghetto North, which was, of course, where the most shattering riots had happened, and where demonstrations of the old sort accordingly took on a deepening edge of menace.

That edge, in fact, had become the basis of a whole new politics of protest in the latter 1960's—an activism no longer aimed at the white man's conscience (the younger militants doubt that he has one) but at his darkest fears. The watchword more and more among the activists was Malcolm X's studiedly ambiguous call to the liberation of the blacks *by any means necessary.* The implied threat was exactly the point; the militants were gambling that the white establishment, in a setting as combustible as the American city of the 1960's, could be frightened just enough to make concessions rather than risk a Watts or a Detroit. The object of the game for most of its players was not, as so many whites imagined, to promote riots but to keep America from forgetting that riots do happen. One of them happened when the police routed a clamorous welfare mothers' sit-in in Boston's Roxbury ghetto in 1967, and two

years later George Wiley, who wouldn't dream of urging anyone to throw a bottle or a brick, could observe mildly, "Well, I
think the question of riots and disorder and tensions in the
ghettos have made the welfare agencies much more responsive
to the welfare-rights movement—no question about that."

The risk, of course, runs two ways. No one on either side
could tell when, or whether, the number of provocations would
pass from some tolerable x to some intolerable $x + 1$ at which
point white repression of blacks might begin. The militants
took this possibility very seriously; many of them were quite
persuaded that the nation had already prepared concentration
camps for the blacks and might in fact be planning some more
final solution still. They kept pressing toward the limits of
toleration anyway, since the alternative as they saw it—acquiescence in the status quo—seemed to them so much worse.
Some of the foot soldiers of the Negro revolt were not ready to
press so far with them, as the poll figures plainly suggest. But
there remained plenty who would, particularly among the
ghetto young. So, increasingly in the late 1960's, demonstrators
disrupted meetings and hearings, blockaded schools, occupied
building sites, traded in the rhetoric of violence and occasionally helped stir violence in fact. The new style in a sense still
presented the Negro as victim. Now, however, the victim was
no longer displaying his scars but his pent-up wrath—and the
possibility that it might not stay pent up very much longer.

The victim, moreover, was sometimes the most favored
Negro of all by the standards of many of his prerevolutionary
elders: the black college student. There were more of them
than ever before, 434,000 of a total college population of 7.1
million, by the end of the decade—a figure that owed partly to
the rapid growth of the Negro middle class and partly to an
access of conscience that moved white universities to admit and
even to recruit substantial numbers of blacks for the first time.
And suddenly, in the late 1960's, the campuses became the
battlegrounds of the black revolt—in psychiatrist Price Cobbs's
phrase, "the dusty Southern towns of today."

The sparks flew first on a series of all-Negro campuses in Dixie—at Fisk, Tennessee A & I, Jackson (Mississippi) State and Texas Southern in the spring of 1967 and in Orangeburg, South Carolina, the following winter, when state troopers fired into a crowd of demonstrating South Carolina State and Claflin College students, killing three and wounding twenty-seven. But the rebellion soon spread to the mostly white campuses of the North and West as well. Blacks led the long, bitter and sporadically violent strike that afflicted San Francisco State College for most of the 1968–69 school year and made its hard-lining president, S. I. Hayakawa, a folk hero for California conservatives. Black demonstrations closed City College of New York briefly and set off three days of brawling between white and Negro students. Blacks at Brandeis and at Duke occupied buildings and proclaimed them Malcolm X universities; Brandeis's MXU departed peaceably after eleven days of negotiation but Duke's was evicted by court order and routed by police billies and tear gas. A classroom boycott at Wisconsin started to turn nasty, and National Guardsmen were ordered in to break up bands of strikers at bayonet point. Images of the revolt filled newspaper front pages and television screens—and none to such chilling effect as the sight of a little platoon of blacks ending the overnight occupation of Cornell's administration building, Willard Straight Hall, and marching out with rifles, shotguns and bandoliers of bullets. Nothing they said after that mattered —not their protests that they had gone in unarmed and had sent for their guns only when they were under attack and in fear for their lives; not even the fact that they never actually fired a shot. All that seemed to count were the pictures of blacks with guns—the victim armed and balefully angry—and their psychic impact was electrifying.

Those pictures measured the distance events had run since the romantic beginnings of the black student movement in the sit-in campaigns of 1960. The sit-ins, said black political scientist Charles V. Hamilton, co-author (with Stokely Carmichael) of the book *Black Power*, were "the first time on a massive scale that students in this country took the lead in anything—except, of course, for those white students who were active in the '30's." That first wave, he noted, tended to be religious, integrationist, raised on Gandhi and King and dedicated to a brotherhood of man that transcended color. "Their tactics were always to be neat, polite and nonviolent. When you sit in at Woolworth's, take your Plato and, by all means, wear a shirt and tie. This gained the support of a large segment of white America: who can fault a cat with shined shoes?

"But then," Hamilton went on, "something happened to begin the transformation to radicalism; the students began to question not only the system but their own tactics." The turning point, as he saw it, came when several hundred white students came South for the SNCC-CORE "Freedom Summer" campaign in Mississippi in 1964—an experiment in brotherhood that abraded the radical black kids while it lasted and which ended in bitter disappointment when the Democratic National Convention refused to give Mississippi's seats to a mostly black challenge delegation of "Freedom Democrats." Thereafter, Hamilton told *Newsweek*, many black students started questioning the legitimacy of The System itself—a disenchantment that accelerated with Carmichael's fiery Black Power circuit-rides of 1966. "Today, they're understanding that they are black," said Hamilton. "And . . . they are not going to be made into little middle-class black Sambos." This central proposition came out, on campus after campus, in the form of "nonnegotiable demands" for black studies programs, more black teachers and students, even black-only dormitories—a new metaphysics of blackness that tended to confuse whites and to blur what Hamilton took to be the central point of it all: "The black-student movement today wants 'in' in the same sense that those kids wanted it in 1960 . . . They're not saying, 'We want to throw over the university.' They're saying simply, 'We want to make it over.' "

Negroes on balance tended to support their young in this enterprise; they believed (by 40 to 32 per cent) that the campus demonstrations were helping their larger cause, with the young leading the cheers and the oldest and poorest blacks—those who rarely got to colleges except to pick up after the white folks who attended them—inclined to disapprove. But the new edge that Cornell put on the campus revolt troubled blacks as well as whites. Demonstrating on campus was one thing, demonstrating with guns quite another—a last symbolic leap for which few blacks were prepared and which an enormous 81-to-11 majority accordingly condemned.

But nearly a fourth of the young, North and South, approved—a martial minority more than adequate to reproduce Cornell a hundred times over. And there were quite enough of them as well to lend an air of implied menace to all the proliferating militant crusades for construction jobs, for welfare rights, for black police and principals, for public-housing rent reductions, for the whole cluster of demands summed up by the phrase "community control."

Or for reparations. James Forman, a thickset, bristly-haired SNCC veteran, put that word into the vocabulary of the Negro revolt one spring Sunday in 1969 when he interrupted a worship service at an uptown Manhattan church and demanded $500 million (or, later, $3 billion) from the nation's white religious establishment in payment for black America's tragic past—the money to be channeled into some specified black economic and community development programs. The idea was not a new one; the concept of a compensatory effort to help Negroes toward real equality was implied in much of the social legislation of the 1960's and in the programs the old-line moderates had been urging for years—in Bayard Rustin's $185 billion "Freedom Budget," for example, or Whitney Young's "Domestic Marshall Plan." ("I said it politely," Young remarked sourly in the midst of the furor over Forman's demands. "I didn't disrupt services. And nothing happened.") What was new was the calculated shock effect of its presentation. "We are demanding $500 million from the Christian white churches and the Jewish synagogues," said the "Black Manifesto" Forman

read at Riverside Church that morning. "This total comes to
$15 per nigger . . . $15 a nigger is not a large sum of money."
The means were quite straightforwardly spelled out: "We call
upon black people to commence the disruption of the racist
churches and synagogues throughout the United States. . . .
We are not saying that [the use of force] is the road we want
to take. It is not, but let us be very clear that we are not
opposed to force and we are not opposed to violence."

Forman's call did set a good many local activist groups plunk-
ing down, disruptively or merely demonstratively, in churches
and church offices around the nation. Yet the real point was
how surprisingly little actual disrupting it took, in the anxious
atmosphere of that spring and summer, to jolt the churches and
synagogues into examining their consciences—and their
budgets. Not many, in the end, gave to Forman and his
colleagues from the Black Economic Development Conference.
But a few did (their biggest score was a $200,000 appropriation
voted them indirectly by the Episcopal Church) and others got
the message, whatever they thought of the medium. "The
churches Forman goes to respond with 'No, never, it's illogical,
it's blackmail,'" remarked Julian Bond, a young man with a
fine-grained sense of irony, "but as soon as he leaves, they increase their commitments to black organizations and community works by a factor of five." A good many moderates
accordingly approved of what Forman had wrought. ("He
should be sainted," said SCLC's Hosea Williams. "When Jesus
Christ went into the temple and saw the money changers, He
brutalized them, and Mr. Forman didn't hit a soul.") And a
good many militants imitated him. George Wiley and some of
his welfare mothers briefly took over a social workers' convention in New York and demanded $35,000; the social workers
said they would try to raise it. Roy Innis and twenty COREs-
men walked in on a bankers' conference in Chicago and
threatened to declare a "warlike situation" unless the bankers
paid six billion dollars in "recoupment . . . for years of oppression"; they didn't.

Reparations, for white America, was an idea whose time had not yet come; a Gallup Poll that summer showed a staggering 94-to-2 majority of whites against Forman's demands on the churches. And the manner of its presentation tended further to blur the line between lawful protest and unlawful violence. Forman had pressed the new militancy a step further, from the implicit threat that violence might happen spontaneously to an explicit threat that it might be consciously employed as a tactic. The fact that Forman and his people didn't actually get violent seemed to count as little in the public mind as the fact that the Cornell rebels hadn't used their guns. It was quite upsetting enough to whites that blacks said they might embrace violence, whether or not they did. Whites by then were too nervous and the ghettos too volatile for many people to draw or even to care very much about the distinctions.

Yet distinctions were still worth drawing, and, late in 1969, President Johnson's commission on violence made the attempt in a report on the contagion of extralegal protest activities by both blacks and whites. The commission considered violent tactics beyond the pale of the democratic process. "It is group protest, not group violence," said the report, amending Rap Brown's dictum, "that is as American as cherry pie." But it went on to observe that protest often turns violent when the hopes of a minority are continually frustrated and when its efforts to press its claims by peaceful means go begging. "What is essential," said the report, "is that when the basic justice of the underlying grievance is clear, an effort to take suitable measures of accommodation and correction must be made. The effort must be made even though other groups feel threatened by the proposed correction, and even though they may resort to violence to prevent it. We cannot 'insure domestic tranquillity' unless we 'establish justice'—in a democratic society one is impossible without the other."

Negroes, as it happened, took their cause into the streets in the 1950's and 1960's not so much because that was their choice as because so few other choices seemed available to them. Black people by and large would much prefer to press their claims as American minorities historically have, through the tidier processes of politics. But those processes for decades were closed to them by law and chicanery in the South and made all but meaningless in the North by a feudal politics built on the apathy, the disorganization and the powerlessness of the black community. Only late in the 1960's, with the voter-registration books opened at last in Dixie and the great cities of the North beginning to go black, did the real possibilities of politics as a means of redress even begin to flower and bear fruit for Negroes. By then, for some of the young, it was probably too late. "As far as I'm concerned," said Fred Hubbard, a tall, well-muscled black anti-machine alderman in Chicago, "politics is where it's really at. But the younger people feel it's too slow a way of bringing about change. And they question whether political position for a black man will ever really bring about change in the white society." What counted for most Negroes, however, was the mere fact that black men *could* seriously aspire to and win political position—an enspiriting discovery even if it did not bring the millennium perceptibly closer to hand.

The first tokens of victory were visible everywhere. Black power sometimes became reality only at the pleasure of white people; so it was, for example, when Lyndon Johnson—a man who understood the very real importance of gestures—named one Negro to his Cabinet and another to the Supreme Court; so, too, when Massachusetts sent Edward Brooke, a Republican moderate of considerable ability and charm, to the U.S. Senate. Yet the real tests of the future of blacks in politics were being run at less exalted levels—in local, state-legislative and Congressional races, where a new generation of black politicians began to practice a new and unabashedly color-conscious style of black politics. And, by the late 1960's, they were making it work.

In the South, in the first four years under the Voting Rights Act of 1965, the number of registered black voters doubled—and the number of elected black officeholders shot up seven-fold. "The Movement *means* political participation," said Charles Evers, the black mayor of Fayette, Mississippi, and one of the principal agents of the new thrust. "We've got to *become* these constables that used to beat us and the sheriff who used to arrest us. We've got to organize for power—not on hate but on working together." Across the Old Confederacy—particularly in the cities and in those Black Belt counties and towns where they were in the majority—blacks began doing precisely that; some few of them did become constables or sheriffs or state representatives or county supervisors or school-board members—or even mayors. The style, if not the sub-stance, of Southern white politics changed glacially to accom-modate them; few statewide candidates dared court Negro votes openly, but even George Wallace learned to say "knee-grow" or even "black people" in public. And Dixie's black Democrats made themselves increasingly visible in the party's national councils. The 1964 Mississippi Freedom Democratic challenge was indeed a failure, measured against the ideals of the children who lodged it, but it did force the Democracy to make a start at democratizing itself. The 1968 convention in Chicago, whatever its shortcomings as a model of open political processes at work, seated a good many blacks from the South, Mississippi in-cluded, and it briefly, if not quite seriously, entertained the nomination of Julian Bond, then an under-age two-term Georgia state legislator, for Vice President of the United States.

The black politics of the North was going through equally profound and promising change. The black caucus in Congress once consisted of Adam Clayton Powell of Harlem, a prodigally talented man who made a politics out of the pleasure principle, and William Dawson of Chicago, an old-school machine pol distinguished mainly for his mutually rewarding alliance with Mayor Richard Daley. By the end of the '60's, however, the number of blacks had grown from two to nine, and the change was more than skin deep. The new black Congressmen—men like Detroit's John Conyers and St. Louis's William Clay—were as tough, as shrewd and as fiercely ambitious as the Powells and the Dawsons. But they owed their position only to themselves and the ghetto. "They're people identified with the black movement," said Clay, who fought his way up through CORE and the rotting politics of St. Louis's Negro wards. "Formerly they had to be acceptable to whites. Now they have to be acceptable to blacks." And, since they were men with no illusions, they did not attempt to trade in illusion. "I've never felt black people had any more reason to have confidence in the political process than white people," said Conyers, an imperturbably smooth young man who, by seniority and sheer presence, is the de facto leader of the new breed. "And God knows white people don't have much confidence in it. But we've just begun to develop an appreciation of making it work."

What was beginning to make it work was the swelling black population of America's central cities—a fact of life that Negroes neither willed nor wanted but which had its political uses. The real vanguard black politicians of the latter 1960's were not so much the Ed Brookes and the John Conyerses as men like Carl Stokes of Cleveland and Richard Hatcher of Gary, Indiana—the first of what was almost certain to become a wave of black mayors in the aging central cities of the North and West. There weren't enough black votes in the cities to control their politics—not yet. Stokes and Hatcher won only by putting together precarious coalitions of the nearly unanimous Negroes and a relatively few sympathetic middle-class whites; Stokes's second-term victory in 1969, indeed, was very nearly as squeaky and as difficult to bring off as his first, despite a solid record of achievement and the real affection of the city's white civic establishment. And other cities weren't ready to go that far. In Los Angeles, Thomas Bradley, a Negro ex-cop who was moderate to the point of blandness, challenged Mayor Sam Yorty and led for a time—until Yorty scared the white majority into line by identifying Bradley with militancy, riots and Negro crime. Other black candidates lost in Detroit, Houston and Atlanta (though Atlanta did elect a Negro vice mayor). But the racial balance in the cities was tipping; several will turn black in the 1970's and 1980's, and their politics presumably will follow. "We have," Conyers observed mildly, "a challenging political future."

Negroes found the prospect exciting. The first successes established Bond and Stokes particularly as authentic heroes of the black revolt, with extraordinarily wide circles of admirers, considering that one was a Southern state representative and the other the mayor of a Midwestern city. When their names came up on the *Newsweek* Poll's list of Negro leaders and organizations (see Chapter 2), Bond was rated excellent by 25 per cent and Stokes by 21 per cent; only the NAACP and Ralph Abernathy among the living did better. (Gary's Mayor Hatcher was not nearly so well known but those blacks who knew of him admired him by better than two to one.) Bond especially attracted Negro America's most activist elements, the young and the middle class—perhaps because of his own past in The Movement (he came out of SNCC in its radical integrationist period) or perhaps simply because he was himself so young, so well mannered, so bright and so stunningly good-looking on television in the bargain.

Far more significant than the personal popularity ratings of three black politicians, however, was what the figures told about the continuing depth of Negro America's commitment to work within the conventional processes of politics. This has been a matter of considerable debate in the black community, with radical intellectuals arguing increasingly that blacks ought to move outside The System and try either to manipulate it somehow to their own advantage or to destroy it. Ernest Chambers, a tough young militant who dropped out of law school to run a barber shop and a grass-roots political revolt in

Omaha, declared for an at-large seat on the city council, knowing, so he said later, that he would lose. "The way I see it," said Chambers, "by participating in the primary and other elections, this would establish a record of our attempts to use their system to bring about solutions to the problems. When we show that all of the peaceful methods have brought no change, then our alternatives will be narrowed to the one that has not been tried—violence."

This is, of course, an enduring revolutionary dream, but it bore little resemblance to the majority will of black Americans. "They look at politics as a tool—not a perfect tool, but any group of people are foolish to ignore a potential source of aid and comfort," Bond remarked. "When I say politics, I'm thinking about having somebody in office who cares about me, and I think that's the way black and poor people think about it." So, indeed, the poll suggested. The number of blacks who disapproved the three political figures on the survey list ranged from Hatcher's 10 per cent to Stokes's 14—one rough measure of how deep the much advertised vein of discouragement with the existing political process actually ran. And there was a closer gauge still: Only 10 per cent thought Negroes ought to operate politically as a separate group outside the two parties—to 68 per cent who felt they ought to stay inside.

This commitment had thinned a bit since 1966; its appeal remained strongest among the most conservative groups—the Southerners, the old and the poor—but roughly a fifth of the middle class and the young in the Northern ghettos opted for an all-black politics. "We need political power," said an 18-year-old Pittsburgh youth, "and that's the only way to get it, instead of working in these antiquated joke systems." Yet even in the ghetto the overriding impulse was to stay inside the major parties. There was a trace of paranoia in this judgment (a Harlem janitor thought Negroes ought to stick "so we can hear what is being said about us") and a healthy strain of pragmatism as well (a Pittsburgh shoe salesman voted for staying because "the white man has got the power"). But most of all, the blacks, after three and a half centuries on the outside, were chary of anyone who promised them salvation through separation. "I don't want a separate *anything*," a 44-year-old maid in Rockford, Illinois, said. "I just want to be an American."

The real peril for the blacks, indeed, lay in expecting too much of The System—an expectation that was almost certain to betray them. The most important single fact about Negroes in American party politics is that they are stubbornly, incorrigibly Democratic: they cast 68 per cent of their votes for John Kennedy, 94 per cent for Lyndon Johnson and 85 per cent for Hubert Humphrey. An edge of cynicism crept into the relationship, particularly among the young, as the Democratic commitment to the blacks seemed to waver in the late 1960's; the number of Negroes who considered themselves Democrats was suddenly a good deal larger than the number who really believed that the Democracy would do the most to help Negroes. Yet black America remained 76 per cent Democratic—as high as at any time during the 1960's. And though the affiliation was reasonable enough, given all the attention the Democrats had paid the blacks, it left the Negro community painfully vulnerable. The Democratic Party could become for them, as it had for other beleaguered American minorities, a source of jobs, prestige and power at the local level. But their deep party loyalty tended to mark them in national politics as the special wards of the Democracy—a fact that was by no means lost on the strategists of a victory-hungry GOP.

The Barry Goldwater campaign of 1964 tried prematurely and ineptly to exploit that fact; Goldwater did manage to steal the Deep South from the Democrats, largely on the votes of whites who were nervous about desegregation and creeping federalism, but he frightened the rest of America into a record Democratic landslide. Richard Nixon and his strategists—his friend, law partner and Attorney General–to-be John N. Mitchell notable among them—learned from that experience, and *their* Southern Strategy for 1968 was quite another matter. George Wallace by then was at play in the machinery of Presidential politics, promising surcease from Negro demands and Negro violence in his own transparent code: "Some *bureau*crats tellin' folks, 'You don't know where to send your child to school so we gonna write some *guide*lines for you.' . . . Well, when *I* get to be President, I'm gonna call in a bunch of *bureau*crats and take away their briefcases and throw 'em in the Potomac Rivuh." Nixon and Mitchell understood that they could not compete with Wallace for deepest Dixie, whose affection for Lost Causes had not dimmed in the hundred years since Appomattox. But they sensed rich possibilities in the Upper South and Florida, and, partly through the agency of South Carolina's Republican Senator Strom Thurmond, they got it across that a Nixon Administration would not push school desegregation too hard or appoint any more liberal activists to the Supreme Court. And they tapped the discontents of the "forgotten Americans" of the North and West with a law-and-order campaign that was nearly as simplistic as Wallace's (Nixon proposed to reduce crime by replacing Ramsey Clark as Attorney General) but ever so much more mannerly. The coalition held together, and it elected Richard Nixon President.

More portentous still for Negro Americans, it suggested a course of strategy that could keep the Presidency Republican for a generation—precisely by isolating the Democrats as the party of the blacks and building the rickety Nixon coalition of 1968 into a true majority of the white center. The principal exponent of this view was a young Harvard-trained lawyer and psephology buff named Kevin Phillips, who worked in the Nixon campaign, followed Mitchell afterward to the Justice Department as a resident braintruster and soon published *The Emerging Republican Majority*—a book proclaiming the advent of a "conservative cycle of American politics" and proposing ways for the GOP to put it to use. He was careful early on to announce that the study "does *not* purport to set forth the past strategies or future intentions of Richard M. Nixon," and the President himself mentioned at a press conference that he had not read it. But Washington noted nevertheless that Phillips had dedicated the work to the new majority "and its two principal architects"—Nixon and Mitchell—and so took the book to be a reasonably authoritative statement of which way the political winds were blowing.

They were not blowing black America's way. Phillips clearly bore Negroes no ill will; it was just that he felt the GOP could get along quite nicely without them. The figure that intrigued him in the 1968 returns was not the 43 per cent of the vote Nixon got but the 57 per cent he divided with Wallace—a rich vein of white power available for tapping by the Republicans, in part because of the love affair between the blacks and the Democrats. "The upcoming cycle of American politics," Phillips wrote, "is likely to match a dominant Republican Party based in the Heartland, South and California against a minority Democratic Party based in the Northeast and the Pacific Northwest (and encompassing Southern as well as Northern Negroes)." The Administration's effort in 1969 to dilute the Voting Rights Act clearly was not Phillips's idea; he argued, quite to the contrary, that the Republicans had a stake in keeping Negroes voting in the South—and thus accelerating the flight of conservative whites from a rapidly blackening Democratic Party. The business of the book was not to draw morals about any of this. Phillips was a technocrat among technocrats, and he followed his numbers where they led him. "Obviously," he concluded, "the GOP can build a winning coalition without Negro votes."

Politics, of course, is rarely so tidy a business as people who spend their days reading bar graphs and census reports imagine. Yet there was something chillingly credible in Phillips's vision. Nor was there great comfort for black people in the fact that, as Phillips himself pointed out, the local Democratic politics of the cities remained wide open to them. The cities—already heavily dependent on help from Washington—are getting poorer as they get blacker, and this central fact tarnished the prize for the new Negro politicians just as they were about to come into their legacy. "The guys who say we'll never be able to work it out within The System are all wrong," John Conyers told *Newsweek*'s Richard Stout. "How do we *know* we can't? We've never been in The System." What The System was about to deliver to the blacks, however, was a cityscape of deepening poverty and decay, shrinking tax resources, rising demand for public services and a chronic potential for explosion. The cities as a consequence would need a friend at court in Washington more than ever—a friendship that neither the first months of Richard Nixon nor the Republican future as limned by Kevin Phillips seemed to promise them. "I don't like Nixon and Nixon don't like me," a Denver factory worker told the *Newsweek* Poll. "He ain't going to do nothing to help me." A two-to-one majority of black America tended to agree—and the judgment, if it proved true, was one of the gravest moment.

Gary's Mayor Hatcher went on a fund-hunting trip to Washington in those early days of Nixon's management. It did not go well, and his mood at the end of a long day, as he tried to unwind in his fourth-floor room at the Hilton, was gloomy. "I know a little more about life than I did a year and a half ago," he said—meaning the day in 1967 when 99 per cent of Gary's black voters combined with 10 per cent of the whites to send him to city hall. "I'm not nearly as optimistic as I was. You're placed in a terrible position of telling people, 'I know we can get something, I *know* we can get it,' and each time coming back empty-handed." He paused. "You know, the power brokers in this country really make a mistake. Gary could be turned into a showplace. They could point to Gary and say, 'Look, all you have to do is go through the election process and you'll get results.' But if Gary is allowed to fail—if it is starved for Federal programs—young people will say, 'Look at Hatcher—what's he been able to do about all those ADC mothers who are starving? What's he been able to do about getting those slums torn down?' If they're able to say that . . ."

His voice trailed off, and he shook his head; he knew quite well what the consequences could be. "We're running out of peaceful techniques," he said. "There will be more and more demands, more and more disruptions of conferences, disruptions of programs, disruptions of services. Black people may not have the power to change their lives, but they do have the power to deny peace to the larger society." There was no trace of threat in Hatcher's voice—only a heavy melancholy. Sometimes, listening to the burners, he had thought to himself, *Maybe the only difference between myself and them is one of time. Maybe in time I'll come to that.* But mostly he labored to make The System work. "It *can* work," he said, his red tie loose, his collar open, his back slumped against a picture-window view of the deepening Washington twilight. "If I didn't believe it would work, I wouldn't be mayor. I still believe it.

"But," he added slowly, "not as strongly as I did a year ago."

Black Americans believe in The System, too; they have always preferred the orderly processes of politics, law and diplomacy to the chancy tactic of protest in the streets. But their confidence in the outcome, like Hatcher's, has begun to flicker a bit, and they do not have the luxury of a wide choice of weapons.

Could whites in the end be persuaded to treat Negroes better because it is right—or would they come around only when they are forced to by black action? There were more voices for persuasion than for action in the 1969 poll, as there had been throughout the revolutionary '60's. But what had been a robust 51 to 24 majority view in 1966 had become a much nearer thing—a 46 to 34 split decision. And far more meaningful was the fact that the balance of sentiment actually *had* tipped from persuasion to action among the youngest blacks in the North and the South—precisely the generation from which most of the action flows. The refusal of the black young to acquiesce in the way things are for Negroes has been one of the decade's most heartening developments. But, if the young give up on the possibilities of persuasion, the consequences for the American future will not necessarily be happy; the action in years to come, whatever form it takes, is not likely to be so gentle as Resurrection City. "There are those," mused psychiatrist Alvin Poussaint, "who honestly believe that the only way to change is to shake things up—that strange situation in this country where it seems that great social progress comes only after great social action. Forman, the universities, the riots. I wish it weren't so. But maybe they're right."

DIRECTIONS:

Jesse Jackson

"I'm just a country preacher," the Reverend Jesse Louis Jackson is fond of telling strangers, slurring the words South Carolina-style. Everything about him says it isn't so: the thickening Afro hair, the temple-to-jaw sideburns, the green turtleneck, the tight gray bells, the desert boots, the soft and vaguely sulky good looks. But put him in front of an audience and it comes suddenly and marvelously true. He is a country preacher, his text the 24th Psalm ("The earth is the Lord's and the fullness thereof") and his message a call to the wretched of the Lord's earth to claim it in His name. Jackson bore that message from Chicago, where he directs SCLC's successful boycott arm, Operation Breadbasket, to Peoria during a spring 1969 circuit ride against hunger in Illinois. His sermon that night to a packed house of 1,500 in a community center free-associated breathtakingly from public policy to private vision and back, but it ended as it always does: "I am somebody. . . . I can see, I can hear, I can feel, I can touch! . . . I am—"

"I am—" the audience responded.

"Somebody!" shouted Jackson.

"SOMEBODY!" thundered the crowd.

"I may be poor . . . but I am—"

"I am—"

"Somebody!"

"SOMEBODY!"

"I may be black . . . but I am—"

"I am—"

"Somebody!"

"SOMEBODY!"

Late that night, Richard Stout, Martin Weston and Jeff Harding of Newsweek found Jackson spent and sleepless in his room at the Imperial 400 Motel. He had stripped down to a blue undershirt and a pair of green shorts and flopped on the bed, his head propped up against the headboard. He was not completely over a case of mononucleosis; retainers fussed about, wishing he would take something for it. "I don't want any of those pills or anything," Jackson said. "There's just one thing I need—rest." He sounded wheezy. But he started talking; the session was not properly speaking a conversation or even an interview but a soliloquy that tumbled on past 2 A.M.

A psychological revolution was going on in black America, Jackson said—a movement beyond survival to resistance. "As I grew up in the Old South," he said, "the whole thing was how much you could endure, and how long you could last, and your manhood was in measure determined by your capacity to endure the stress without breaking. Now the change is how well you can resist, and that's a qualitative adjustment. . . . Fifteen years ago, we were operating, as Du Bois would say, behind a veil. We were alive and we were climbing, but we were in a pit behind a veil. The world outside of us was moving, and we saw it, and we knew we could not reach our fingers through the veil. And the effect of Dr. King's era was that, in our marching, we marched down that veil. One has to understand that it was a psychological veil that was held up by military suppression and economic denial; that is, it was held up by fear. But in the Montgomery movement and the sit-ins and the Birmingham movement and the Selma movement, we developed an inner power that could absorb beatings and jail cells. For we could suffer, and rather than the sight of our blood frightening us, it began to inspire us, and that blood began to fertilize the soil." Jackson shifted heavily on the bed. "The simple object then

was that men could ride anyplace on a bus and we couldn't—
therefore we were not considered men. Men could eat anyplace
or recreate anyplace and we couldn't—therefore we were not
considered men. Men could vote when they were twenty-one
and we couldn't—therefore we were not considered men. We
marched until those redefinitions took place. And so the veil
is down, and we can touch the world we've only seen."

The far harder task now was to move into that world, not
singly but as a people among peoples, and this required first
that blacks become a people. "The continuity between our root
in Africa and our fruit in America has been broken," he said,
"and in part we are now trying to establish it. Because when
there's a gap between the root and the fruit—when it's broken—
that is death." He pushed himself up into a sitting position.
"There's a strong move now for ethnic assertion on the part of
the black man. It is a move toward independence as opposed to
separation. Independence means just what it says—non-depend-
ence. It means you control at least the vital elements of your
life: your school boards, your church, your cultural tastes and
habits, and your holy days—the days you set aside to maintain
some continuity with your history en route to your destiny."

A trace of fire flashed in Jackson's heavy-lidded eyes. "When
we say we want independence, people say, 'Well, y'all want to
be separate.' Well, we're already separate, and we didn't do the
separating, and we did not have the power to do the integrating.
The fact is the white community is separate. The difference is
that they are separate and independent, and we are separate and
dependent. They control us. And that is what you would call
the state of colonialism. What the sociologists traditionally call
the ghetto, we now know to be a colony. And when you understand that your problem is colonialism, you ask for independence. As opposed to moving toward horizontal integration, you
move toward vertical liberation." He saw no necessity for deny-
ing The Movement's past to arrive at this view of its future.
"All the great freedom leaders knew we were evolving toward

higher levels of understanding. The analogy that Dr. King used to use all the time was that it was like going around a mountain. And for a while you'd be going toward the city, and as you'd rise up the mountain, you could see the city very clearly. But then you'd go around a curve and you couldn't see the city— same as if you were going away from it. But the fact that you were dynamic and still moving, you were just that much closer to the city . . .

"Today," he went on, slumping down on the bed again, "we are at the point where the children of Israel escaped Egypt, and before they could move too far economically and politically, Moses had to ask the question, 'Who am I?' Who are we as a people? What are our historic roots? What is our purpose, what is our role? Are we beautiful? Are we really ugly? Or did we just see our faces reflected in dirty water?" And today, too, he thought, black people were beginning to ask questions, and demand answers, of the larger society. "There is," said Jackson, "nothing essentially wrong with airplanes flying from New York to Chicago in an hour and fifteen minutes, but there's something terribly wrong with making an abundance of those planes while you fly over rats in Harlem. There's something terribly wrong with paying a white girl who is nothing but a waitress in the air $200 a week and allowing her to live in first-rate hotels when a black woman does the same job and works even harder down on the ground, and she can't make $40 a week and lives from rat to rat. There's something wrong with a society that produces doctors whose value commitment is more to personal wealth than public health; lawyers more concerned about a judgeship than justice; a teacher who teaches for a living rather than for life. Black power at its best is not jealous of white power—it is sick of white power and seeks to become an antidote to it. As I guess Du Bois would have said, it is unfair for people who are in a struggle for their own survival to accept the priorities of somebody else's agenda."

The form of black power that absorbed Jackson, and Breadbasket, was buying power—the critical margin between profit and loss for a whole range of products from salt to sports cars. "To have that power and not know it," Jackson said, "is to be exploited. But to realize it is to begin to make demands in relationship to that power, and therefore, in feeling ourselves and in seeing new things, we become a new people. Because power has a way, though it may be crude and brash and young, of forcing doors to remain open. And impotence has a way of always being told, 'Just wait a while longer.' "

Jesse Jackson plainly is not the waiting sort. "America," he said, "is nothing but a giant economic corporation that was built by both slaves and slavemasters, and for the slaves now to go to the bank and be told that no money's there for them and they know they're living in the richest nation in history—a $900 billion GNP moving toward $1 trillion—is to create an adverse reaction." He smiled faintly at the understatement. "Riots are inevitable, and other forms of discontent. And riots may be considered illegal, by virtue of the laws established by men who make laws for their own interest, but riots are not illegitimate. Riots are real. They are reactions to the pain and the frustration and the sense of hopelessness that exists among the people. And the only antidote to their cry for education is education. The only antidote to their cry for a job or an income is money or a job. The only answer to their cry for respect is respect, and recognition."

All at once he was sitting up again. "Fifteen years ago," he said, "we wouldn't have been involved in a poor people's campaign, because we didn't think we had the right to eat if we couldn't work and didn't own the farm. Now we know that this land is our land. From a social point of view and a theological point of view, it's God's land. Rockefeller and that bunch didn't discover the oil—they found it. That's God's oil. And Jefferson had something to say about the oil, but Genesis had more to say about the oil. And that's ours. The fertile land is ours and the oil is ours and the gold and the mines really belong to everybody. This is God's world. Not a few who developed squatters' rights and enslaved blacks and killed Indians—this is our land . . ." His voice trailed off; he sat shadowed in the half-light; and, in the sudden silence, it was as if everyone in the room could still hear the voices of those 1,500 poor blacks shouting "I am somebody" and by that act asserting that some little piece of God's world was their own.

CHAPTER 4

"We in a War—
Or Haven't Anybody
Told You That?"

THEY ROARED ON TWO WHEELS into Burma Road—Harlem's unaffectionate nickname for its stretch of Lenox Avenue—and burned to a stop outside the Royal Flush Bar. The car belonged to Joe-Joe, a chunky ebony 20-year-old who earned it by sticking through high school and graduating into a job at the post office. But the dude who led everybody into the artificial midnight of the Royal Flush and popped for beers all around was just naturally J.B., a young man of obtrusive flash and dash in hip-hugging black gabardines, a crisp yellow shirt and a new stingy-brim straw hat. J.B. was 20, too, but he had quit high school early and got himself a hustle. He was a numbers runner, with a bankroll built out of Harlem's dimes and quarters, and he had it made.

Outside, the streets cooked in the August sun; the bloods were idling on the corners and the stoops, slugging wine from bottles wrapped in brown paper bags; the talk, as it did every summer now, fastened mostly on the latest news of riot and retaliation in the ghettos of urban America. "The Man, he worried now," J.B. was saying, "cause he know we ain't takin' no more his shit. Anybody come rollin' into a city with tanks *got* to be afraid of somethin'. Anyplace you see a tank, you

113

know there got to be a war goin' on, right? And that's what this is, baby—war!"

"That's right, that's right," said Skeeter, a spindly kid who quite clearly neither expected nor demanded anything of life except a place at J.B.'s heels. Skeeter was 19 and nowhere, a jobless dropout living with an aunt and a sister. A fierce stammer helped shame him out of high school when he was 14, and he still wasn't talking much. Except when J.B. said something; then Skeeter would say, "That's right."

Someone wondered what Rap Brown was into those days. "That's my man!" J.B. exclaimed. "Ain't nobody in the world gonna get nothin' if he don't fight for it. The black man's been takin' low too long."

"That's right," Skeeter blurted. But Joe-Joe half disagreed—not on the necessity of making a fight but on what the fighting was really about. "I used to watch ole Stokely up there on TV tellin' off the white people," he said. "I thought he was crazy, cause I thought he was gonna get hisself killed—like Malcolm. But you know, when a man says what all the time you been thinkin', you wonder if maybe *you* ain't crazy. I mean like if you feel inside knotted all the time, maybe it's better if you make some noise." He sipped at his beer. "Like the time I broke my big toe cuttin' the fool [roughhousing] out at Coney Island. I went on limpin' around grinnin', not lettin' on to nobody I was hurt. But I finally had to tell 'em cause I couldn't stand it no more. And like, you know, these two cats crossed their arms and made like a seat and carried me to the beach clinic. Now supposin' I hadn't said nothin'?"

So Joe-Joe guessed that if Harlem ever rioted again he would join in. "Man," he said, grinning broadly, "you know my sister wouldn't let me in the street that last time. But I bet I'm goin' to get somethin' next time. I just might break me some windows, grab me some rags and throw me some bottles."

J.B. didn't know. "I wouldn't mind knockin' me some cracker heads together," he said—but, like any budding entrepreneur, he worried that rioting might be bad for business. Still, in the end, he guessed he would join in, too. "I mean," he said, "that's where it's at."

"That's right," Skeeter said. "That's right."

White America had, by the end of the 1960's, accumulated a vast literature on rioting in the ghetto, some of it intelligent, some banal, some provocative, some pedantic—and hardly any of it quite so educational as an hour in any black slum in the nation. Joe-Joe had it right—the riots were the black man's desperate cry to whites that he was hurting and that he couldn't stand any more. But rioting is the most primitive form of communication; it evoked shock, fear, guilt, anger and finally a sort of numb acceptance of periodic violent insurrections in the casbah as an ordinary part of urban life. "What shocked me most," said a Detroit matron in the midst of the devastating riot there, "was how *normal* it seemed to have those soldiers standing outside Hudson's department store when I went shopping." To be so inured to rioting was finally and tragically to miss the message of the rioters. For what Joe-Joe and J.B. and the kids on a thousand corners were trying to tell America was that, for them, life as their elders had lived it simply was no longer supportable. When a young man growing up in the suffocating emptiness of the ghetto reaches that unhappy pass, the issue is no longer whether or not riots are moral. The question becomes whether or not they will be useful—or at least be fun while they last.

It was a judgment on America that so many of the ghetto young came to that pass and acted on it in the middle and late 1960's. A "white racist" when the decade began was somebody who put a bedsheet over his head and said "nigguh" in public in a Southern accent. When the '60's ended, America *as a society* had been pronounced racist by President Johnson's impeccably responsible riot commission—a verdict which may or may not have accurately stated the nation's collective intent but which most certainly described the results. That some white Americans finally asked themselves the question was no doubt a hopeful sign. That black Americans were able to raise it only at the most terrible cost—by resort to violence at a pitch and a frequency without precedent in the history of this violent land—may have been the sorriest fact of all.

The cost was devastating indeed. The fire this time flared first in Harlem in 1964, burned high in Watts in 1965 and roared to a crescendo in the ten months between July 1967 (when Newark and Detroit exploded) and April 1968 (when Martin Luther King's assassination set off what amounted to a single coast-to-coast rebellion). The statistics of those five years were unreliable and in the last analysis nearly meaningless. It was enough to record that more than 200 people, most of them blacks, died in the streets; that at least 10,000 were injured and 60,000 arrested; that whole streets were plundered, whole blocks laid waste by fire; that the occupation of American cities by soldiers armed for war became an everyday spectacle of summer; that, by the end of the decade, hardly a city or a town with a black enclave big enough to be called a ghetto had escaped at least a brush with catastrophe. The epidemic touched not only such acknowledged urban disaster areas as Newark but such progressively run "model" cities as Detroit and New Haven—a spread that suggested how little such distinctions mean to black people as against the everyday desperation of ghetto life.

Desperation was precisely the point of the riots; they were important not so much for the physical damage they wreaked as for the social and the psychic damage they revealed. Harlem began it all but Watts was the watershed—the revolt of the colonials in a sun-washed, palm-shaded paradise a continent's distance from the stifling tenements of black Manhattan. The ashes there were still warm when Martin Luther King ventured in to try to make peace, and his first speaking stop in the ghetto told everything about the way the currents were running. "We must join hands—" he began. "And *burn!*" a black kid whooped, and everybody laughed. King struggled through his speech, but he canceled the rest of his schedule in Watts and soon left town. Neither he nor The Movement was ever quite the same again. A whole ideology of rioting flowered in the ghetto after Watts; Rap Brown and SNCC proposed celebrating August 18, the anniversary of the uprising, as Independence Day—the day when the blacks "stopped moaning 'We Shall Overcome' and started swinging to 'Burn, Baby, Burn.' "* And where the ideology didn't take, the fever did. Whites were recurringly shocked not only by the fury of the riots but by the unbridled joy of the rioters. "It's like laughing at a funeral," said New Jersey's Governor Richard Hughes, haggard and hollow-eyed after a pre-dawn riot tour of Newark's Central Ward. Not quite. "The chronic riot of their day-to-day lives is, as far as they're concerned, no better than the acute riots," Kenneth Clark, the black psychologist, observed. "They don't have anything to lose, *including* their lives. It's not just desperation—it's what-the-hell."

The riots were all the more ominous for the very fact that they flared in a community so heavily inclined to nonviolence as a strategy of protest—and so stubbornly hopeful that nonviolence would carry the day. Nearly two-thirds of the Negroes in the *Newsweek* Poll believed that the blacks had more to lose than to gain by resorting to violence and that, in any event, they could win their rights without it. This faith, for all the devastation of the latter '60's, was as strong at the end of the decade as it had been at the beginning. "You can catch more flies with honey than with vinegar," a 42-year-old Pittsburgh housewife told a Gallup interviewer. "We have nothing to fight *with*," said a Denver printer, 41 years old. "Violence," a 29-year-

---

* The battle cry actually was the signature phrase of a locally popular black disc jockey, and, before Watts, it had nothing to do with Molotov cocktails. To "burn," in the black argot of the day, actually meant something like to "groove" or to "wail"—to improvise brilliantly in singing, soloing or just living.

old steel-mill worker in Kansas City offered, "will only get a lot of people killed without winning anything. We *are* winning without violence."

Yet there was peril in taking too much comfort in the great sentiment for nonviolence. It ought to surprise no one that black people, like everybody else, preferred war to peace; the far more stunning figure was that fully a fifth of all Negroes—and more than a third of the Northern ghetto young—simply did not believe that their struggle could be won by peaceful means. They remained a minority within a minority—but there are quite enough of them, in James Baldwin's phrase, to ring down the curtain on the American dream. "We aren't going to get anything unless we take it," said a 21-year-old student in Baltimore. "The white man has no reason to give us anything when he can keep us where we are." A college freshman in Pittsburgh: "It's gonna be *three* eyes for an eye." A machine operator in Philadelphia, 42 years old: "There's a time for everything. Sometimes a brick must be thrown." A Pittsburgh housewife: "We got to get to *all* white people, and some of them, honey, only listen to violence." A waitress of 39 in Kansas City: "I used to feel that nonviolence was the way. But I'm changing and I don't know why. I think violence may be the only thing they understand."

There was, moreover, a painful ambivalence in black America's view of the rioting of the summers just past. Negroes on balance shared the white man's abhorrence of the burning, the thieving and the killing. But they parted company on what those acts meant. Lyndon Johnson probably spoke for the white American consensus when, in a stricken TV report to the nation on the Detroit riot, he said, "First—let there be no mistake about it—the looting, arson, plunder and pillage which have occurred are not part of a civil-rights protest. That is crime—and crime must be dealt with forcefully, swiftly, certainly . . ." Black people were by no means so certain. They agreed that the *actions* of the rioters were criminal, but they tended to see the rioting very much as a political act—an outcry at the just and widely shared grievances of the Negro community. So, for them, the riots in fact were continuous with the civil-rights protest of the 1950's and '60's. And so the fire and the blood were not simple criminality run rampant; they were, for many blacks, the more or less regrettable excesses of a righteous struggle toward freedom.

A poll can only begin to suggest what so traumatic a train of events meant to Negro America. But the *Newsweek* survey figures were nevertheless revealing as a post mortem on five riot summers:

· *Negroes on balance did not believe that the riots were justified, but very nearly a third did—a reservoir of black anger deeper and more desperate than most whites dreamed possible.*

Americans—for all their revolutionary beginnings as a nation—grew up believing that no level of grievance, however broadly based or acutely felt, could justify resorting to violence. Negroes share that article of democratic faith with whites; it was accordingly less startling that 48 per cent of them said the rioting was not justified than that 31 per cent felt it was—a riot constituency equivalent to nearly 4 million of America's 12.5 million adult blacks. For a comparable fraction of the nation's whites to feel pressed to the point of rebellion would surely be recognized as a disaster demanding the most drastic relief measures; the New Deal did not wait for the cities to start burning. No such effort has yet been mounted in the ghettos, however, and the ideology of rioting as a legitimate expression of discontent could only be strengthened as a result. That notion by 1969 had already become the prevailing view among Northern middle-income blacks—the leadership class in the ghetto. And there was evidence in other surveys that many Negroes who did not consider rioting justified were in fact deploring the acts of war—not its underlying motives. A 30 per cent minority of the Watts Negroes spoke favorably of the riot there in a UCLA poll, but majorities of two and three to one thought that it had been a purposeful act of protest and that its targets—police, merchants and whites in general—deserved whatever they got. "People want *recognition*," a Watts filling-station worker told *Newsweek* long afterward, "and the only way they were gone get it was riot. The *only* way. See, we don't want to overthrow the country—we just want what we ain't got."

· *Negroes do not think of the rioters as hoodlums—the common judgment of white Americans—but as a representative slice of the black community; as people, in short, much like themselves.*

White people, as one of UCLA's riot-study papers accurately observed, have squandered a good deal of time and energy constructing a mythology of "bad Negroes" (a tiny minority who make riots) and "good Negroes" (the vast long-suffering majority who are said to cower before them). This comfortable fantasy ought to have been punctured by warfare on the scale of Watts, Newark and Detroit, in which at least 10 to 20 per cent of the ghetto actually tasted combat and many more were approving or at least acquiescent spectators. The rioters, as psychiatrist Alvin Poussaint once put it, "range from the plain damn angry to those with fantasies of taking over, to those who want a TV set, to those angry at their father and mother, to those caught up in hysteria, to those who will act only when they see the cops shoot someone . . . Rage is common to all of them." That is a far cry from dismissing them as the dregs of black society—a view indulged by many white and few blacks. Who riots? A fourth of the Negroes blamed mostly hoodlums. But fully as many thought that the rioters were mainly "good people"—and 41 per cent guessed that both sorts were involved. What this collective verdict announces to white America is that conditions of life in the ghetto are so oppressive that the law-abiding as well as the lawless—the "good Negro" as well as the "bad"—may feel driven to rebel. Ernest D., a foundry worker at decent wages and with no criminal record, was driving home in Milwaukee's ghetto when a pride of rioters swirled by. "I got out of my car," he recounted later, still plainly surprised at the fact, "and asked 'em what was goin' on. They said they wanted their freedom. I asked what kind of freedom and they said black power. So I just started fightin' too."

· *The widely held view of the ghetto—against the weight of the evidence—is that rioting works.*

"This nation," Bayard Rustin once remarked sadly, "is teaching the poor that they *ought* to riot lest they get nothing. Tell them in the spring that you are going to riot in the summer and they will vote money. Or after a riot. In Watts they wanted a hospital. They didn't get it. They rioted. Now they have one; it's not up yet and it's not very good, but after the riot they came in with plans. In Chicago, the children wanted sprinklers on the fireplugs. Riots. Then Mayor Daley came along personally with eight-dollar sprinklers." The victories, as Rustin went on to note, are usually cheap and often meaningless, and every riot increased the risks of bringing down repression on the heads of the blacks. But the balance of sentiment in Negro America in 1969 was that, like them or not, the riots had not hurt and probably had helped the cause. The feeling was by no means unanimous. The poorest blacks, contrary to much of the folklore of the day, felt rather strongly that the rioting had done more harm than good. But the relatively affluent were even more firmly convinced that it had advanced the struggle, and their view prevailed, 40 to 29 (with an additional 16 per cent doubtful that rioting made much difference one way or the other). That their optimism bore so little tangible relation to reality did not shake those who shared it; some notice from white people, and some attention to the problems of the blacks, was for them clearly better than nothing—even if it had to be bought at the great pain and the greater peril of insurrection. "Black people," Watts community worker Ferman Moore said cheerlessly, "now know that if you burn down a city or two, the power structure is going to dump a bushel basket of money on top of you to try to quiet you down. And they realize that the white boy who *built* the power structure did it by violence and force—by kicking the shit out of the British, then the Indians and now the black and brown people. Yes, sir, we have a fine example to follow, and who can fault us? It's in the finest American tradition."

· *The restraints on rioting are crumbling among the young in the Northern ghettos—the children of the city of destruction.*

The under-30 generation in the ghetto came of age during a decade of black revolt. They were witness to the televised affluence of white people and the real-life defeat of their own fathers; they were exposed daily to the bright promise and the bitter disappointments of the Negro revolution; they were schooled in the work ethic and then graduated into a job market frozen at depression unemployment levels; they lived in a milieu where racial hatreds and revanchist passions that had been suppressed for decades were suddenly out in the open. They were precisely the blacks who had, in Clark's phrase, passed beyond desperation to what-the-hell. "I can't lose by rioting," said one of them, an Oakland gang kid. "Done lost. Been lost. Gonna be lost some more. I'm sayin' to The Man, 'You includin' me in this game or not?' An' I know his answer, so I'm gettin' ready to get basic." He might have been speaking for a generation. The under-30 Northern blacks believed by 47 to 32 that the riots were justified; by 74 to 18 that the rioters were partly or principally "good people"; by 50 to 20 that rioting helped the cause. And one in six said he would join a riot if it happened—an extraordinarily large pool of combatants waiting for a war and utterly reckless of the odds against winning it. "I don't mind gettin' killed," a street-corner kid in Chicago told *Newsweek*'s Marvin Kupfer. "When I'm dead, they'll tell my kid, 'He died for a good cause.' "

So, in sum, the poll reveals sizable numbers in every sector of the black community—and most of all in the volatile age group that makes riots—who see the street mutinies of the late '60's in something quite like revolutionary terms: a series of explosions that were broadly based, purposeful, rooted in real grievances and helpful in the common cause of Negroes everywhere. What polls cannot tell about riots is their emotional content for the individuals and the communities who actually experience them—a psychic dimension even more disturbing than the statistics in what it told about the state of mind of black men in white America. "At the level of individuals," Frantz Fanon once wrote, discussing the Algerian rebels, "violence is a cleansing force. It frees the native from his inferiority complex, and from his despair and inaction; it makes him fearless and restores self-respect." The vices and virtues of comparing the situation of Negroes in America with the lot of colonials in Africa can, of course, be debated inconclusively forever. Yet there is eyewitness evidence aplenty that rioting, for many American blacks, may in fact have been an exhilarating and even a liberating experience—an expression of power by the powerless, an act of revenge by the vanquished, an assertion by the Invisible Man that he really exists.

New Jersey's Governor Hughes glimpsed that inner reality in the carnival gaiety of the Newark looters; what he saw as laughing at a funeral may have been more like rejoicing at a birth. Ernest D., the Milwaukee foundry worker, experienced it when he poked his fist through a shattered store window in search of an intangible piece of goods called freedom. And Dr. Frederick J. Hacker, a white psychiatrist from the University of Southern California, recorded it in a remarkable report on the Watts riots in the West Coast magazine *Frontier*. "For the Negroes," said Hacker, who interviewed some of them before and after the riot, "what happened . . . *was* justified legally and morally. Where the police saw black criminals tearing apart law and order with a cascade of Molotov cocktails, the Negroes of Watts watched freedom fighters liberating themselves with blood and fire." Hacker found widespread acknowledgment

that burning, looting and lawbreaking are bad things to do—
and surprising little shame, guilt or regret about having done
them. Quite to the contrary, the riot in important ways was
"psychologically analogous to the Hungarian Revolution and
the Boston Tea Party." It was plain damned fun ("Violence
makes you feel good—at least for a while") and far more: "It
was the metamorphosis of the Negroes of southeastern Los
Angeles from victims—historical objects—to masters . . . The
people of Watts felt that for those four days they represented
all Negroes; the historical plight of the Negroes; all the rebellions against all injustice." Most of them, Hacker wrote, knew
that they couldn't win; all that mattered to them was the
exercise of their will and their stunted pride. "What must be
understood by the rest of America," he said, "is that, for the
lower-class Negro, riots are not criminal but a legitimate
weapon in a morally justified civil war."

The exhilaration, as Hacker noted, is a function of action and
does not long survive the war. But the pride does. Watts
Negroes began throwing an annual summer festival on the
anniversary of their rebellion well before Rap Brown suggested
it, and independence was precisely what they were celebrating.
And in postwar Detroit, with the acrid scent of smoke still
souring the air, *Newsweek*'s John Dotson found a few of the
children of the city of destruction sitting on a rail and staring
idly across Dexter Avenue into a solid block of charred ruins.

"Those buildings goin' up was a pretty sight," said one of
them, a lanky spidery-legged kid whose hand-me-down pants
ended a shin's length short of his shoes. "I sat right here and
watched 'em go. And there wasn't nothin' them honkies could
do but sweat and strain to put it out."

"Yeah, man," a pal chimed in, "it's about time those honkies
started earnin' their money in this neighborhood."

"You know," the long-legged kid said, "we made big news.
They called this the worst race riot in history."

"Yeah," another boy, mountainously beefy, echoed, "we got

the record, man. They can forget all about Watts and Newark and Harlem. This where the riot to end all riots was held."

They were silent for a moment.

"That little girl that got shot, man," the long-legged boy said. "She shouldn't of got shot."

"That's the breaks, brother," the beefy youth replied, absently patting at the deep waves in his processed hair. "We in a war—or haven't anybody told you that?"

Everyone laughed.

The language of war, by the end of the 1960's, was common currency in the ghetto—and so was a deep, fatalistic assumption that acts of war would keep recurring in the years to come. Would there be more riots? Two-thirds of the nation's blacks thought so—a level of expectation verging on that point where possibility can become probability. And there was talk everywhere of a turn from the spontaneous violence of the riots to the strategic violence of revolution. Malcolm X, Stokely Carmichael, Rap Brown and the Black Panthers successively urged Negroes to take up arms; by 1969, no fewer than a fourth of all Negroes—and a third of the ghetto young—agreed that they ought at least to have guns, whether or not they used them. Police periodically aborted what they said were terrorist plots— one to blow the head off the Statue of Liberty, another to dynamite Macy's, still another to assassinate Negro moderates like Whitney Young and Roy Wilkins. Street battles broke out with all the surface appearances of guerrilla warfare—the worst and most notorious of them a summer 1968 shoot-out between police and a little troop of armed nationalists led by a half-hinged street astrologer named Fred (Ahmed) Evans. Three cops and seven blacks died; Evans was sentenced to the electric chair for murder; tales flew, in and out of print, that the blacks had gulled police into a carefully plotted ambush.

It mattered little that the evidence for this theory was flimsy, or that most of the proliferating reports of sniping by supposed ghetto *guerrilleros* in the late 1960's proved on close examination to have been minor or plain fictitious. What mattered was what people believed was happening, and the combination of incendiary black rhetoric and inflamed white imaginations was quite enough to lead them to believe the worst. "May the deaths of '68 signal the beginning of the end of this country," Rap Brown wrote his followers from jail early that year. "Resistance is not enough. Aggression is the order of the day." Blacks as well as whites took such prophecies at face value. Were newer, more exotic forms of violence on the way? "There *couldn't* be any more, could there?" an elderly Houston man replied. "Lord have mercy on all of us if something else happen." But the widespread expectation was that something else would. "Racial war," said a Philadelphia electronics plant foreman, 34 years old. "Suicide squads," said a 28-year-old Harlem housewife. "Real revolution," a Denver schoolteacher ventured. "Sabotage," a middle-aged Pittsburgh woman predicted, "and whites intimidating Negroes, and child, all hell will break loose when that happens—bombings, shooting, fires . . ."

Tactical violence remained a possibility for the 1970's; whites tended greatly to overestimate the number of practicing revolutionaries in the ghetto, but a very few *plastiqueurs* could wreak very considerable havoc. Neither was the nation safely past the riot era. The rebellions percolated down in the latter 1960's from the big cities into small-to-middling towns and suburbs; they spread from the streets into the schools; they started earlier and died out later until the "long hot summer" stretched from winter to winter. And tensions tightened dangerously between militants and the police. The militants, said Terry Ann Knopf, research associate at Brandeis University's Lemberg Center for the Study of Violence, "really believe the police are out to kill them all. They stockpile arms. The police infiltrators learn of the stockpiles and law enforcement gets nervous. They begin surveillance. The spying makes militants more nervous and more sure of extermination. The stage is set for battle." And battles flared in the late 1960's: the Evans shoot-out in Cleveland, a duel between the cops and a group of black separatists meeting at a ghetto church in Detroit, the running and generally lopsided combat between police and the Panthers.

Yet there were signs by the decade's end that rioting on the cataclysmic scale of Watts, Newark or Detroit might at last be passing into history. The riots over King's assassination were like some last furious Walpurgisnacht in the ghetto—a transcontinental firestorm on a scale with the trauma that set it going. Street disorders in the days and months thereafter were at least as numerous and as widespread as in the summers before. But their intensity was considerably banked; it was almost as if the worst of the fury had spent itself in those terrible April days and nights after King died. The *Newsweek* Poll a year later asked blacks whether or not they would join a riot. Eleven per cent said they would. That is, of course, a startlingly large number to confess so violently angry a cast of mind to strangers. But the more telling fact may be that the number was down significantly from the 15 per cent who said yes in the days three years earlier when insurrection in the ghetto was still relatively new.

There were a number of theories as to why this should be so, each with some claim to credibility. Among them were these:

· *The Inoculation Theory.* This view holds that a riot is an act of catharsis—a spontaneous rising that may be satisfying once but is too harrowing and too exhausting to go through a second time. "Cities which have had the bath of full-scale rioting are likely to have been washed out," said a black Federal intelligence source with well-laid wires into the ghetto. The record of a half-dozen years of rioting was indeed suggestive: lightning rarely struck twice with deadly force in the same place, and by the end of the decade, most places had been struck once. The riots, in short, were running out of cities to happen in; the ghetto, having tasted war, began to reassert its deeply grained will for peace.

· *The Hangover Theory.* A related hypothesis is that the

ghetto wakes up the morning after a riot to discover that it has sustained most of the death and all of the destruction—and that it has achieved little if anything for its pain. The riots were a kamikaze assault on white America's conscience; the results—a faltering white liberalism on one hand and a quickening white backlash on the other—set many blacks wondering whether white America really had enough conscience to justify the cost. "The stupid thing about riots," said Earl Raines, a tough-minded young lawyer who headed the Los Angeles NAACP, "is why should you burn down your own home? The man in the ghetto lived in despair for so long—he just couldn't communicate with The Man downtown. To him, picking up a Molotov cocktail was his way of grabbing The Man's attention. The Watts riot was a time of glee for black people. But later they tallied up the damage and found out they'd lost the game. It wasn't even close."

· *The Police-Are-Getting-Better Theory.* The riot commission was appalled by the "indiscriminate and excessive force" often used to put down riots—a rather delicate phrase for a form of collective madness in which panicky cops and militiamen fired on anything that moved or made noise, including one another; in which densely populated tenements were powdered with .50-caliber machine-gun fire; in which the dead included not only looters and fire-bombers but old men, women and children. The police-are-getting-better theory presumed that lawmen had learned from disastrous experience. Their response to the King assassination riots was, relatively speaking, a model of sophistication—a show of maximum force at maximum speed and with a minimum of random gunplay. (The national death toll was 43 scattered among a dozen cities—still high, perhaps, but that many were killed in Detroit alone in 1967.) And department after department got religion about riot-prevention as well as riot-control measures: sharpened intelligence operations, serious community-relations programs and increased use of mobile commando units trained to nip riots surgically before they start.

· *The Police-Are-Getting-Worse Theory.* This view insisted that, for all the appearance of reform, the police were in fact arming for Armageddon—an overt war of repression against the ghetto. The notion, of course, was most inflamed among the militants: the withering police pressure that destroyed some of them and drove others into exile persuaded them that Armageddon was already on. But the view was surprisingly current among ordinary blacks as well. At the height of the Newark rioting in 1967, a ghetto kid stood on a street corner watching the white firepower parade by and screamed in helpless rage, "The Man have *everything!*" Not yet; there were, in the wake of that angry summer, tales of the police stockpiling still more: high-powered rifles, machine guns, tanks, gas, helicopter gunships and miscellaneous other exotica of war unheard of this side of Vietnam. And none of it eased the paranoia which is one of the afflictions of life in the ghetto. "These people aren't stupid," said Los Angeles's Raines. "They know The Man is just waiting for them to do something wrong so he can come in and mow them down."

· *The Lull-Between-Storms Theory.* Some black spectators read the winding down of the street war less as a turning point than as a pause—a time for the Negro community, in its own argot, to get it together and consider which way to move next. Militants and moderates alike in this period preached against the spontaneous insurrections of the past—the moderates because they had never believed in insurrection and the militants because they no longer believed in spontaneity. Various groups channeled the energies of the young into conventional politics, or community organization, or militant protest; even the Panthers stacked their guns out of sight and laid on their breakfast-for-children program. Yet a vein of pessimism underlay the lull-between-storms theory—a presumption that all these moral equivalents to war would fail and that violence in some form, probably but not necessarily more organized and more selective than the riots, almost certainly would follow. "All blacks are angry, very angry," said William Grier, a black psychiatrist and co-author (with Price Cobbs) of the book *Black Rage*. "Every black person in this country is a smoldering keg of dynamite. I would say the big riots are over. But the riots were not an end point by any means."

All of these elements no doubt were at play in the ghetto by the end of the 1960's, operating at least temporarily as a check on mass violence where the normal restraints had been overrun by events. None of them, naturally, guaranteed that the danger had run its course, or would so long as grievance remained the norm of the ghetto. J.T., a wasted young man of 23, came home from Vietnam to Chicago's West Side with no skills, no job, no future and so no vista beyond the street corner where he spends his days and nights jiving with his friends. "All you guys want to give is a dollar an hour," he said bitterly. "Man, I can *beg* more than that right on this corner. They didn't tell me I was going to be just another nigger when I got back home." So J.T. was indeed a keg of dynamite waiting for a match. "I want to burn down every building in this town," he said. "Let me do that and I'll be grateful to The Man for the rest of my life."

There are thousand of J.T.'s in the ghetto; they are bitter, alienated and potentially destructive, and, as Rap Brown once noted, matches only cost a penny. Yet the evidence is that their numbers are diminishing—at least partly because the riots turned out, in one important sense, to have worked after all. They scarred black America, to be sure, and they carried the very real risk of white backlash and white reprisal. But they created even as they destroyed, wakening a sense of community among the blacks—and giving many of them, often for the first time, a sense that they actually did have something to lose by rioting. Whites have always had a tendency somewhat to overstate the disorganization of the ghetto; blacks over the centuries have been forced by the fact of exclusion and the hard necessities of survival to develop their own parallel structure of churches, colleges, fraternal orders, burial societies and black betterment organizations. But their history in white America has always encouraged a sort of atomization of the Negro community—an ethos of Making It in which the object has been the escape of the talented few from the ghetto and from the shame of blackness.

The riots changed black America. They were, however, ugly and terrifying, a rare communal experience, a series of explicitly racial rebellions that cut across the wide class divisions of the Negro community, and their net effect tended more toward fusion than fission. The fleeting exhilaration of action, as USC's Dr. Hacker noted, was succeeded in Watts "by a strange sense of pride and accomplishment which is actually the finding of a national and racial identity. . . . The riots welded them together, and now they feel capable of carving a new fate, not just passively enduring their present existence." Detroit's Mayor Jerome Cavanagh, an urban politician of rare sensitivity, thought he detected a movement from "the militancy of despair" before the insurrections to "a militancy of hope" afterward. That rising militancy heightened the new introspective mood called black awareness; it brought many of the Negro middle class to the pained rediscovery of their kinship with the ghetto poor; it flowered in the explosion of community organizing efforts in the slums. Despair fragments; war unites. Before the riots, said psychiatrist Grier, "it was rare for a black man to use the term 'brother' to another black man and have each share a conception of its meaning. The secular meaning of brotherhood rose out of the riots."

Men who discover the fragile beginnings of community will not lightly risk them in war. Yet, to America's shame, it took war for those beginnings to be discovered, and the decision as to whether war would recur did not rest exclusively with the blacks. "In the ghettos of America," Hubert Locke, a black former police official, wrote in an unpublished epilogue to his book *The Detroit Riot of 1967*, "the fear of violence itself is tempered by a deep-seated desire, conscious or unconscious, to see white America pay dearly for 300 years of white injustice. . . . Unless the nation wages a vigorous and massive campaign to eradicate its injustices, the ability of or the basis for black people to decide clearly against violence and for a stable and just social order is virtually nil."

And the clock was running. In Watts one summer, while much of the community was celebrating its rebirth by riot, an authentic American ruin named Henry J. lay flat on his back on a lot in the burnt-out block called Charcoal Alley No. 1, sipped at a 50-cent bottle of Applejack wine and delivered a soliloquy to a sunny and utterly indifferent sky. He had, he announced, spent 12 of his 28 years in jail; as a consequence, he could not find work; there was a car-wash job in Torrance, but Torrance was 20 miles away and he had no car. So he lay in the grass and drank Applejack and told the sky, "Fuck whitey. I don't believe in nothin'. I feel like they ought to burn down the whole world. Just let it burn down, baby."

DIRECTIONS:

The Black Panthers

"America is up against the wall," said Eldridge Cleaver, the gifted voice of the Black Panther Party, to a luncheon gathering of young, buttoned-down and uniformly uneasy white lawyers in a gracious San Francisco dining room. Across the bay in Oakland, a jury was deliberating the case of California vs. Huey P. Newton, the Panthers' Minister of Defense, who was charged with murdering a policeman in a predawn street shoot-out. Newton was and is the ranking saint in the party's pantheon, and Cleaver, anticipating his imminent martyrdom, was fuming. So he dressed all in black for his date with The Barristers Club and fastened a tiny pearl earring to his left ear and came down on the lawyers in the language of the street.

And what he told them was that America was up against the wall. "The reason Huey P. Newton is a hero in the black community and the reason he turns people on is precisely because he's been given the credit by the racist power structure of Alameda County for killing an Oakland policeman. . . . The people dig that. When action is taken, like [patrolman] John Frey's death, it's a source of enthusiasm and hope for the black community. We say we won't be a witness to the execution of Huey P. Newton but that we'll be witnesses against it. We say there's nothing so sacred in America, nothing so dear to us, that we won't lay down our lives with Huey. This whole apparatus, this capitalistic system and its institutions and police . . . all need to be assigned to the garbage can of history, and I don't give a fuck who doesn't like it. If we can't have it, nobody's gonna have it. We'd rather provoke a situation . . . that will disrupt cities and the economy so that the enemies of America could come in and pick the gold from the teeth of these Babylonian pigs. . . . The right of revolution can't be taken from the people. What Huey Newton symbolizes is the right to self-defense. We can go nowhere unless we have the right to defend ourselves against the pig cop . . ."

The lawyers were looking at one another and toying with their salad forks, and Cleaver shouted at them, "Up against the wall, motherfucker! You may think you're riding in luxury liners, that you can put a fool like Richard Nixon or an unconscionable man like George Wallace in the White House, but none of those pigs can solve the problem. . . . I could go into the White House poor and come out fat fucking rich, but I'm too young. [Cleaver at the time was running for President on the 1968 Peace and Freedom ticket but was, at 33, two years under age for the job.] So I have to say fuck the White House, fuck the electoral system, and fuck all the pigs, and fuck the power structure. You're all chasing dollars, but there are other people here who are chasing dollars to buy guns to kill judges and police and corporation lawyers. We need lawyers today who have a lawbook in one hand and a gun in the other . . . so that if he goes to court and that shit doesn't come out right, he can pull out his gun and start shooting. . . . If I could get two machine guns out of this crowd I wouldn't care if you applauded me or threw glasses at me. I'd get my black ass out of there . . . I meant all my insults to those who won't choose my side—the right side. You people can take your wallets, credit cards, and cut your motherfucking necks. . . . You people on the other side, I love you . . . I hope you'll take your guns and shoot judges and police." Some of the lawyers applauded. In the question-and-answer period, one of them asked what white people could do for the blacks. "Kill some white people," Cleaver said. "Or make them act in a prescribed manner." Afterward, as everyone was filing out, a pale young man in a pin-striped suit remarked to a companion, "His speech certainly reflects the growing polarization between the races, doesn't it?"

On September 8, 1968, the jury found Huey P. Newton guilty on a reduced charge of manslaughter, and he was sent to prison for two to fifteen years. Cleaver himself, a few months before, had been arrested in a police siege in which another Panther, Bobby Hutton, was shot and killed. He was then on parole from a 13-year sentence for assault; the authorities revoked the parole, and not long after Cleaver's speech to the Barristers, his last appeal failed. "I didn't leave anything at San Quentin except some of my mind and some of my soul," he said. "They can have that. There's nothing I want that I left there. And anything more they want from me now, they're going to have to come take." They were coming when, in late November 1968 Eldridge Cleaver fled the country.

On September 24, 1969, Bobby G. Seale, chairman and co-founder of the Panthers, was brought to trial with seven white radicals in Federal court in Chicago on the charge that they conspired to foment the disorders attending the 1968 Democratic National Convention. Their arrest and trial under the Rap Brown Law, a recent act of Congress which proposed to stop the ghetto riots by putting a few Outside Agitators in prison, did not strike people who care greatly about such matters as a glorious chapter in the history of human liberty in America. And the inclusion of Seale struck some as particularly odd, since he had spent only two days in Chicago during the convention and made only two speeches, one of which in fact urged demonstrators not to try to march on the convention hall. A Chicago officer of the American Civil Liberties Union chanced to be on a plane with a Justice Department official shortly after the indictments were returned and asked him, Why Seale? "Look," he quoted the man from Justice as saying, "these Black Panthers are just a bunch of hoodlums and we've got to get them."

Seale, in any event, did go to trial with the others. His lawyer, Charles R. Garry of San Francisco, had just undergone surgery and could not be present; but Judge Julius Hoffman decided that Seale was adequately represented by the principal defense lawyer, William Kunstler, and refused either to grant Seale a delay or to let him conduct his own defense. Seale tried anyway, and through the early weeks of the trial was constantly on his feet interrupting the proceedings, demanding the right to cross-examine, calling the judge and the prosecution racists and worse, once yelling at Hoffman, "Every other word you say is 'denied, denied, denied, denied,' and you begin to oink in the faces of the masses of the people of this country. That is what you begin to represent, the corruptness of this rotten government [for] four hundred years. . . . This racist and fascist administrative government with its Superman notions and comic-book politics. We're hip to the fact that Superman never saved no black people—you got that?" The judge repeatedly had his marshals sit Seale down; later ordered him bound and gagged; and finally, on November 5, 1969, hailed him before the bench and held him in contempt on sixteen separate counts—at which point Seale, to his great surprise, was given a chance to speak.

"Wait a minute," he said. "Now are you going to . . . punish me for attempting to speak for myself before? Now after you punish me, you sit up and say something about you can speak? What kind of jive is that? . . . Is this a court? It must be a fascist operation like I see it in my mind, you know—I don't understand you. . . . What am I supposed to speak about?"

About his impending punishment for contempt of court, Judge Hoffman told him.

"Punishment?" Seale exploded. "You've punished black people all your life. I mean, you, they even say you own a factory that produces raw materials to kill people in Vietnam, you know, so it's nothing—death is nothing, I mean, if that is what you're talking about, or putting me in jail, or prison, or hanging people, and all that stuff. I have nothing to say about that. I have something to say about the fact that I want to defend myself still. . . . The first thing, I'm not in no contempt of court. I know that. I know that I as a person and a human being have the right to stand up in a court and use his Constitutional right to speak in behalf of his Constitutional rights . . . and I will continue to make those requests, hoping that once in one way along this trial, you will recognize my rights as a human being, a black man living under the scope and influence of a racist decadent America where the Government of the United States does not recognize the black people's Constitutional rights, and have never recognized them. . . . Oh, yes, you're acting in the same manner as those courts acted in those periods of slavery history, and you know it. That's what you're doing. If a black man stands up and speaks, if a black man asks for his rights, if a black man demands his rights, if a black man requests his rights, what do you do? You're talking about punishing . . ."

Seale wound down. The law requires that a person charged with contempt be granted the right to a jury trial if the possible penalty will be more than six months. Judge Hoffman sentenced Seale to three months on each of the sixteen counts—a total of four years—and directed that he be tried alone later in the conspiracy case. "I still want an immediate trial," Seale was shouting as the marshals carried him out of court. "I'm put in jail for four years for nothing?"

"Free Bobby!" some Panthers in the gallery started chanting. "Free Bobby! Free Bobby!"

Bobby Rush sat at a desk at Illinois Panther headquarters on Chicago's West Madison Street, under a photo poster of his friend Fred Hampton. HE CAME DOWN INTO THE VALLEY, the poster said, SO HE COULD KEEP SAYING—I AM A REVOLUTIONARY. They had founded the Illinois party together in December 1968. Hampton, all fire and dash, was then just out of the NAACP youth division in the Chicago suburbs; Rush was a dropout from an all-black West Side high school—one of those demoralized ghetto custodial institutions where kids get passing grades just for showing up, which some do and some don't. "It was the same old story of a brother leaving school because there wasn't anything in there," he told *Newsweek's* Donald Johnson. "Let's just say I outgrew the situation." He tried the Army next, but that didn't work out much better. His obvious talent kept getting him promoted (he made specialist 4th class) and his rebel streak kept getting him busted, once for growing a mustache and refusing to shave it, once for moonlighting as a SNCC organizer. So he dropped out of the Army, too, after five years and started clerking for $3.46 an hour at the B & O, which didn't work out either. He had, in service, fallen under Stokely Carmichael's spell—"I heard him speak once and I dug the relationship he had with the brothers in the South"—and Stokely had made him a revolutionary.

Rush was wearing the uniform of the revolution the day Johnson called on him—black leather jacket, black pants, black fur cap, black Afro and mustache and goatee—but it didn't entirely seem to fit. Johnson thought him a gentle man, introverted, with a low hoarse voice and a furrowed face that looked ten years older than it should have at 23. Rush spoke about how he dug Coltrane and wished he had more time for music, and how he was forever reading adventure stories when he was a child—Kit Carson or Davy Crockett or Geronimo or Bill Bridges, Mountain Man. "I remember I used to get pissed off because there was nothing left to discover," he said. He grinned, and it was possible for a fleeting second to see him as a shy little boy buried in a book and dreaming of Kit and Davy and the Alamo. But only for a second. He still read a lot, but now it was Malcolm and Eldridge and Marx and Lenin. He would go to the revolution every morning the way most men go to offices or factories, except that while their wives were telling them goodbye at the door, his Sunny always had to say, "Be careful." He learned not to smile very much, but he did one day when his own little boy, Jeffrey, 3 years old, grinned up at him and said that when he grew up he wanted to be a revolutionary, too.

"We're prepared to struggle countless years for our liberation," Rush said softly. But the struggle kept getting deadlier. The law was raiding Panther offices and cribs with increasing frequency and fury. In the latest raid, just before dawn on December 4, 1969, the Chicago police had stormed a Panther apartment in a "gun battle" in which the raiders came out miraculously unscathed while two Panthers were killed and four wounded. One of the dead was Mark Clark from Peoria. The other was Fred Hampton, his body sprawled face down in his bed, his mattress turning red, his Frantz Fanon and his Malcolm X and his three-volume life of Lenin scattered on the floor around him.

The police came looking for Rush at his place the next morning, but he had gone briefly underground with his family, and the assault party captured an empty apartment. When he gave himself up the next day, he picked a time (broad daylight) and a place where no one could touch him: on the stage at the Capitol Theater, where the Reverend Jesse Jackson was preaching his regular Saturday morning sermon to several thousand of the Operation Breadbasket faithful. He came out on bond in time to bury Fred Hampton; Ralph Abernathy came up to preach the funeral ("We are going to take up your torch, Freddy") and, afterward, Rush got the mourners to repeat after him, "I am a revolutionary!" And then he went back to the revolution—back to his desk and the photo poster of his dead friend and the zigzag line of bullet holes in the office wall. He seemed untroubled, but he took to working indoors in his astrakhan and his jacket, as though he might suddenly have to start running somewhere. "I don't want to die in no accident or from lung cancer or nothing like that," he said. "I want to die struggling." Did he think he would? Rush looked dully at Johnson, and he said, "I'm convinced of it."

CHAPTER 5

Black Folks,
White Folks

You been leaning on others to be your keeper
That's why they call you Negroes and colored people
Better change your strut and get in the swing
Find yourself and do your own thing
I don't know whether you realize
Before you get some respect you got to be Blackenized . . .
—A hit soul record, 1969

AMERICA, OF COURSE, had been Whitenized from the very beginning. White people today argue, with some justice and great heat, that none of them is old enough to have owned slaves and that therefore they ought not to be held guilty for whatever damage was done the blacks by that ancient wrong. A racist society? The idea offended them, particularly after a decade in which they had, as they frequently said, *done so much for the Negro.* Yet the middle-aged, middle-class and thoroughly decent American of the 1960's grew up in a culture whose language itself identified white as good (*white hopes, white hats, Snow White, the White House*) and black as bad (*blackmail, black day, black mood, black magic*); which, with endless invention, referred to Negroes as nigger, nigra, coon, darky, dinge, smoke, spook, spade, shine, *schvartze*, jig, jigaboo, boo, boot, boogie or boy, sometimes to their faces; which baked angel's food cake, which is white, and devil's food cake, which is black; which populated its Africa with Tarzan and Jane, Little Black Sambo and cartoon cannibals stewing missionaries in iron pots; which read its children those quaint old Uncle Remus tales, rarely suspecting that Br'er Rabbit was probably America's first black revolutionary; whose history textbooks commonly insulted the Negro* when they remembered to mention him at all; whose public schools graduated generations, black and white, who could tell you with authority that Booker T. Washington came Up from Slavery and that George Washington Carver was the Father of the Peanut but were otherwise illiterate in Negro history; which distinguished those black heavyweight champions who were a Credit to Their Race (Joe Louis, Floyd Patterson) from those who were not (Jack Johnson, Sonny Liston, Muhammad Ali); which dressed brides in white and undertakers in black; which outgrew coon songs ("You'll find no common second-class nigs/In the gentlemen coons' parade") but not darky jokes ("Know what they said when the first colored astronaut blasted off? The jig is up"); in which it was white of someone to do someone else a kindness; which sang "Shine" and "Mammy" and "The Darktown Strutters Ball"; in which people sent one another postcards of black children ("pickaninnies," the captions called them) eating watermelons; whose pop culture was crowded at the edges with Negroes in blackface (Uncle Tom, Aunt Jemima, Old Black Joe, Sportin' Life, De Lawd, Rastus, Kingfish, Rochester, Beulah, Farina, Stepin Fetchit, Butterfly McQueen, Bojangles Bill Robinson, the Harlem Globetrotters) who were required to

---

* From the 1940 edition of *The Growth of the American Republic*, by the eminent historians Samuel Eliot Morison and Henry Steele Commager: "As for Sambo, whose wrongs moved the abolitionists to wrath and tears, there is some reason to believe that he suffered less than any other class in the South from its 'peculiar institution.' The majority of the slaves were adequately fed, well cared for, and apparently happy. . . . Although brought to America by force, the incurably optimistic Negro soon became attached to the country, and devoted to his 'white folks.' "

grin relentlessly, sing hotly, dance sinuously, misbehave incorrigibly, be afraid of ghosts and say things like "Who dat say who dat?" or "Feets, get movin';" in which imitation Negroes (Al Jolson, Eddie Cantor, Amos 'n' Andy) came to seem more authentic than the real thing; which agreed that black is beautiful and produced Lena Horne and Harry Belafonte to prove it; which finally wrote black leading men into movie and TV scripts but rarely let them get or show any interest in getting the girl; which sent a segregated army to fight Nazi racism in Europe; which quoted its maids and manservants as saying the civil-rights movement was a mess that most Negroes wanted no part of; which probably suspected all along that Sambo one day would stop grinning but which managed nevertheless to be surprised in turn by The Movement, the riots and the judgment of the riot commission that we are a nation decisively shaped by our racial prejudices.

For whites to survive this assault with their sensibilities even relatively undamaged was, for those who managed it, something of a feat. For black people, it was probably impossible. White America has always spoken about its Negroes as though they were not in the room. They were, of course; they heard it all; and the psychic impact over generations was devastating. The Negro American, W. E. B. Du Bois wrote long ago, has always been afflicted by a "double-consciousness . . . [a] sense of always looking at one's self through the eyes of others, of measuring one's soul by the tape of a world that looks on in amused contempt and pity." He lived surrounded by evidence of what white people thought of him; his color was like some terrible judgment that he could not escape; he was, in the words of an old street saying, "black all day long" in a world whose standards of worth and beauty were created by whites. And in a hundred subtle ways the judgment of the world became his own. He bought skin whiteners and hair straighteners, fled the ghetto if he could and paddled his children if they "acted nigger," meaning any of various sorts of mugging, singing, dancing, noisemaking and horseplay that were thought to be

stereotypically colored. The worst thing white people ever did
to blacks, Malcolm X said accurately and often, was to teach
them to hate themselves. That so much of the teaching was
innocent in intent did not diminish the damage. Its innocence
in fact was precisely the tragedy; it suggested how deep and how
reflexive color prejudice in America had become.

And then, in the 1960's, Negro America began to get Blackenized. Malcolm himself was the harbinger—the first furious
prophet of a black revivalism unmatched since Marcus Garvey's
heyday. "Malcolm," said Price Cobbs, "brought the realization
that the white man is not going to save us." Stokely followed,
bitter and disenchanted, the voice of the combat-worn black
kids who had taken too many lumps and grieved at too many
funerals for too little gain in Mississippi and Alabama and
Southwest Georgia. The rise of a free Africa charged Negroes
with a sense of contact with a lost past and an expansive future.
"Suddenly," said a Washington poverty worker, "it wasn't all
Tarzan and Jane flying through the trees the way we'd been
taught. Suddenly these people were talking about independence." Black athletes, in the two decades between Jackie
Robinson and Lew Alcindor, came to dominate most American
spectator sports. James Baldwin heralded a brilliant and angry
generation of new black writers—and a flowering of black arts
and letters unexampled since the Harlem Renaissance of the
1920's. The riots, grave as their cost may have been, asserted
their own sort of black power—the very real power to loose
chaos at the heart of America's cities. The buffets of the
1960's—the assassinations, the rumors of backlash, the faltering
of American liberalism—eroded the white man's capital in the
ghetto. Negro students forced college after college to put
together instant "Black Studies" programs; even Harvard,
which was then 333 years old, discovered and announced in
1969 that the history, culture and peculiar problems of a ninth
of the American nation were a "legitimate and urgent" field of
academic interest.

And out of it all flowed a surging current called black

consciousness, or black awareness, or simply thinking black—a struggle to escape the old double vision and create a proud, positive and independent identity for blacks *on their own terms*. The quest struck even sympathetic whites as frequently overheated and shrill, occasionally violent, more often merely scholastic, sometimes silly, at moments quite mad. Yet even when it most outraged their sensibilities, thinking black commanded their attention to the terrible sanity at its core—the necessity for Negroes at last to define themselves instead of being forever defined by whites. "You don't have the same kind of Negro now," said the Reverend Arthur Brazier, the head of Chicago's activist Woodlawn Organization. "He isn't the bubble-eyed buck-toothed clown who was only good at stealing chickens and tap dancing on a barrel by the docks the way they always showed us we were in the movies. I would see those movies in the Army in World War II and I hated it, and I hated being segregated in that army, and I hated the word they printed in big letters across my record folder: C-O-L-O-R-E-D." The new mood demanded that Negroes do the spelling themselves—and for increasing numbers of them the spelling came out B-L-A-C-K.

Thinking black was not a unanimous style of mind in Negro America; its roots were deepest among the young and the middle class, frailest among the old and the poor, whose principal ideology is survival. But it was spreading fast. It decreed that bubble eyes and buck teeth indeed were out. So were skin creams and konked hair. ("A broad nose, a thick lip and nappy hair is *us*," cried Stokely, "and we are going to call that beautiful whether they like it or not. We are not going to fry our hair any more. But they can start wearing their hair natural to look like us.") Africa was in. So were Dashikis, Frantz Fanon, *The Autobiography of Malcolm X, The Battle of Algiers*, the vocabularies of nationalism and revolution, and that sweet-and-sour way of seeing, doing, eating, drinking, singing, dancing, walking, talking and thinking called "soul." Even a plate of chitlin's became an epiphany in the new metaphysics of blackness. "When black consciousness takes over," a black teacher at Atlanta's Morehouse College said solemnly, "you eat your chitlin's with an air of ceremony. The eating of that soul food is a sacrament because you are aware that you are eating it and that this is a thing that is unique to your people. When you sit down to take tea, you are losing your identity. Tea is not your bag, man."

And waiting for Whitey, in the new militancy of color, was out. It became suddenly, luxuriously possible to curse white folks, call them honkies, sass them mercilessly, even threaten their imminent destruction. "The biggest difference between being known as a Black man or a negro," H. Rap Brown wrote in his memoir, *Die, Nigger, Die!*, "is that if you're Black, then you do everything you can to fight white folks. . . . If white folks say it's more cultured to whisper, you talk loud. If white folks say gray suits are fashionable, you go buy a pink one. If they say america is great, you say america ain't shit." It even became possible to laugh at The Man. Carmichael, evangelizing the ghettos in 1966 and 1967, used to tell the one about the white U.S. Air Force pilot ("with a Harvard Ph.D. in military science") who crashed in Africa and was rescued by a native tribe. "Well," the chief asked the pilot, "what's happening with this bird?" Replied the pilot: "Well, that's a war plane and we're engaged in a war." Was his side winning? Why, yes, said the pilot, he himself had killed thirty of the enemy—"three-zero men, by myself, and these are the medals."

"Wow, baby," said the chief, "you must have had some feast."

"My good man!" said the pilot. "Where I come from, we're *civilized*—we don't eat people."

"Well, baby," asked the chief, "why you kill them?"

To tell white people to their faces that they are not entirely civilized was a new phenomenon for the ghetto in the 1960's. To think it was not. Whites, who had so long overestimated the Negro's affection for them, tended now equally to overstate his hostility: not all black people hate all white people all of the time. But, as the *Newsweek* Poll makes clear, they do look on The Man with the deepest ambivalence. They understand their continuing dependence on him. But their hope that he can be persuaded or forced to treat them better is shadowed by the old curdling suspicion that he does not really mean them well.

The findings of the survey:

· *The great majority of blacks do not particularly trust most white people.*

Twenty per cent of the sample believed that whites generally wanted to see Negroes get a better break. But fully 69 per cent disputed the white man's good intentions—argued, that is, that he actively meant to keep black people down or at best did not really give a damn what became of them. And the tide, particularly in the ghetto North, was running against a charitable view of The Man: the majority who considered whites either hostile or indifferent was up 15 points in three years. Southern blacks were a shade less bleak, a shade more willing than Northerners to make fine distinctions. They still felt kindly toward the much-abused "white moderate"—a people so long ill-used are grateful for small favors—and nearly half of them still imagined that whites Up North were nicer to Negroes than whites down home. Northern blacks dissented on both counts. Having seen the promised land at first hand, they were not easily persuaded that its white folks were friendlier than the ones they left behind—or that the beneficence of white moderation was worth waiting for. "White people," said one of them, a 41-year-old Philadelphia truck driver, "have never planned to help the Negroes. They pretend all the time. But white people just can't stand black people."

· *Negroes nevertheless believe, in the face of mixed objective evidence and their own deep misgivings, that white people are warming to them.*

This view was not quite so widespread at the decade's end as it had been in earlier, happier days; the number who doubted that white attitudes toward black people would soon improve very nearly doubled in the space of three years. "White people," said a dissenter, a 45-year-old woman who makes a living chopping cotton outside Estelline, Texas, "don't care much about colored folk—only for their work." Yet black hope remained buoyantly high. The sample believed by 54 to 40 that white folks had got better in the five years just past—and by a rosy 61 to 28 that they would get better still in the five years just ahead. Some thought this would come about by force ("When somebody keeps pounding on your head, you have to listen sooner or later") and others by friendly persuasion ("I think most white people would really like to do the right thing, but they don't know how"). And some simply believed that if whites would only get to know black people nature would take its benevolent course—that the thaw, in fact, had already started. "White people," said a Philadelphia schoolteacher, 36 years old, "are beginning to dig us."

· *Negroes are discriminating about whites but do not stereotype them; they feel generously toward anyone they think has behaved generously toward them.*

Militants tend to overestimate the hostility of ordinary blacks toward the "white power structure"; the majority of Negroes actually have nothing against white power where they believe it has been responsive to their needs. Their faith in the Federal government verged on collapse with the advent of Richard Nixon; his Administration got a bare 25 per cent favorable rating, to 83 for Jack Kennedy's in 1963 and 74 for Lyndon Johnson's in 1966. But, out of a list of a dozen other white groups and institutions, blacks rated only two—real estate companies and the police—more harm than help to their cause.* Their misgivings about all the rest, to be sure, had

---

* The mass media did not fare quite so well in a separate question. Only newsmagazines and television got favorable ratings for covering the black community truthfully and accurately. Newspapers, radio and the movies did not.

increased significantly since 1966—particularly among the young, the middle class and the ghetto dwellers of the North. Yet the balance of sentiment remained on the whole rather benign. Most popular of all were the anti-poverty program (with a 68 to 9 per cent favorable rating) and the Supreme Court (at 64 to 8). Congress's rating was down but still high (at 52 to 16) in the afterglow of its civil-rights and social-welfare labors of the middle 60's. Catholic priests, white churches and Jews all fared nicely. Business and labor alike won more good will with their positive gestures than the worst among them lost by discriminating against Negro job seekers. White college students were widely admired, though far more in the North than in the South. Perhaps one black in a dozen utterly despaired of getting help from The Man or any of his institutions. ("It isn't in their nature to help anyone if they don't profit something by it," said a 44-year-old maid in Rockford, Illinois.) But most grass-roots Negroes were more than willing to suspend their disbelief; the advice of the militants to the contrary notwithstanding, they held to the view that some of their best friends are white liberals.

· *The breadth and depth of black anti-Semitism has been greatly overblown by black militants and overplayed by the white media.*

It exists; a vein of Negro anti-Semitism is probably as old as the ghetto, where landlords, storekeepers and welfare workers—next to police the most visible and least loved whites in the ghetto—are so often Jewish. What made it a *cause célèbre* in the national press, however, was the bitter fight over the Ocean Hill–Brownsville school decentralization experiment in Brooklyn, when both black militants and leaders of the two-thirds-Jewish teachers' union discovered and exploited black anti-Semitism for their own purposes. The result was a good deal of hysteria in the press and the Jewish establishment—and a crisis between old allies that was the sorrier because it bore so little resemblance to the actual beliefs of the black community. The *Newsweek* Poll figures:

WHITES AND JEWS: THE BLACK VIEW

	% of Blacks Who Agree
Most whites want to keep Negroes down	43
Most Jews want to keep Negroes down	19
Most whites want a better break for Negroes	20
Most Jews want a better break for Negroes	28
Most whites don't care one way or another	26
Most Jews don't care one way or another	32

The Jews, in sum, were substantially more popular with Negroes than white people generally were. It was tempting, indeed, to conclude that what animosity there was against them existed less because they are Jewish than because they are white.

· *The animosity of Northern ghetto blacks toward the police has not been exaggerated at all: it is real, it is critical and it is getting worse.*

The importance of a détente between the cop and the ghetto can hardly be overstated; police malpractices were No. 1 on the list of grievances underlying the twenty-four ghetto uprisings covered in detail by the riot commission report—and police incidents actually triggered half of them. And nothing police did thereafter materially diminished black America's suspicions. Southern Negroes tended, though not very enthusiastically, to support their local police. Northern blacks did not. They were persuaded, 56 to 34, that police were not doing a good job of preventing crime in their neighborhoods. They believed, by 50 to 34, that the stories they hear about police brutality are true. And they felt, by 57 to 18, that the police all in all are more a harm than help to Negroes—a stunning vote of no confidence in the men entrusted by the larger society to enforce its laws in the ghetto. To so mistrust the police is to begin, whatever the merits of the case, to see them as the militants do—as an occupying army sent not to protect but to contain and pacify the natives. It clearly will not be enough for the police merely to tell black people that this is not so. The ghetto wants to be shown.

· *Anti-white feelings run highest of all among the most violently inclined blacks of all—the young bloods in the inner-city black preserves of the North.*

A casbah psychology has taken root among the under-30 generation in the ghetto—a baleful feeling of isolation in a hostile white world. A clear majority believed that most whites are anti-black; barely one in ten considered them friendly. The ghetto young, unlike the rest of the black community, did not think the white man had got any better in the past five years— and they were considerably less certain than their elders that he would be any nicer to Negroes in the '70's. ("A white person," said a young file clerk in New York, "seems to think he has to be superior to something, even if it's nothing but a dog. He feels if he gives us a break he loses his superiority.") They do not like Northern whites any better than the Southerners their parents fled. They rated Jews, white moderates, business and the churches as more harm than help to Negroes; a steady fourth of them, in fact, were so turned off that they saw nothing helpful about *any* group or institution on the survey list. And they gave the police a next-to-unanimous 70-to-12 negative rating—a level of hostility so pervasive as to verge on a psychic state of war.

War remained a step farther than the ghetto young were prepared to go in 1969. But they were powerfully tempted by the imagery of mobilization—an imagery of sides chosen and gauntlets flung down and lines drawn in the dust. By a narrow but no less disquieting margin of 45 to 43, they agreed that whites would never help Negroes voluntarily and that accordingly they had to band together *as blacks against whites* to get what they wanted. This, of course, is a central premise of the black power heresy, and the Stokely Generation found it enormously attractive. Said a 23-year-old factory worker in Baltimore: "As long as the black man has to *ask* the white man for something, he'll never get it." A 25-year-old graduate student in New York: "If whites had any intention of helping Negroes, they would have started helping long before now." A 26-year-old poverty worker in Oakland: "They haven't given us equal opportunity in the past three hundred years, and they won't now. Our only power is in our numbers."

Their elders had spent too much of their lives constrained by color lines drawn by white people and so were not easily persuaded to begin drawing their own. A two-to-one majority rejected the idea of organizing around the single fact of race—and *their* position, of course, is a central premise of black moderation. "We don't need someone to fight in order to get ahead," said a credit clerk in Kansas City. "Some whites have been helping for years on the advances we as a race have made." A jitney driver in Philadelphia: "We need each other." A garbage collector in Cincinnati: "How can we band against them? We got no jobs for each other." An aging housewife in Pittsburgh: "How we gonna get something when we ain't got nothing? Niggers won't help you—they can't. When you ain't got nothing and white folks got it all, you got to work with them to get what they got."

Getting what whites have got remained the object of the game; to be Blackenized did not really change that. But it did alter some of the basic terms of play. "The highest priority," said Price Cobbs, "is a change in the basic attitude of this country so that when Americans think of themselves, they will think of more than just a white man in an Uncle Sam suit." And it altered the habits of mind of some of the players. Whitney Young of the Urban League was not given to standing on ghetto street corners railing against Whitey; he would look all wrong eating chitlin's, ceremonially or otherwise; he let his hair grow out only just long enough for a discreet dash of the new natural style. But in the spring of 1969, he sat in his midtown Manhattan office, from which he maintains daily diplomatic contact with some of the most powerful white men in the nation, and told a visitor softly, "White America needs some of our soul to survive."

*   *   *

Soul was the cry in the ghetto in the latter 1960's—a joy in blackness as passionate as the shame of blackness had always been in white America. Whites had long been accustomed to thinking of the Negro as, in Cobbs's phrase, "an imperfect white person"—simple, carefree, emotionally, spiritually and sexually unbuttoned, periodically blue but innately happy and, yes, naturally rhythmic. His impulse was assimilation; the implied price was the forfeiture of his blackness. But the soul renaissance of the 1960's said no sale—not on those terms. "Just when we were almost white," said black historian Vincent Harding, "we found out we didn't want to be." Soul rejected some of the ancient stigmata and stereotypes, embraced others and proclaimed them virtues. (What was wrong with rhythm anyway?) It defied codification: it was red beans and rice and James Brown at the Apollo, tambourines in church and hollers in a jailyard, nappy hair and a diddybop walk, Oscar Robertson and John Coltrane and Eldridge Cleaver, Saturday night on 125th Street and Mother's Day once a month when the welfare checks arrive; it was rage and wry humor and a gift for survival against odds; it was the sudden heretical discovery that black is beautiful and that white is not necessarily right; it was a card of identity, a passkey to a private club, a membership in a mystical body to which Negroes belonged by birthright and from which whites for a change were excluded by the color of their skins.

And soul, in the late 1960's, was sweeping the country. The black revival was most of all a phenomenon of the young and the middle class but it reached Negroes everywhere. They agreed by two and a half to one that black people in fact partake of some special grace called soul. Their attempts at explaining what soul is varied widely. But taken together they approached a definition:

It's the bringing up of the two races—there was more warmth and love in our people because they had nothing else to give

*their children. . . . It's something inside of you that keep you
going even though you know you're being mistreated and taken
advantage of. . . . We are a more compassionate people. . . .
The white people can do the Watusi but we are the Watusi.
. . . It's the ability to laugh in the face of adversity that would
drive the average white to suicide. . . . I think it's more a
happy and contented feeling—I've always gotten joy from being
black for a reason I can't explain. . . . They don't have the gift
of religion that we have, try with all their might. . . . It's a
feeling of black nationalism—a kind of common destiny for
survival. . . . You meet other Negroes and speak to them, you
don't have to know them—there's just a kind of understanding. . . . Whites have had no problems, therefore no soul—no
sincere feeling for anything at all. . . . Our belief in God is
different—I think they believe God is white. . . . We have
heart, whites just don't have it. . . . They can stand the cold,
we can stand the heat. . . . Sure 'nough—swinging and being
happy. . . . They try to copy the Negro people—they see us
dance and they wish they could do it too. . . . We like spirituals and jazz, they like way-out things we can't understand.
. . . We got more rhythm—they don't move like us. . . .
We're happy with the least or less. . . . It's more experience in
life—the average Negro lives more in five years than the whites
do in ten. . . . I wonder how the white man would survive if
he were to be told all of his life that he isn't as good as the
black man or made to feel he isn't human. . . . It's from being
down so long. . . . It's like you get to feeling the spirit. . . .
It's so sweet. . . .*

And: *I can't describe it, man. You just have to be black.*

And: *Soul is the colored person.*

And: *Soul is you. Yourself.*

And soul, by the end of the decade, was insistently black.
The word black was a painfully acquired taste, and only a
minority, by the end of the 1960's, had acquired it. Into the

middle nineteenth century, black Americans rather preferred "men of color" or "colored people"—terms which thereafter faded but remained acceptable in the twentieth. (It was Colored People the NAACP proposed to advance at its birth in 1909.) "Freedmen" was in fashion briefly during Reconstruction. But "Negro" was by all odds the most popular over the century between the Civil War and the black revival of the 1960's. It came periodically under attack as a badge of inferiority; during one such flurry in the 1920's, W. E. B. Du Bois wrote, "Suppose we arose tomorrow morning and lo! instead of being 'Negroes,' all the world called us 'Cheiropolidi'—do you really think this would make a vast and momentous difference to you and me? The feeling of inferiority is in you, not in any name. . . . Exorcise the hateful complex and no name can ever make you hang your head." "Negro," in any event, survived; the real battles around it came during the 1920's and '30's when blacks insisted on and won the capital N and pressed for the pronunciation *knee-grow* as against *negra, nigro, nigra* or *nigger*. None of the alternatives seemed very attractive at the time. There were, of course, the African Methodist Episcopal Church, and the Baltimore *Afro-American*—but names that suggested Africa did not easily catch on in a country that, until recently, thought of Africans as cannibals with grass skirts and bones through their noses. And black? Black was an insult to a community that had acquiesced in the tyranny of color and had enshrined "bright" or "clear" (i.e., light) skin as its own ideal of beauty.

To call oneself "black" in that climate meant that one accepted the stigmata; it was therefore an act of some pain. What was surprising in the late 1960's was not that "Negro" was still the most favored name but that so large a minority had embraced what had so recently been a fighting word. Malcolm and the Muslims began the rehabilitation of "black" in the late 1950's and early 1960's, and a few kids in the Southern civil-rights movement tried it on and liked it. Yet the vogue did not

really take off until 1966, when first Willie Ricks and then
Stokely Carmichael of SNCC began hollering "black power" at
freedom rallies in Mississippi and discovered how deep a chord
they struck. Stokely more than any single man transformed the
move from "Negro" to "black" from an exercise in semantics
into an act of liberation—a declaration to whites that their label
was no longer acceptable, that the most important single fact
about black people was the fact that they are black and that
they would henceforth insist on "black" as their rightful name.
Others dusted off "Afro-American" out of a similar impulse; it
had a parallel revival though a smaller one—partly for want of a
Carmichael to promote it.

The enormous investment of energy in the matter of a name
confused whites, and the returns in the *Newsweek* Poll were an
uncertain guide precisely because the issue, in the spring of
1969, was not yet settled. The interviewees were asked which of
four words (Negroes, colored people, blacks, Afro-Americans)
they liked most and which they liked least. The figures:

OUR RIGHTFUL NAME

The Most Liked		*The Most Disliked*	
Negroes	38	Colored People	31
Colored people	20	Blacks	25
Blacks	19	Negroes	11
Afro-Americans	10	Afro-Americans	11
Don't care	6	Don't care	6

The overall returns show, not surprisingly, that "Negro" was
still the most liked and the least disliked name of all, and that
more people rejected "black" than accepted it. "I hate the word
black," said a Pittsburgh housewife. "I resent it." But "Negro"
was no longer a majority choice. There remained substantial
dissent among the most conservative elements—the oldest and
poorest blacks, particularly in the South—to whom "Negro"
had always been too close to "nigger" and who felt more
comfortable thinking of themselves as colored. And now "Ne-

gro" was under challenge by the most militant elements as well—the young and the middle class in the Northern ghettos. "Black" topped their list, and their choice carried weight beyond their numbers because they were so well placed to influence the vocabulary of race. The young and the middle class together provide much of the leadership and most of the activism in the ghetto; their people are regularly on television and in print; and by the end of the 1960's practically all of them, from the Urban League to the Panthers, were using "black."

Black was a style as well as a name. The old esthetics of color decreed that hair was "good" if it was straight and fine like white folks'; if it wasn't, the next best thing was to straighten it with lye-based Congolene or electric frying combs, neither a particularly pleasant experience. But black consciousness held that kinky hair was natural and therefore good and that "processing" it was quite literally a slavish imitation of The Man. "Now you see my wife with her hair in curlers to make it look like white folks' hair?" Ralph Abernathy asked a visitor to his Atlanta home. "Well, my children wouldn't do that in a million years. They've got their Afros. That's the difference these past fifteen years have made for blacks—they look black, they think black and they want freedom now." Afros indeed were all the rage. Roughly half the nation's blacks—and three-fourths of the ghetto young—approved them; cosmetics companies sold hair straighteners on one page of *Ebony*, sprays for naturals on the next; the look got so faddish that Rap Brown, whose own shock Afro helped get it going, remarked sourly, "I'd rather see a cat with a processed head and a natural mind than a natural head and a processed mind."

Afro-style clothes—Dashiki blouses, for example—seemed more eccentric to Negro Americans and so were less popular. Yet, even at that, a third of the blacks liked them and nearly a fourth said they would wear them—a minority but a large one for a people who had only slowly come to real pride in their

African past. A Dashiki, like an Afro haircut, was a political statement—a declaration of the right and the necessity to be different. "Why should everyone have to wear a tuxedo for some event?" the psychiatrist Alvin Poussaint once puzzled. "That's a form of Western European tyranny. It's also a way of keeping out poor people, because tuxedos are expensive." And Dashikis, more important, announced the discovery that "black is beautiful"—a proposition that ought not to have been startling but was in a nation where gentlemen prefer blondes, where sin is what the darkest Negroes are said to be as black as, and where practically everyone regardless of race dreams of a White Christmas. Is black beautiful? Three-fourths of the Americans who chanced to have been born black said yes—an extraordinary affirmation of color for a people who had squandered so much energy and cash trying to bleach it out, rub it off or otherwise disguise it.

"Black is beautiful" had thus passed from slogan to article of faith. And blackness as a faith, like any other, had not only a body of perfectly sensible believers but a train of monks, cultists, fabulists, schoolmen, exegetes and crazies, all impelled by the necessities of creating a race of men. White people had effectively blacked out Negro history and then clucked and smiled when many blacks, in the rush to construct a new one, made every African a prince or a scholar and every slave a Nat Turner. Fastidious scholarship is a luxury of the settled and the comfortable; blacks plunged on, writing their own history and rewriting the white man's in the bargain. (George Washington begat nine illegitimate children with slave women, former CORE chairman Floyd McKissick lectured a somewhat startled convention of white bankers, "so maybe he *was* the Father of Our Country. . . . Sherman didn't know his ass from a hole in the ground—black scouts led him to Atlanta. . . . Abe Lincoln didn't free the slaves, he *fired* the slaves. . . .") Black students pursued black studies, shut off from whites, where they could manage it, in separate classrooms, separate dorms, separate

campus hangouts, separate tables in the cafeteria. "When I first
came here," a black campus editor at Wayne State in Detroit
remembered, "it was vogue to dress and talk boojy [bourgeois].
If you were light-skinned, you were in. But now people can say,
'I'm black and always have been. This is me, the real me you're
seeing now.'" And sometimes it seemed that nothing else
mattered. "Oh, we still have parties and things," said a Wayne
classmate. "But the whole atmosphere for blacks, even at a
student party, is about their being black."

There were perils in all of this, of course—not the least of
them the possibility that, for some, the celebration of blackness
would become an end in itself. Not all blacks shared the almost
obsessive preoccupation with what was in a name: "Negroes,"
the black historian John Hope Franklin told *Newsweek*'s
Lucille Beachy, "have been called everything including sons of
bitches. I don't care *what* you call us so long as justice is done."
Or the politics of natural hair: "There are people with konks
with more pride than people without," said the novelist Ralph
Ellison. "Don't convert an esthetic gesture into something
metaphysical." Or the taste for soul food: "Eating chitterlings,"
wrote Eldridge Cleaver, "is like going slumming to [the black
bourgeoisie]. Now that they have the price of a steak, here they
come prattling about Soul Food. The people in the ghetto want
steaks. *Beef steaks.*" Or the faith of the kids in the *relevance*—
their word—of black studies curricula. "Black studies makes as
much sense as European studies," Sterling Tucker of the Urban
League insisted. "Society tells these young people they're nobody and their parents tell them they're somebody. They're
trying to find out who they are." But Bayard Rustin, for one,
remained unconvinced: "What the hell are soul courses worth
in the real world?" And Gary's Mayor Hatcher was fretful that
the black young might miss the real point—"that they'll ro-
manticize so much about blackness and pride that they won't
move into the places where the power is."

The black revival loosed a good deal of honky-baiting as

well—a tendency among the Jacobins who appear in any revolution to tease, curse and threaten whites for the sheer indulgent pleasure of seeing them scared. There comes a time in the making of a revolutionary, one Brooklyn militant said, when "you realize you're black and although your people have done nothing wrong, you must live this way. So you start realizing you hate the white man because he is responsible. You know it is he you'll have to reckon with." The realities of numbers, armaments and power in America do not permit very many opportunities to reckon with him violently. But, up to a point, they do allow a sort of surrogate violence of language; if one is not permitted to kill Whitey, one can at least say *boo!* and make him jump. There are obvious satisfactions for the man who says it and a very real psychic profit for the blacks in his audience, so many of whom had been brought up prisoners to their awe and their fear of The Man. But rhetorical violence requires continuous escalation. It proceeded rather quickly from its classic style (Malcolm X telling cautiously Aesopian tales in which dogs, foxes, wolves and snakes were forever catching hell) to baroque (Rap Brown threatening to shoot Lady Bird) to rococo (David Hilliard of the Panthers hollering about President Nixon at a San Francisco peace rally, "Fuck that motherfucking man! We will kill Richard Nixon! We will kill any motherfucker that stands in the way of our freedom!").* And, in the process, the rhetoricians began to bump against the limits of words as weapons. Some whites were frightened into buying guns, some policemen into using them; Congress passed a law which proposed to end riots by putting Stokely Carmichael and Rap Brown in jail (it accomplished neither purpose); liberals fell back from the field, their ranks decimated and their feelings hurt. And finally honky-baiting grew so

* Hilliard was shouted off the stage by members of the crowd of 200,000 chanting, "Peace! Peace! Peace!" The government, which was then actively pursuing Panthers, chose to take him literally and had him arrested a few days later on charges of threatening the life of a President.

commonplace that whites stopped jumping or even listening; there was, after Hilliard, so little with shock value left to be said.

Yet it would be a tragic mistake to judge the black revival of the 1960's by its extravagances and its excesses. "The search for identity is growing up," said Rustin, who passed through his own bitter black period as a young man. "It will be partly painful and partly foolish. But the moment the society restores the Negro's faith and hope that something will change, the sense of self-pride will fall into place. Most of the kookiness is a reaction to not being accepted: 'You don't want me. OK, well, let me tell you, I don't want you, your hair, your food or nothin' to do with you.'" And the growing pains, at their most exaggerated, tended to hide the real creativity in Blackenization: an impulse toward pride, manliness, unity, independence, self-help, community development—toward precisely those traits, in short, that whites had urged on the ghetto in countless debates, dissertations, conferences, symposia and white papers on The Negro Problem. Getting there was painful for everybody, but the trip was worth taking. "I used to hate Whitey with a fucking passion, man," said Ferman Moore, a Watts community worker, "but I've gotten to know a lot of groovy white people. Now I know it ain't a matter of white or black but a matter of oppressed people."

Ferman Moore could hardly be said to love Whitey today. But there was too much to be done getting Watts together, and hating Whitey had suddenly become a waste of energy and time.

So Moore had moved beyond getting Blackenized, which is to discover oneself, to black power, which is to begin to act on one's discovery. The resources of the ghetto were notoriously frail. It had lost generations of natural leaders who had fled as soon as they achieved middle-class status; most of what it had— its tenements, its businesses, its politics, even the numbers—was owned by whites. But the élan was there in the late 1960's. Blacks were so persuaded of their possibilities that they lined up eight to one against preferential treatment to make up for their ill treatment in the past. Whether they were being realistic or not was another question. No important Negro leader, "responsible" or otherwise, accepted the proposition that whites owed blacks nothing more than a scratch start in the race for diplomas, jobs and a taste of America's plenty; they uniformly insisted on some form of compensatory effort by The Man, whether it was advertised as "reparations" or a "Domestic Marshall Plan" or merely a "War on Poverty." Ordinary blacks quite obviously would not turn down any such assistance, but it clearly was important to them to believe that they are ready to compete on equal terms with whites right now.

And the will was there, too—a new sinew, a rising assertiveness, a quickening of the pulse at the cry "black power!" That slogan was born in a time of riot and racial tension; its creators in SNCC were sure only in retrospect what they meant by it; it quickly became the property of demagogues of every sort. Whites took it badly from the beginning, on the presumption that "black power" meant rioting or separatism or blacks taking over America. The earliest reaction among Negroes was negative, too, though far more ambivalently: the *Newsweek* Poll in 1966, when the slogan was still new, audacious and very controversial, returned a 37-to-25 split decision against it. A "black death," Roy Wilkins called it that anxious summer; what he and most of the other mainstream leaders saw in those first superheated Carmichael rallies was a carnival-mirror reflection of the white racism they had spent their lives battling.

But "black power" aged well. The Whitney Youngs as well as the Stokely Carmichaels started using it, each for his own dissimilar purposes. And the more black people heard it, the more they came to like it. The balance of sentiment turned about in three years: the 37-to-25 vote against "black power" in 1966 became a 42-to-31 split *for* it in 1969. The South, still uncertain, split even. But Northern blacks (at 50 to 28) liked it—and the youngest among them (at 68 to 16) liked it best of all.

Black power was no more easily codified than soul: it meant what the listener chose to hear in it. What it did *not* mean to those who embraced it was black hegemony over whites or black violence, as so many whites imagined; the Negroes who took that view were the ones who rejected the slogan. "I think they're talking about taking over, having their own country or something," said a shoe salesman, 26 years old, in Pittsburgh. And a neighbor, a 63-year-old housewife: "I'm scared of it. I don't believe in stealing and robbing. I don't uphold them. Don't mean nothing to me but trouble, and I ain't no soul sister either."

People who approved the phrase told quite another story. What they heard in the words "black power" was a call to pride and manhood, a summons to unity, a demand not for the destruction of America but for a rightful share in its life and plenty. This was *their* black power:

It's a sense of standing up and being counted as a man. . . . Equality, rights, liberty, freedom, peace, unity, black people uniting and accepting each other as brothers. . . . Helping your brother, standing tall and together. . . . The liberation of our black brothers and sisters. . . . It's money, baby, and success. . . . It's we shall overcome—right now. . . . It makes me feel like I am somebody. . . . It's black people uniting to attain the rights that most whites take for granted. . . . It's the way James Brown sings it—I'm black and I'm proud. . . . It's black strength, courage and recognition. . . . The only thing better than black is more black. . . . It's black people getting justice. . . . It's just to live like decent human people. . . . I think it means to get all the people to the polls—that's where the power is, the ballot box. . . . It's freedom now—or else war. . . . It means blacks controlling their lives in their area.

. . . The black people get together and do for himself. . . . It means identification with the blacks and pride in oneself. . . . It's "I am me"—a sense of strength. . . . It means a lot to me because I am black power. . . . It's black people getting a place in the world. . . . It's beautiful!

"Sure, black is beautiful," an auto mechanic in New Orleans told a Gallup interviewer. "Any color is beautiful. Isn't a rainbow?" Negro Americans did not abandon the rainbow quest when they started talking about black power. Quite to the contrary, they were still pursuing it; but they had discovered that the terms of the quest would be rather different than many of them once imagined. "I've seen my wife come home crying because of the police stopping her on the street and asking her if she's a prostitute," an Indianapolis poverty worker said. "As a human being, I believe in human power. As a black man, I have to believe in black power because I've lived under white power too long." He had gone to bed one night a Negro and woke up the next day a black man, marching to a different drum, singing a different tune:

You better go to a natural school
Negroes get hot, black people get in the pool
I don't know whether you realize
Before you get some respect you got to be Blackenized . . .

DIRECTIONS:
Bayard Rustin

Bayard Rustin may be the nearest thing we have to a renaissance man—a blend of thought and action, grace and rage, sense and sensibility in dizzying kinetic balance. It is typically Rustin that he taught himself the lute while doing twenty-eight months in prison for resisting the draft in World War II: his life has been that way. He was a three-letter athlete (football, tennis, track) in high school—and a twenty-four-arrest campaigner against segregation long before going to jail got fashionable. He migrated from communism to pacifism, from pacifism to civil rights. He read Gandhi in India; he was CORE'S first field secretary; he organized the first Aldermaston peace walk in England and a ban-la-bombe march into the French Sahara; he was with Nkrumah in Ghana and King in Montgomery. He is a gourmet raised on leftover tastes of pâté and Roquefort that his grandfather, a caterer, brought home from white folks' parties. He plays piano, harpsichord, guitar and lyre as well as lute, and he sang with Leadbelly and Josh White at Café Society Downtown. He is a student of formidable learning in history and economics, a connoisseur of formidable taste in African art and European antiques: a magnificent West African Sulofo mask breathes fire on an Italian Renaissance sideboard in his office on Park Avenue South. And Rustin is beyond doubt the best impresario The Movement ever had—the master logistician who put on, among other spectacles, the enormously affecting March on Washington of 1963.

"Bayard," a friend once said, "has a way of popping out of the shadows when he's needed." But he has always insisted on approaching the problems of black people as though they were principally economic and therefore economically soluble by a sort of inchmeal evolutionary socialism. His strategy was coalition—with Democrats, unions, churchmen, liberals, intellectuals or anyone else who at a given moment would vote with the blacks for Medicare, say, or public works, or a two-dollar minimum wage. This increasingly put him in what were, according to the mood of the times, all the "wrong" positions—campaigning for Hubert Humphrey, supporting the New York teachers' strike against ghetto control of ghetto schools, opposing black studies and black-power sloganeering. And so, in his sixtieth year, he was in a sense back in the shadows the day Newsweek's Tom Mathews called on him in the autumn of 1969; many of The Movement kids who had once revered him were not sure that they needed him any more.

And Rustin understood that, because everywhere they had been, he had been and gone. "What I think people seldom understand," he said, leaning forward over an expanse of glass desktop, "is that the March on Washington in 1963 was the culmination of one period and the beginning of another. Essentially what the march symbolized was the end of the period of the struggle for a legal basis for justice in the United States and the beginning of the economic struggle which was to come. Naturally, as long as people were concerned with the struggle for the achievement of legal rights under the Constitution, there could be unity; because as long as there was discrimination in hotels, theaters, restaurants, swimming pools, it affected everybody. But as far as Negroes were concerned, once we were in the present period, there had to be splintering. You are not now asking the simple question 'Are you in favor of Negroes having the right to use public accommodations and the right to vote?' You are asking, 'Are you in favor of Negroes having economic freedom?' The answer to that is very simple—

'Yes.' But as to how to bring it about—well, people will answer according to their philosophy, according to their class outlook, according to many other things."

Rustin leaned back and touched his index fingers briefly to his lips. "Some Negroes," he said, "would believe that the least important aspect is cooperation between blacks and whites in the labor movement. I would argue that it's the most important. Others are in favor of black capitalism as the answer to the problem; I think the ghetto cannot be made economically viable— you cannot use poverty to make nonpoverty. There are also people who will argue that American capitalism is going to solve the problem. Well now—if white capitalists have permitted white poverty to exist in Appalachia when they have millions and billions of dollars, how are Negro capitalists with fifteen cents going to eliminate poverty in Harlem? It's silly. And then there are people like myself who believe that only investment on the part of the Federal government can solve the problem. Billions of dollars, for housing, schools, jobs, a guaranteed income."

The sound of buses and taxis rumbling and honking drifted up from the street six stories below. Rustin shifted in his leather chair. "Now," he said, "let's look at this from the point of view of white people. It was very easy for white people to be in favor of God and motherhood and civil rights for Negroes in 1963 because it didn't cost them a damned penny. Negroes were paying all the price, Negroes were going to jail, Negroes were being beaten. But you can't say, 'Give Negroes housing, schools, jobs, medical care and a guaranteed income' without saying, 'You must take some money out of my taxes to do it.' That's the difference now."

Rustin's instincts are political: he understands power, that is, to mean majorities in Congress, not control of the ghetto. He is neither enamored of whites nor ashamed of blackness; he let his hair grow natural and read up on the Zimbabwe Empire before many of the black-power kids of the middle 1960's were born.

But he saw neither esthetic merit nor political gain in declaring that black is beautiful. "Sometimes I'm very beautiful, sometimes I'm quite depraved, like every other human being," he said. "Black is not beautiful. White is not beautiful. Simply because white people have been stupid enough to think that because they were white they were beautiful doesn't mean that now I am going to turn around and make a similar stupid error and consider myself beautiful because I am black." He understood why people should say that. "It was inevitable. We had to go through this. Any time you've told people for three hundred years that they are ugly because they are black, that they are depraved because they are black, sooner or later they have to revolt. And when the revolt comes it's not going to be a tea party—it's going to be more irrational than rational. But that doesn't mean that voices of sanity shouldn't point out the irrationality, because the sooner we get through this period, the better."

Better, he was saying, for all concerned—whites and blacks alike. "White liberals," Rustin said, "are really saying now, though quite unconsciously, 'Isn't it nice that the blacks are saying that they are superior because now we can feel better about having said it ourselves about ourselves.' I find that white guilt is the most sickening of all diseases. I loathe white people who are guilty—who want to take on all the burdens of their fathers and the sins of three and four generations. I have never in the forty years I have been in the civil-rights movement known anything creative at all to come out of guilt feelings on the part of whites or blacks." He spread his long fingers on the desktop and looked absently at them. "When people are called honkies—when they go to see the so-called new drama of black people in which whites are cursed from the stage and told that they stink and they sit there self-flagellating themselves and are delighted to hear it—well, that's sick. Or when they are prepared to give Mr. [Roy] Wilkins three hundred dollars to talk and then are prepared to give Stokely Carmichael or Rap Brown fifteen hundred in order that they can be told what bastards they are, I think that is simply sick. That's exactly where guilt will lead one.

"And down the road guilt will lead to even worse. Because having spent all their energy in self-flagellation, when the time comes to put their energy into the development of an economic and social program which will really free black people, they won't be there." The fingers came down—thwunk!—on the desktop. "It's happened many times in our history. The abolitionists are a good example. We must beware of men who have a single moral drive independent of an economic and social program. The abolitionists were so happy at having spent their whole lives seeing that Negroes were free; but after they were free and they were asking for forty acres and a mule—an economic program if there ever was one—the abolitionists were so tired that they all went home"—thwunk!—"and did not put up any fight. Mark my words—the so-called peaceniks today, who are out here screaming, 'We want the war ended so that the money can be used in the ghettos,' they will be the last people to fight once they have achieved their so-called moral victory."

Rustin had even less patience with the white camp followers of the Black Panthers. "The Panthers," he said, "know nothing about power—otherwise all their leadership would not be in jail or their secondary and tertiary leadership on the way to jail. They have much more of a following among whites than they do among blacks, which ought to define something for you. Again, it's part of this whole guilt thing. Great numbers of white people really feel, 'Oh, isn't it nice, we are lazy bastards, and privileged, all going to college, all living in Westchester, all getting money from papa, but we can talk revolution.' Those people are what Lenin and Rosa Luxemburg described as the most dangerous element in society. They want to play radical while preparing to buy homes in Westchester and working for their Ph.D.'s in order to make as much money as they can. And what they are really saying is, 'You sic 'em, nigger Panthers. You bring about a revolution for us while we go on living our nice little jolly lives. You niggers do it. Oh, aren't they cute. We'll be right behind you—at a considerable distance.' Now, they are the most immoral people on the face of the earth."

Rustin has spent forty years in another sort of black revolt entirely. His revolt is in its own way profoundly black-conscious: he has been in four African revolutions, collected and read a private library of black writing, surrounded himself with prime African art and artifacts. "And therefore I profoundly appreciate my heritage," he said. His arms stretched over the desk; Mathews glimpsed a black bracelet made of hair from an elephant's tail, a talisman of good luck and potency given Rustin by Jomo Kenyatta. Rustin wears it with style and sentiment and pride; but he will not dissociate his heritage, or his destiny, from America's. "I've worked too long," he said. "I've been in jail too many times. I've seen too many people killed and lynched for integration." He knew what it was to feel so bitterly toward white people that one does not want to be around them; he had been there, too. But he had not stayed. He swiveled his chair and briefly contemplated a potted plant stretching up toward the ceiling; then he turned back and said, "Black people cannot be viable separate from white people in this society."

CHAPTER 6

Integrate or Separate?

HARLEM IS A DAILY REBUKE to America—a crowded, crumbling, rat-ridden, doom-haunted barren in upper Manhattan that stands as a metaphor for every black ghetto in the nation. White New York relegated its Negro menials there roughly with the turn of the century; it built subways under them, a commuter line over them and expressways around them; it held them out of sight and largely out of mind for sixty years. A casbah often seems a picturesque and vital place to outsiders, and Harlem, more than most, created a style out of its poverty and a soul out of its desperation. But Harlem knew all along why it existed, and why it was poor and desperate. Rage ran in its blood—a rage that is smothered most of the time in the low-grade depression of everyday life within the walls but which, at intervals, explodes. Harlem exploded one muggy July night in 1964, the first in the cycle of native uprisings that would haunt America for years to come. Bricks and bottles flew. Windows disintegrated. Children made Molotov cocktails from recipes in crude mimeographed flyers ("Take any bottle. . . . Fill with gasoline. . . . Use rag as wick. . . . Light rag. . . . Toss and see them run!") Looters and burners battled cops for control of the streets. "Go home! Go home!" a sweaty red-faced police captain pleaded at the height of it, pointing his bullhorn into the blackness. "We *are* home, baby!" a voice echoed back, taunting and shrill—and that simple statement of fact was perhaps the most terrible indictment of all.

For the Harlems and the South Sides and the Wattses *are* home for the nation's urban blacks, not by their own choice but by white America's. The ghetto has romantic periods when it celebrates its own warmth and verve and hardihood; the Harlem Renaissance of the 1920's was one, the soul revival of the '60's another. But what the ghetto can never escape is the fact that it is the white man's devastating judgment on the blacks— a second-class preserve into which he has thrust most of them by the conscious design and the unconscious cruelties of decades and centuries. James Baldwin, who spent (or survived) a boyhood in Harlem, came to think of it as a cage and discovered in himself what cages do to their inmates: "I hated and feared white people. This didn't mean that I loved black people; on the contrary, I despised them, and the ghetto from which they could never escape. In effect, I hated and feared the world." Baldwin fled into exile, to Greenwich Village and Paris and Istanbul, before Harlem could destroy him. Others, equally angry, stayed behind and fought—at first to disperse the ghettos, then to rebuild them, lately to bring them politically, economically and socially under black control.

The best-known name for this last impulse was "black power," and, to the extent that it summoned black people away from integration and toward separatism, it dismayed assimilationist Negroes and liberal whites. They tended to look on the history of postwar American race relations partly if not entirely as a continuing effort to put as many Negroes as possible in the company of white people. The struggle, in this view, had made measurable progress—slowly, to be sure, and at great cost in the blood and treasure of both blacks and whites, but progress nevertheless. The black power movement said no, however, and offered Harlem, or any of a hundred places like it, as prosecution Exhibit A.

And Harlem was not easy to get around. Separatism was a fancy indulged by a minority of Negroes; separation was a fact ordained and plainly desired by the great majority of whites.

The government of the United States, for all the civil-rights legislation and court decisions of the 1950's and '60's, has never seriously attempted the integration of large numbers of blacks with large numbers of whites except in the armed forces and in the public schools of the South. On the contrary, its housing policies, public and private, tended for years to promote segregation, not deter it. Neither has any major metropolitan area even made an important beginning at the dispersal of the ghetto. By the end of the 1960's, indeed, there was reason seriously to question whether the cities *could* any longer be desegregated even if white people wanted to—and the existence of the Harlems on one hand and white suburbia on the other suggested rather powerfully that they did not. "The *real* separatists," argued Floyd McKissick, late of CORE, "are not the blacks—they don't have the power to be separatists. The whites moved out of Harlem, moved out of Watts, moved out of South Chicago. *They* left *us*. They left us separated and isolated, and there's only one salvation. Nationhood. We've got to become a nation."

The idea of becoming a nation—of seceding from white America in spirit if not in formal political fact—has been an enduring undercurrent in Negro life. "I'm sure," Julian Bond said, "that at one time or another every black person has been a separatist and said, 'If these people would just get away from me and leave me alone, I wouldn't have most of the problems I do now.'" The temptation runs highest at times of maximum frustration among the blacks and maximum stress between the races. Some few blacks before emancipation joined the colonization movement, which proposed resettling America's Negroes in the Caribbean or in Africa. Booker T. Washington, around the turn of the century, preached racial solidarity, black economic development and a moratorium on agitating against segregation—a gospel of withdrawal that flourished in a period when anti-Negro riots were commonplace and lynchings almost literally an everyday occurrence. Marcus Garvey, Provisional

President of Africa by his own ordination, reached his zenith during and after World War I—a period when Woodrow Wilson told darky jokes to friends around the White House, Warren Harding came out publicly for segregation, and returning black doughboys were roughly and sometimes bloodily reminded of their place. Garvey and his Universal Negro Improvement Association claimed four million followers. That was no doubt an exaggeration. But it was true that, as Bayard Rustin put it, hundreds of thousands and possibly millions of Negroes who would never have followed Garvey back to Africa wanted nevertheless to pay him dues. "Up, you mighty nation," Garvey told them, "you can accomplish what you will!" His love was all they really asked of him; they were paying dues to themselves.

Rather too much has been made of the parallels between the Washington and Garvey ideologies on one hand and the black power movement of the 1960's on the other; the riot commission report, which was otherwise extraordinarily sensitive for a government document, wrote black power off entirely too casually as "old wine in new bottles." Washington and Garvey appealed largely to the most conservative Negroes, black power to the most radical—the second- and third-generation young in the ghettos of the North. Washington proposed accommodation, and Garvey flight. Black power argued for confrontation on issues chosen by Negroes; it just happened that integration was no longer one of them.

Yet there were in fact kinships between the old movement and the new. Black power, like the earlier appeals to turn inward, was born in frustration—in the exhaustion and the disillusion of Movement kids who had fought at great hazard for an open society and discovered how little difference their few victories had made in the lives of the masses of poor blacks. There were psychological and, not infrequently, sexual tensions between blacks and whites within The Movement itself—especially when white middle-class college students streamed south-

ward on their summer vacations to join the struggle and too
often came to dominate it in ways they neither intended nor
understood. (They were, Stokely Carmichael scoffed in retrospect, a "Pepsi generation," trying to come alive by association
with the most soulful people and the most vibrant cause in
America.) And there was hardening white resistance, North as
well as South, as The Movement's goals moved beyond the
relatively simple questions of Southern Jim Crow and as its
language and its tactics grew correspondingly more abrasive.
What was advertised in America's press and politics as "the
white backlash" seemed to the children of The Movement
really to be the surfacing of a deep white racism that had been
there all along.

And so black power preached withdrawal in some degree
from the society of whites. CORE, which had only recently had
two white members for every black, and SNCC, which had
always had a few white field men, got rid of them. A revisionist
history insisted that integration had never been what The
Movement was about. ("When we went to Mississippi,"
Carmichael said, "we did not go to sit next to Ross Barnett. We
did not go to sit next to Jim Clark. We went to get them out of
our way. . . . We were never fighting for the right to integrate,
we were fighting against white supremacy.") What integration
had been achieved to date, in this jaundiced view, consisted
entirely of the token rewards of The System to those few
Negroes who scrubbed up, straightened their hair, wore Ivy
League suits, aspired to wealth and acted in all ways "boojy"—
those, in short, who made themselves into imitation white
people. But whites clearly did not want and would not permit
the black unwashed to share their schools or neighborhoods. So
black power argued that integration, whether or not it was
desirable as a long-term goal, was irrelevant to most black
people today—and that to beg for it was degrading because it
meant acquiescing in the notion that white schools, white
neighborhoods and therefore white people were in fact superior.

What the new movement proposed instead was that black people pull back behind their own lines and concentrate on developing their own pride and their own political and economic power. A few, like CORE and the Muslims and the Republic of New Africa, made total secession into a separate black nation their ultimate goal. To far more, black power meant giving up confronting whites over integration, at least until that distant day when blacks are ready to demand it as a coalescence of equals, and to concentrate instead on making the best of the ghetto—which after all was the central fact of black life in white America. ("We do not want a nation," LeRoi Jones once wrote, "we are a nation.") And the first priority in making the ghetto better, in the new ideology, was to get white people out of it and put black people in control. "We oughta give all the white men passports and send them back to white countries," SNCC's Willie Ricks said pleasantly. "There's just no way you can live with a white man. We tried to live with the white man for four hundred years. We didn't reject him—he rejected us." But now all that had changed. "Now all we want is what we got coming—forty acres and a mule. All we want is for the white man to let us alone, stop exploiting us, get out of our communities and let us live in peace."

That the old Movement vision of a beloved society should have come to this was tragic—and, given the circumstances, probably inevitable. "You could say it is a failure of the American dream," said Robert S. Browne, a black economist who chooses to call himself a "commentator" on the possibilities of a separate black nation on U.S. soil. "But the American dream has never attempted to deal with us." The American liberal tradition argues that Browne overstated the case; the realities of American life in the 1960's were prima facie evidence that he did not. "You're not really a part of America," said a New York City poverty warrior who is by no measure a radical. "You're not really hooked into the real world. White is here and black is there and there ain't no way to bridge that gap. So there's a real belief today that white America isn't serious. You sit in and you lay down and you wade in but white America goes along its merry way. You struggle for integration, and then, when the white man says you can have a little bit, you discover that you don't want it any more."

But most Negro Americans do want it. They are, when they speak of integration, dealing largely in abstractions. White America was not ready to consort with Negroes in any significant numbers. The Nixon Administration was prepared even less than its predecessors to force the issue. Those blacks who led or presumed to lead the Negro community were decreasingly inclined to push for it. Yet despite all this—despite the deepening resistance of whites and the deepening recalcitrance of many Negro leaders—black people still want integration. They want it across the board. And they want it, if anything, more deeply and urgently than ever.

This was not an unmixed vote of confidence in America. Something between a tenth and a fifth of all the nation's Negroes, depending on how the question was put, did want out—a vein of alienation that indeed raises the question of how well the American dream has accommodated the blacks. Fourteen per cent of them—and 31 per cent of the Northern ghetto young—said flatly in the *Newsweek* Poll that they would not consider America worth fighting for in a world war. "Take the same poll at Harvard and see what you get," one staffer in Nixon's White House said when he heard those figures. That wasn't the point. It is one thing for Harvard's privileged young to opt psychically out of America, quite another for every seventh Negro in the nation, and every third among the ghetto young, to do so. Those figures reveal a stunningly high level of disaffection—a level that had more than doubled in three years.

And the ancient separatist dream of a black Zion, though still distinctly a minority phenomenon, was more widely shared in 1969 than it had been probably since Garvey's finest hour. The

idea of a separate black nation was approved by only 4 per cent of the blacks in the *Newsweek* polls of 1963 and 1966, and by 6 per cent in the riot commission's fifteen-ghetto survey in 1968.*
But *Newsweek*'s third poll a year later revealed a sudden leap forward for black zionism: 12 per cent thought there *would* be a separate Negro nation within the U.S. someday—and fully 21 per cent thought there *should* be. One can argue that any displaced American minority would like its own Israel and that the blacks, in any event, are talking about an abstraction. Yet separation is hardly more abstract for most Negroes than integration, and the contention that everyone would like a homeland somewhere does not explain why the blacks had got so much keener on the idea in so short a time. A likelier explanation lay in the impact of the black revival. A detailed reading of the poll figures showed that those who favored a separate state were far more likely than the integrationist majority to swing with the slogans "black power" and "Black is beautiful." The secessionists are, in any event, a disquietingly large minority; for a comparable pool of spiritual dropouts to materialize among whites would surely be thought a national crisis of faith.

Yet faith continues to sustain the overwhelming majority of blacks today—a tough, hardy, invincible belief that the American dream was meant to include them, too. The levels of alienation are important. But so is the fact that four-fifths of the blacks did consider the nation worth fighting for, and that two-thirds were against establishing a separate state. By far the greatest number of Negroes do not want out of the United States; they want in very badly, in every aspect of life. The findings in the poll:

· *Black people want to work alongside whites.*

* The earlier *Newsweek* polls asked Negroes about a separate nation "in this country or Africa." Including Africa may, of course, have loaded the question. But the riot commission got similar results asking whether Negroes wanted a black nation "here," which suggests that only a marginal minority—up to now—was interested in secession on any terms.

Integration at work is the most widely sought-after kind, partly because Negroes think it is right, partly because there is no other way for them to get at the good jobs. It is, moreover, the target of least resistance, at least in good times; it is not so much the company of Negroes that white workmen fear as their competition in the job market. The blacks, in any event, stood 82 to 11 in favor of working in mixed rather than mostly Negro groups—a level that held high and steady through the '60's.

· *Black people want their children to go to school with whites.*

The rude fact of the matter was that segregation in the schools was getting more acute in the North even as it abated at last in the South. A 1970 analysis by the U.S. Department of Health, Education and Welfare found the progress of desegregation across the nation "shockingly low." Yet it remained a first-priority goal for the nation's Negroes. They were persuaded at least as strongly as ever that their children would do better work going to school with whites: 70 per cent said yes. They were a bit ambivalent about busing their children across town to white schools. Southerners approved integration by bus, but Northerners, who once favored it strongly, had soured on it in six years. What counted for blacks in both regions, however, was not the means but the end. And the end most definitely was integrated education: 78 per cent wanted it—up 8 points in three years of sustained agitation against suing for integration—and only 9 per cent said no.

· *Black people want to live with white people in mixed neighborhoods.*

The reality once again was dismaying. Negroes were so clumped in America's cities that, according to the riot commission, 86 per cent of them would have to move if the ghettos were truly dispersed. This amounts to an informal apartheid in the land of equality—a conflict between myth and fact which Gunnar Myrdal described a generation ago as the American Dilemma. Whites have lived with it partly by telling themselves that Negroes really prefer to stay among their own kind—a long-standing folk view that has lately been reinforced by the widely publicized separatism of some of the younger black leaders. Stereotypes often bear some relationship to fact, and there is a minority view among blacks—particularly in the South—which holds that the comfort of the ghetto is preferable to the dislocations, the hostilities and the real dangers one may experience if one moves out. Some of them spoke up in the *Newsweek* Poll:

You can't get along with whites—one would haul off an' call you nigger. . . . I guess I'm prejudiced too. . . . Negroes understand each other, we've been through the same trials and tribulations. . . . I like living with Negroes—they're my own people. . . . I know them better. . . . I hate white people. . . . I can be more relaxed—more like myself—in a Negro neighborhood. . . . White people are nasty, I know. . . . I'd feel more comfortable around Negroes—you never know how a white person feels about you. . . . I worked with white people so long and I know they are hard to get along with and I wouldn't want to live next to them.

But the main current of Negro American thought was insistently for integrated housing, more so in 1969 than at any time in the decade:

HOUSING: TO LIVE NEXT DOOR

	1963	1966	1969
PER CENT WHO PREFER:			
A mixed neighborhood	64	68	74
A Negro neighborhood	20	17	16

The number who want to live in mixed company thus has been increasing and the number against it actually decreasing, for all the swing away from integration as an official goal of The Movement. Support for integrated living was particularly high in the North (where 80 per cent favor it). The black South was charier of moving in with white folks, but the pro-integration majority nevertheless climbed from 55 to 67 per cent in six years. The pattern held, indeed, in every sector of the black community. Even the Northern young, among whom anti-white feeling ran so high, were massively in favor of racial togetherness; part of their hostility may in fact owe precisely to the white man's resistance to integrating with them.

The enormous thrust toward integration was not entirely due to an access of brotherly love. Some Negroes in the poll quite candidly said they preferred living with whites because white neighborhoods seem to them better, or at least better kept, than black ones:

I want to enjoy some of the good things they have, and this is the only way I can. . . . If it's all Negro, it might not be as nice a place to live. . . . The property wouldn't depreciate as quickly—by the whites fixing their houses up, the Negroes would catch on. . . . I believe living in a mixed neighborhood would help Negroes learn more how to be citizens—uplift our morals. . . . When you call the police in an all-Negro neighborhood, they won't come, but if you live in a mixed neighborhood, they will, because they don't know if it's a white or a Negro that needs help.

Yet the will for integration runs far deeper. Black people have been held apart all their lives, and the reasons are quite brutally plain to them; still they cling tenaciously to the belief that it has all been a case of mistaken identity, that the white man would like them if only he would let them come close enough for him to see them. So they want integration as a proof of their common humanity; they want it so their children will grow up free of its crippling weight; they want it because it is right. And these were *their* voices:

I love everybody. . . . Whites say we're wild and loud and dirty—we need to show them we're human, too. . . . My

*children will never be able to understand white people unless
they live with them. . . . All whites aren't alike—some like us,
some don't. . . . I believe I could really feel like a first-class
citizen living in a mixed neighborhood. . . . Children playing
together don't usually end up fighting each other. . . . I believe in an integrated society—I think a man is a man. . . .
Whites think they are better than we are, but if we live
together, they'll see they are no better. . . . I go along with
anybody if they're nice to me. . . . It's really not doing good to
separate—togetherness is best. . . . I prefer a mixed neighborhood because I am people.*

Nor did black people finally despair of reaching white
America's better nature. Black power argued that there was no
such thing, that American society functions not on conscience
but on power and that blacks ought therefore to go get some
instead of depending on whites for their redemption. "Perhaps
the failure of integration has been an unexpected blessing," said
Warner Saunders of Chicago's Better Boys Foundation. "It's
made the black person realize that he's got to do his own thing
because Whitey ain't going to care what happens to him." Yet
ordinary blacks are not yet persuaded that integration has failed
or that Whitey is beyond the reach of reason or compassion.
They responded strongly to the idea of black power. But to the
extent that black power meant giving up working with whites at
all and going it alone, Negroes weren't buying: they rejected the
proposition by a resounding 72 to 16.

The notion had picked up some followers in three years.
"Before the whites recognize us as equal," said a Baltimore
laborer, "they must first recognize us as powerful." A retired
Chicagoan: "The white man, if you lean away from your color
and toward him, that's what he want you to do. You'll be in the
palm of his hand then." A Pittsburgh housewife: "You can't be
a monkey and a cat too. If you want to be something, you got
to be your own. You can't work with the white folks and expect

to do something for colored. You just can't." But the prevailing sentiment was that there was no other way—that the realities of power in America dictated that Negroes maintain their alliances with those whites who were disposed to help them. Said one Harlem pensioner: "They ain't enough of us." A Savannah truck driver: "Ain't no way for us to get anything without the whites helping us." A young factory worker in Louisiana: "Some white people will help Negroes some. So we need all the help we can get, so if they're not against us, use them if you can." A garbage collector in Andrews, Texas: "You are always going to have to go back to whites to get what you want because, right now, they got it."

So the blacks in effect were putting the choice to white people: either they were serious about opening America to Negroes or they were not. Negroes looked forward to the outcome with a confidence based more on faith than on the visible evidence. "The white man," said a 52-year-old Baltimore longshoreman, "is beginning to realize that we're human." Or was he? Black people who wake up every morning in a Harlem or a Watts must constantly ask themselves that question—and try to deal with the obvious answer. For the Harlems and the Wattses in the end were monuments to white separatism. It was not the masses of blacks who refused the society of whites—quite to the contrary. "Trouble is," a 62-year-old Negro maid told a Gallup interviewer in Detroit, "they keep running from us."

That, of course, was catch-22 for the blacks—white people keep running from them. The evangels of The Movement for years organized Negroes and confronted whites on the issue of segregation. They made headway as long as they were talking about lunch counters, motels and even jobs. But the closer Negroes got, the more whites dug in their heels—or disappeared to the suburbs. And finally The Movement got tired of beseeching, and in its exhaustion it began to accept the ghetto as given and to demand that the blacks, since they could not escape it in meaningful numbers, ought at least to be allowed to run it. "The whites," argued Floyd McKissick, "say, 'We don't want to be bothered with Harlem, we don't like niggers, we don't want to go to school with them, we don't want to associate with them'—that's fine. It's a damned cheap price for them to pay to let the blacks control their own communities. And it ought to make the suburbs happy."

It didn't make the ghetto especially happy; the blacks, in a straight choice between community control and integration, opted for integration by roughly six to one. But black power contended that no such choice existed in the real world—that the only alternative to moving for control of the community was not integration but acquiescence in the disastrous order of things as they are. "Integration is something in the past," said Watts community organizer Robert Hall, whose Operation Bootstrap assiduously maintains its independence of government money and government control. "Not that we don't want to—we tried and it didn't work. We don't want to be separate either. We just want to rule our own destiny." That central premise led some of its advocates into extravagances of language and style—a rhetoric of nationalism and national liberation which borrowed heavily from Mao, Che, Kwame Nkrumah and other anti-colonial heroes of the Third World and which inevitably came out sounding to whites more like outright revolutionary separatism than it actually was. "The whole issue of separatism," said Walter Bremond of Watts's Brotherhood Crusade, "is a phony issue. Black people have always been separate."

The real point was the impulse toward autonomy—the demand of the powerless for a voice in deciding questions that affect their own lives. Black people did not have to look very far for evidence that the ghetto schools were a failure—nor did they have to pledge allegiance to some fantasy Republic of New Africa to imagine that they might do better running the schools themselves. They could not do very much worse. "Whitey," said a Philadelphia ghetto lawyer, "comes on to you to get an education and you'll get a job. But he runs the school system, and he doesn't run it for us, and so a lot of us drop out, and that's his fault—he's running things. Sure, there's a chance for the black person—just like playing the numbers. But the numbers give the caveman more genuine hope than this messed-up system. Maybe we should give the caveman the money, and if he wants to gamble it away on the numbers, okay. If the mistake is going to be made, let him make it."

Community control was far more talk than reality in the late 1960's; power is not easily created out of the debilitation of centuries of dependency, segregation and absentee rule. The war on poverty was launched with a proviso decreeing the "maximum feasible participation" of the poor, although no one, including the authors, was sure exactly what that meant. What it did not mean, in the event, was that the poor were really to run things; some of those who tried were ill-tempered, ill-mannered and even at moments revolutionary, and Congress wrote their "maximum feasible participation" out of the poverty law after three fractious years. New York City, with backstage encouragement and engineering help from the Ford Foundation, turned over a few ghetto schools to neighborhood boards in the latter 1960's. But the boards and their white godparents made mistakes, too, some of which precipitated and inflamed a series of three teachers' strikes, and the state ultimately moved to call off the experiment by enacting a watered-down decentralization plan of its own. Some of the most intriguing ventures in developing black community power, indeed, were those which were able to operate independently of outside authority and which therefore *could* make, and profit by, their own mistakes. The proliferation of community uplift organizations in hundreds of ghetto storefronts and walk-ups was a particularly hopeful sign; so was the birth and growth of a farm cooperative movement among Negroes in the Black Belt South.

None of this, of course, amounted to a great deal of power;

the resources of the ghetto were too frail and the task of reconstruction too large for blacks to create their future entirely on their own. Yet the demand for community control came increasingly to dominate the agenda and the vocabulary of race relations in the late 1960's. "Community control, down here with the black folks, that's really where the black movement is at," said Warner Saunders. He did not suggest that it was the majority will of the blacks; he guessed that no more than a fourth of them supported community control now, to 1 per cent or under for revolution ("If there were any more, they'd blow this fucking town up") and 75 per cent for integration. But, given the depth of white resistance to integrating, Saunders saw it as inevitable that more and more black people would be moved to tell The Man that if they couldn't live with him, he would no longer be allowed to run them. And what Saunders did not need to add was that a majority is not necessary to control the terms by which the problems of the blacks are discussed and acted upon. Black people, it is true, do not have very much power. But they do have the power to disrupt—a power which, in the hands of a minority prepared to use it, can throw the white man's best-laid plans for the ghetto awry unless he includes Negroes in on the planning. It was significant that community control had its largest following among the Northern young; roughly a third of them preferred it to integration, at least for now, and they are the most inclined to take their predilections into the streets.

The impulse is not at all difficult to understand. The Irish experienced it; so did the Italians and the Jews. It is true that they did not go about making other people nervous by shouting about Irish (or Italian, or Jewish) power—but it is equally so that they sought and achieved power, in part by maintaining their identity and their connections as groups in a pluralistic society. They began with the stores and the politics of their own communities. "The only place where that doesn't happen," Gary's Mayor Richard Hatcher observed, "is in black neighborhoods, which are run like a kind of colony. What's so unusual about people saying, 'We're going to control our own turf'? That's not separatism—that's good old-fashioned Americanism."

Yet there is a strain of danger for black America in investing too much of its hopes and energies in the issue of control; power can be an illusory goal in a community which has so little to assert power over. The vocabulary of decolonization may be helpful, at least to a point, in understanding the psychology of the ghetto, but its economy is another matter. The ghetto has no basic industries to nationalize—the factories have been following white people to the suburbs—and no capital to develop any; Negroes could take over all of Harlem's corner markets, carry-outs, night spots, pawn shops, easy-credit stores, even its vices and its hustles tomorrow and still not significantly diminish its poverty. Nor could black political power of itself deliver the ghetto. No one could seriously argue that Negroes should not control their own politics and use whatever leverage it gives them to better their common lot. But black politics can be a snare, too, if one does not understand its limits in a society in which whites finally have the power. "I'm for the black communities staying intact," said Jesse Gray, a militant tenants' rights organizer in Harlem. "If they disperse the communities, they'll only create smaller ghettos subservient to the white middle class. If they remain intact, they'll have some power." The thought can be powerfully tempting to blacks, particularly when control of not only the Negro wards but city hall itself was coming within their reach. But the question remained: Power over what?

The riot commission ventured some answers in its report, and they were not comforting. It saw an America drifting toward permanent division into two separate societies—a trend which could only continue and accelerate unless the nation undertook massive simultaneous efforts to upgrade and to disperse the ghetto. The burgeoning black population of the cities indeed opened to Negroes the sort of political power the Irish had used to great effect in New York and Boston. But a city turning black would have fewer and fewer tax dollars as whites and white businesses defected to the suburbs—and more and more demand for services as rot and poverty advanced outward from the ghetto. The squeeze would soon reduce city hall nearly to bankruptcy, whether whites or Negroes ran it—and it would fairly invite insurrection. "A rising proportion of Negroes," said the report, ". . . might come to look upon the deprivation and segregation they suffer as proper justification for violent protest or for extending support to now isolated extremists who advocate civil disruption by guerrilla tactics. . . . If large-scale violence resulted, white retaliation would follow. This spiral could quite conceivably lead to a kind of urban *apartheid* with semimartial law in many major cities, enforced residence of Negroes in segregated areas, and a drastic reduction in personal freedom for all Americans."

Even an all-out effort to improve the ghettos, the commission thought, would be "unacceptable" without a simultaneous commitment to integration. The notion that everything could be set right without moving people out of the casbah was far more attractive to whites than Negroes, the black power ideology of the '60's notwithstanding. A *Newsweek* poll of white Americans in the early autumn of 1969 showed, for example, that only 25 per cent favored integrating the public schools to 64 per cent who opted for some separate solution—either improving ghetto schools with outside help or letting the blacks run them as the new leadership demanded. But, said the commission, to undertake the enrichment of ghetto life without trying to disperse black people would be consciously to choose a permanently divided society—and to sentence the blacks to second-class status for life. So enrichment, the commission held, could be "no more than an interim strategy. . . . The primary goal must be a single society, in which every citizen will be free to live and work according to his capabilities and desires, not his color."

The riot report insisted that this could actually be brought about. Americans are an optimistic people. We do not appoint blue-ribbon study commissions to tell us that we have irretrievably failed; it is understood that, after we are taxed with our sins for several hundred pages, we will be told that our redemption is possible if we will only pass the appropriate laws and spend appropriate amounts of money. The riot commission was true to its craft. "This deepening racial division is not inevitable," it said. "The movement apart can be reversed. Choice is still possible."

But the possibility was not quite so clear from the evidence published by the commission; the choices may already have been made. Roughly 12.1 million Negroes were clotted in the nation's central cities at the time; the commission conceded that it would be "extraordinarily difficult" merely to give them the option of breaking out of the ghetto, even assuming that many and perhaps a majority would stay together by choice at first. And the task was not getting any easier with the passage of time. The black population in the cities, the commission figured, will have grown nearly twofold to 20.8 million by 1985 if present trends run on unchecked—by which time what was merely difficult in the latter 1960's would "quite clearly . . . be virtually impossible." The commission, given the implied terms of its contract, did not ask itself whether real integration was more than technically possible today. One could, of course, imagine the logistics being worked out, particularly if one thought of the separation of the races in urban America not as a city but as a metropolitan-area problem in which the suburbs were equally implicated and which they were therefore equally responsible for correcting. But logistics are meaningless until someone makes a policy choice—and policy choices in a democratic political order usually must bear some resemblance to the will of society. "The major need is to generate new will," the riot commission said. There was little in the years immediately following to suggest that any such surge of commitment was about to happen or that the nation's elected leadership had any idea how to bring it about.

And so black people, who had waited so long, began in the late 1960's to alter the terms for reconciliation. The great debate over separatism, to the extent that it absorbed and confused white people, was a diversion from the real issues. "Blacks," said Alvin Echols, head of Philadelphia's North City Congress, "can only talk about separation. Whites can do it." And the fact that they have done it remained a daily affront to Negroes. "Why in hell can't we live together?" puzzled Watts community organizer Ferman Moore. "I got skin and bones and a heart and a soul and you got skin and bones and a heart and a soul. Now if you could flap your arms and fly"—his long arms flailed the air ludicrously—"and I couldn't, then okay, baby, stick me in my own place, I got no place being with you. But my grandmammy and grandpappy picked cotton for these bastards and I've earned my right to be an American and live decently among Americans, white and black."

He is close to the black American consensus: Negroes still want to bring the walls of Jericho down. Yet their leadership is increasingly adamant on the point that they will no longer seek the company of whites for its own sake, as though there were something particularly uplifting in proximity to whiteness and particularly degrading in immersion in blackness. "There's bigger fish to fry here than integration," said a Los Angeles Movement youngster. "Integration is an indication that black people want to sit next to whites. That fogs the issue. That's not it. It is that they want to sit in a chair that's upholstered the same as the white man's. We want an equal slice of the pie." And Negroes, having discovered a beauty in their blackness, were equally insistent that they will not surrender it as the price of leaving the ghetto. "Integration up to this point meant blacks have to act like whites," said Charles V. Hamilton, the black political scientist. "That's a lot of nonsense."

So the poll suggested. It returned enormous majorities for

integration—yet questions about blackness evoked a powerful current of feeling among Negroes that they are different from whites, possibly even superior in matters of love, faith and the human spirit, and that the differences are important to them. And these two facts taken together suggest that, for them, a little piece of the American dream has in fact died—the part of it that says America is a melting pot and that no minority is finally unassimilable. That had not worked out for black people —not in a hundred years of prayer, petition and struggle for even the most trivial freedoms of movement and choice. And so the black American was asking white people to respect his color, since they could not seem to forget it; to include Negroes into a genuinely pluralistic America as a group on a footing with every other group; to let them stay together and develop their own communities or move out among white people as they chose; and not to run from them any longer. "We do not seek integration," said Whitney Young, "we seek an open society. Discussions about separatism and integration are irrelevant." Young lives in a white suburb and spends much of his professional life among white men who have what black people need; and now he was telling them that there was nothing inherently more gratifying or elevating or ennobling in their company than in the society of Negroes.

Times have profoundly changed in America when Whitney Young announces that integration is no longer a relevant item for the nation's agenda. One might argue that it *is* relevant for white people, who after all created Harlem and what Harlem stands for and who alone have the power to decide whether blacks and whites will integrate or separate. Negroes overwhelmingly vote for integration. But a black man need not be a separatist to believe, from the evidence of his everyday life, that the decision is already in and that his wishes in the matter never really counted. "Whites," said Elma Lewis at her black cultural center in Boston's Roxbury ghetto, "are always seeking to pin labels on black people. I suspect that most of them are still searching for 'The Good Nigger.' Well, I can tell them that 'The Good Nigger' is gone forever." She waved vaguely in the direction of the ghetto's burying ground. " 'The Good Nigger,' " she said, "is over in Mount Hope Cemetery."

DIRECTIONS:
Ferman Moore

His eyes came open a minute or so before 6:30, beating the alarm, and he slipped out of bed carefully so he wouldn't wake up Bernadine. He showered, got into a pair of gray striped slacks and a blue gypsy shirt, ran a brush over his short Afro and his beard and hooked on his Ben Franklin glasses. He pulled a few records out of a stack and put them on: Ramsey Lewis, soft and jivey; 'Trane, tumbling and probing; and Jimi Hendrix, his voice tearing high like a cry of pain—"The night I was born/I swear the moon turned a fire-red/My poor mother cried out Lord, the gypsy was right/And I see her fell down right dead . . ./'cause I'm a Voodoo Chile . . ."* Ferman Moore, 20 years old and not so long ago a wine-slugging, pill-popping, buck-hustling, low-riding blood in the streets of Watts, Los Angeles, California, dragged on his first du Maurier of the day and nodded in recognition. "Yeah," he told Newsweek's Nicholas Proffitt, "that's right. That was early Ferman Moore. A voodoo child."

A bad child, white people kept telling him; he remembered that from early grammar school on—"all the way back in the second grade." A kid from a decent family of the working poor,

* Excerpt from the song "Voodoo Chile" written by Jimi Hendrix. Copyright © 1968 by Bella Godiva Music, Inc., c/o Arch Music Co., Inc., a Division of A. Schroeder Music Pub. Co., Inc., 25 W. 56 St., New York, N.Y. All rights reserved. International copyright secured. Used by permission.

with a daddy who usually worked two custodial jobs and a mother who took in sewing, but nothing on his mind except trouble. "All I wanted, man, was to be a pimp. When I was coming up he was the only cat who had some bread. He was the only one with money. The one who got a lot of attention. He had bucks. He learned how to shoot pool. He wore a diamond ring on his pinkie finger. He wore nice silk shirts and ties and suits and drove a Cadillac." Moore crushed out the du Maurier and lit another. "I wanted so much because there was just so little to have. And the pimp had it all."

Moore nearly made it. The street taught him how: "Lie and cheat. Do the dirty thing like everybody else was doing just to get yours. Because I knew what I wanted. I wanted everything I could get my hands on." He started moving with a gang and soon was running it, because he was so big (pushing toward 6-feet-2 and 225 pounds) and so gifted at rapping and because he could drink more Thunderbird than any kid on 99th Street. He learned how to hustle girls while he was still in junior high. He was busted out of four high schools five times—once for changing his marks in a teacher's gradebook, once for turning a scrap over a white girl into a baby race riot, once for selling Red Devils (the drug underground name for Seconal), once for taking them. ("Ferman Moore," the teacher who caught him wrote the principal, "asleep in class due to addiction to narcotics.") And no one really tried to turn him around. It might have helped, he thought, "if the school system would have sat down and took that little minute to say, 'Hey, you messed up in class today,' and give me a good swat, then sit me down and give me a cold drink and say, 'You know, Ferman, you got potential, you're bright, but you fuck up too much in school. I'd like to see you come up and be somebody, but what you're doing now is bullshit.' But that didn't exist, man. It was just, 'Ferman, shut up and sit down.' "

So he wound up adrift in the streets, and, when Watts rioted, he was there. "Man," he said, "I sure grabbed a lot of loot. It was

something completely different for black people. It was great to
know there were all those kids out there and their daddies
wanting to kill the white man for all the shit he had done. Now
I know it was a disaster for black people. Who got killed? Black
folks. Whose homes were burned? Black folks'. Who had to
live in this ravaged community when it was all over and Whitey
had pulled his guns out? Black folks. But I dug it then. I thought
it was really cool." Only not much happened afterward. Moore
did grow a long funky Afro, a beard and a revolutionary line of
talk; but he kept on dropping pills, soaking up wine and
thieving, and somehow a whole year disappeared before the day
in the summer of 1966 when he wandered into a barber shop
for a trim.

"The barbers and the old men were still talking about the
riot, saying things like, 'Dem niggers ought to be dead, causin'
all that trouble.' It really got to me. I went to war on them,
screaming about Vietnam and why black kids were pissed off."
He remembered a young black man in the next chair listening
quietly, then walking over in mid-monologue and asking, "You
need a job, son?" Moore did, and said so. "Tell you what," the
man said, "you get a haircut and a shave and I'll give you a job."
Moore was merely irritated at first ("Shit, no, ain't no way!")
but he needed a dollar, so he chased the man out of the shop
and got his card and a Monday appointment. The card said the
man was Ted Watkins, and the job was at the Watts Labor
Community Action Committee—a labor-sponsored black-run
outfit organized after the riot and dedicated to reconstructing
Watts with everything from job training to summer camps to
instant vest-pocket parks. Moore went to work, started out at 17
running a clean-up crew of thirty youngsters and moved through
a succession of jobs (and a year back at high school getting his
diploma) until, at 20, he was put in charge of WLCAC's major
job-hunting and job-training program.

The last record on the stack was over. Moore got up, switched
off the phonograph, kissed Bernadine and the baby good-bye

and started out for his parents' home—he visits them for a few minutes every morning—and then work. On the way, his English Ford purred past a wino sitting on the curb, head in hands. Moore frowned. "It's a hell of a thing," he said, the words fast and angry, "for kids to be brought up in the kind of shit they have to around here. Winos on the corner—what kind of shit is that for a kid to see on the way to school? You go into the markets, man, and the markets are filthy. No jobs—except for whites. The only jobs left in the community are not in any permanent fields but just pacification jobs in the poverty program." And even poverty money was running short. "Now The Man says, 'You fools have allowed us four years to get ourselves together after your silly little uprising. Now we are going to cut you off and let you do whatever the hell you want to. If you want to throw some goddamn bricks, you come right on out here and we're going to show you what we got prepared for fools who want to do that kind of shit. In 1965 we weren't prepared— we thought you fools out there in Watts were going to act nice and not get angry. But you got angry, so we figured we got to pay to keep you in line for a while. We paid for four years. But now we ain't got to pay no more. We're prepared. We got it together. In twenty minutes we can put seven thousand police on your ass, and we can run tanks down any goddamn street you want. In twenty minutes. We got guns in the racks we don't even use—they're for riots, not for shooting suckers who run a red light. These guns are for killing babies who want to throw a brick.'" Moore's eyes were flashing. "Yeah, The Man made those guns in four years, and he's satisfied now. Because the same time he was giving us three billion dollars for coffee money, he gave his own self ninety billion to prepare for any kind of trouble we want to start."

He paused, and in that moment he seemed surprised at his own anger; Proffitt, beside him in the car, could almost see him wind himself down. "You know," Moore said, softly now, "I used to hate white people. All white people. I don't hate them

any more. I like to think I love all men now. But I used to hate
Whitey. I can still see through him. But I don't hate any more.

"You know, man, it's so hard to tear down this shit that
Whitey has built up for years and years and years. I mean we're
just getting the chance to move up across La Brea Avenue in
Los Angeles. Here's Mighty Whitey moving up onto the moon
and we're just getting across the goddamn street." He reached
for another du Maurier. "He's so damn far advanced, you really
can't hate him. What you gonna hate him for—because he's
powerful? Damn, you got to respect power. You go around
hating a guy because he's powerful, you ain't shit. He's powerful
because he was born that way. He's done it himself for generations—nobody can come in here and say what Whitey's got he
didn't do for it. Hey, man—he cut throats for it. He killed for it.
They talk about the Apaches torturing prisoners—they won't
tell what the white boy did to the Mexicans. Or the Indians.
That white boy rolled in, man, and talked that Seventh Cavalry
bullshit to those tribes and told those Indians they had to live
on a damn reservation. 'Hey, why?' 'Because Mighty Whitey
wants to come from Europe and own a big ole nation, that's
why. So you gotta live on a reservation.' And you know what's
the crazy thing, man? There's time for us. Time for us all to
live together. I mean, hey, there's some beautiful white cats,
beautiful Mexicans, beautiful all kinds of people—they're just
groovy, you know? But what's so cold, man, is that the conservative white boy done overpowered all the liberal white boys."

The blocks slid by; people who are accustomed to thinking of
the ghetto as someplace cramped like Harlem are commonly
surprised at the vast bleak distances in Watts. And Moore was
rapping on. "Hey, man, like everybody wants to go to Africa."
He grinned. "I don't blame the white boy for wanting to go—
he knows how much oil and gold is there, and copper. But I
can blame black folks, because any time we spend four hundred
years building a nation for somebody else and then want to go
elsewhere to live and start building all over again, that's bull-

shit." And so was separation, whoever proposed it. "Why in hell we got to be separate? You know, we're not animals, man. We cannot be separate and live together in this country. To be separate, white folks are gonna have to put niggers on a reservation. You talk separation and you're talking about enslaving me again, and I'm not gonna be enslaved."

The car slid up to WLCAC's project center. Moore spent half the morning there going through files and rattling out questions ("Who's in jail? . . . What'd he do? . . . Did you go by and visit Mr. So-and-so and find out why he didn't make that damn job interview I set up for him?"); then he toured his job sites, conferred with Watkins, looked in on some classrooms and counseled with his staff into the early evening. And finally, in the settling twilight, he was driving home. He was tired, and quiet at first, but then he passed two cops arguing with a Negro driver, and the anger rose again. "It's an awful thing to have to say, man, but I hate the police department. I'd hate to have to live without police, but, goddamn, I hate to have to live with these dogs." Only a week before, two white policemen had chased two black girls into WLCAC's building, revolvers drawn, and briefly arrested Moore when he asked them what was going on. A crowd gathered; the cops got nervous and told Moore they would let him go if he would clear the street; he did, and the LAPD later sent two black officers around with apologies. "So how can you like somebody like that?" he asked. "How do you make kids like policemen? The cop never comes around to talk to you unless he's gonna hassle you. He's got but one thing to say to us—'You're a nigger and you ain't shit and you kiss my ass or you go to jail.'"

At home that evening, Moore seemed gloomy. He poured Proffitt a glass of wine, and one for himself, and put Cannonball Adderley on the phonograph while Bernadine was fussing over dinner. "I'll tell you one thing," he said, "it's all gotta stop—this hassle with people. Someday people are gonna get sick of it and they're gonna start some real fighting. A lot of black kids want to see that happen. I hope and pray to God it doesn't. I pray to God white folks can get off without bloodshed. I hope we can all get it together without a bloodbath. Because it's gonna be awful if we have to get out and shoot and kill." He sipped at his wine. "I hate violence. I can't stand it. Some of our people say Mighty Whitey took this country by violence and that's the only way we're going to get anything. That's bullshit. Violence got people killed in Watts—black people . . ."

He spoke slowly. "You know, we came from Africa and in Africa we were cool. We were just mellow. We just sat back and were happy. We didn't hate. There wasn't all that bullshit. And then they brought us over here and started treating us like dogs, man, and before you know, we started hating. We didn't want to hate no-goddamn-body. We'd never hated. White folks were always hating folks because they were always wanting to take something that wasn't theirs. . . . But even when they brought us to the plantations, the white boy would whup us with a whip and all we'd do was sing spirituals. Because we loved. But now, man, you can't hardly talk love no more. Who gives a goddamn about loving any more?"

The wine was warm, and Adderley cool, and Ferman Moore gave himself to the glow. "You know," he said, "I want to take white folks to the park and eat watermelon and drink Kool-Aid. Eat greens and cornbread and turn you on to my black sisters. I'd love to stage a national black and white feast day—not sponsored by blacks or whites but together. A huge national barbecue in towns all over the country and invite everyone—rednecks and black folks and everyone. No discussions of problems, just a good ole feast. Break a little bread and drink a little wine. People that break bread together don't hate each other. White and black women trading cooking secrets and the men playing softball or horseshoes together. Wouldn't that be nice."

The idea pleased him; the edge of gloom vanished, and, after dinner, he hoisted the baby so her face was inches from his, and they mugged and beamed at each other. "A little boy is born a prince and a little girl is born a princess," he said, "and only through cultivating do they become a king or a queen. It'll be so groovy to raise a queen. I'll teach her to love, teach her to help people. I don't want her to be a typist or a nurse—I want her to be a queen. With all of the funkiness, it's still cool to bring children into the world. Because they are the ones who will set it right. Maybe mine will be a leader in the struggle. Maybe my child can sit down with white kids and get it all together." He grinned at Karma Chablis Moore; Karma, two months old, grinned happily back. "You know, man," said Ferman Moore, a voodoo child who grew up, "if these kids can do that, I'll fall down dead right now and go gladly."

EPILOGUE:

Black America
in the 1970's

MARLO STEWART and his friend Elijah Brooks lay on the hood of an abandoned pick-up truck in black Chicago, gazed lazily up into the sky and talked about what they wanted to do if they grew up. It was hard, seeing their eyes, to think of either of them as a child, and harder still to imagine that either had a future. Marlo had already spent three of his thirteen years in reform schools ("Sometimes I would steal 'cause I was hungry but mostly I would steal 'cause there was nothing else to do") and Elijah, at ten, had just been busted for the first time for thieving from a restaurant. Yet there was boy enough left in them for dreaming. Elijah thought he might like to be a policeman—"That's the only way not to be bad." And Marlo? "Well, when I grow up," Marlo said, "I want to be a train engineer and then go on a ship and then go on a plane. And then I want to buy a big grocery store so any time I'm hungry I can get my own food." But most of all he wanted to get out of Chicago. "Chicago," he said, "ain't hittin' on nothing."

Marlo Stewart's Chicago is West Madison Street, a cauterized slash across the West Side where a generation of children dies a little every day. West Madison is still spaced out with blackened boarded-up storefronts—the scars of the native risings of summers gone by—and posters on every second or third building shout out for armed insurrection. ("Your God better have a rod," says one, taped to the window of the Soulville Pool Hall. "Mine does.") But the suffocating banality of ghetto life blunts every human feeling, even rage; the truth is that nothing much ever really happens on West Madison Street. Children get in trouble and disappear. Despairing men drink away the daylight to get from night to night. Hustlers succeed; working people fail. Preachers pray for deliverance. Black Panthers plot it. And everybody waits. "It is in the street that the people really live," wrote Johnathan Rodgers, a young black *Newsweek* reporter who melted into the life of West Madison for a few weeks in the spring of 1969. "The dirty littered thoroughfare is the PTA, the bridge club and the playground—where, for want of anything else to do or any place to go, blacks stand and watch America pass them by."

And yet, at the dawning of the 1970's, people on West Madison Street still dared hope that things might be different. There was little in their everyday life to encourage this belief—and much to discourage it in the ebbing resolve of white America to set matters right between the races. Whites had listened when The Movement was talking about nonviolence, Christian love and the rudimentary civil rights of Southern Negroes. But their mood soured as the rhetoric turned nasty, the ghettos started burning and the black bill of grievances got longer, costlier and closer to home. "White America," said a disheartened Presidential staffer in the late days of Lyndon Johnson, "is fed up"— an accurate reading of a mood which had already sapped the Johnson Administration's nerve and which soon thereafter helped to elect Richard Nixon. Negroes did not precisely fall from grace at that juncture, but they did go out of fashion. Nixon's Forgotten Americans were in, and so were their concerns, which included Vietnam, inflation and crime in the streets but not a special solicitude for black people. Whites in a 1969 *Newsweek* poll rejected even the basic premise that the ghetto's slum housing and recession unemployment were due to discrimination and not some failing of the Negroes themselves; they were therefore inclined to doubt that most of black America's complaints were justified. And suddenly even the most circumspect Negro leaders had the uneasy feeling that it was 1877 all over again—that the Remembered Americans and their President were about to forget the blacks again, that Northern white liberalism was in retreat and Southern white conservatism in favor and that the Second Reconstruction had come like the first to the verge of collapse.

Perhaps so. But this time, in contrast to the last, Negroes will not go quietly; they have come too far in their struggle to stop now. Ten to twenty per cent of them do despair of their future in America—are persuaded, that is, that the nation is not worth defending in a world war; that Negroes should withdraw into a separate black nation; that their salvation by peaceful means is impossible and that it will sooner or later come down to black against white, an eye for an eye, a tooth for a tooth. ("They'll tell you they want jobs and education," said one Mississippi Delta black leader, speaking of some kids who were trying to keep a boycott campaign going past its useful life, "but deep down they want revenge.") Ten to twenty per cent comes to a stunningly large number—perhaps as many as 2.5 million of the nation's 12.5 million Negro adults—and some of them may be alienated past recall by any gesture whites are likely to make. And yet the great majority of the blacks still want to become part of America, still imagine that they can bring it off nonviolently—and are still convinced as they enter the 1970's that they will in fact overcome some day.

Their optimism does not promise white America surcease from the demands and the dislocations of the 1960's. Far from it: the millennium keeps receding beyond the reach of the blacks ("To Whom It May Concern: Keep This Nigger-Boy Running") but their pervasive feeling that they are moving toward it demands that they go on. Negroes still feel discriminated against; their sense of grievance is at least as high as it has ever been. They agree that they have made progress toward a rightful share in America's affluence. But, in an age and a culture whose special genius has been the creation of the infinite consumer appetite, black people think less about how far they have come than about how far they still have to go; and, by that measure, most of them do not think they are going fast enough. They still mourn Martin Luther King. But they have the strong feeling that an era of nonviolent loving-kindness ended with his death, and they are beginning to show signs of impatience with others of the old-line moderate leadership. Their goal is still integration; their mood, even so, is increasingly nationalistic—not a formal nationalism of territory but a spreading community of disbelief in the good intentions of white people and of belief in the beauty, the power and the soul of black folk. And a substantial minority of them feel that what whites perceive as riots are in fact rebellions—the morally legitimate and tactically sound revolt of the oppressed against their oppression. What all of this describes, of course, is a community psychically in a state of revolution—a revolution against the tyranny of caste and color, not the political or economic order, but a revolution nevertheless.

And the revolution will continue into the 1970's. It is likely to be unpleasant and abrasive and sometimes violent; the Selma-to-Montgomery march of 1965 may have been the last of the great parades, but Watts and Newark and Detroit most certainly did not exhaust the possibilities for destruction at the heart of urban America. Yet it surely would be worse for America if the Negroes were to quit their revolution now. It is the despairing ones on West Madison Street who acquiesce in the death of children; even a riot for them is hardly more than an acute stage of the desperation of their everyday lives. A revolution by contrast is an act of hope; and a revolution which prefers negotiation to war, which seeks not to destroy but to reform America and which continues in spite of everything to operate on the premise that it is winning is the most transcendently hopeful act of all.

*   *   *

Hope, of course, is not an indestructible state of mind; it must be periodically rewarded if it is to survive—and the rewards must quicken as expectations rise. White America may or may not have had the resources to keep pace with black America's vaulting hopes in the 1960's; what it lacked, or rather lost along the way, was the resolution. So the going got slower for Negro Americans. Hope yielded to impatience and impatience bred militancy—not the old-fashioned hymn-singing march-to-jail militancy of the early 1960's but a tough new strain which thought black, demanded power and suspected that violence might be useful and even necessary to the cause. Mass opinion shifts glacially in the black community or any other, particularly where the currents go counter to old, accepted verities. Yet a subsurface trend toward militancy was clearly running among young and middle-class blacks in the urban North—two catalytic groups to whom The Movement looks both for its leadership and its foot soldiers. The two together may or may not be able to carry a majority of Negro opinion with them; it hardly matters. They are the activists, the leading edge of the black revolution, and what they think will have everything to do with the language of race and the terms of race relations in the 1970's.

The radicalization of the young is the less surprising development of the two: Americans rather expect their sons to rebel against them and are in fact a bit nervous when they do not. And so it is with the blacks—particularly in the North. Those who are under 30 today were children when the Supreme Court struck down school segregation and when Martin Luther King mounted the Montgomery bus boycott—the two events that signaled the arrival of the Negro revolution in the middle 1950's. That revolution has now been going on all their lives. Because they are young, they believe that it ought long since to have been won. Because they are black, they know that it has not been. And so they are angry, and their anger has opened a wide and dangerous generation gap between them and their elders:

THE BLACK MOOD I: THE YOUNG

THE PERCENTAGE WHO:	Northern Negroes	
	Under 30	Over 30
Believe that Negroes have soul	79	52
Like natural hair	76	37
Approve the idea of black power	68	43
Think blacks must band together against whites	45	26
Believe whites want to keep Negroes down	51	41
Consider the pace of progress too slow	70	58
Think violence will be necessary	36	20
Believe the riots have been justified	47	30
Believe the riots have helped	50	32
Prefer community control to integration	30	9
Would like a separate black nation	27	18
Don't think the U. S. is worth fighting for	31	11

The figures profile the Stokely Generation: a generation among whom practically everybody is in some measure black-conscious, majorities or near-majorities are hostile to whites and amenable to rioting—and nearly a third have psychically dropped out of the American dream and gone separatist. A similar generational split has begun in the South but is not nearly so pronounced there; it is the manchild already arrived in the promised land who has discovered how little promise it really holds and who is acting today on his sense of betrayal. And the bitterness of the young is full of peril for the peace and good order of the nation's cities. They are the volatile ones— well placed either to create or to destroy—and there are troubled blacks and sympathetic whites who fear that a generation of them may have been lost already. Lost to the streets: unemployment and crime run fearfully high among the ghetto young. Or lost to the romance of violence: "If I were the mayor and a riot started," said a University of Chicago coed, 19 years old, "I would call all the white policemen off the street. I'd put all the black policemen in plain clothes and have them man ambulances to help the people. I would make a public statement about the causes of the riots and I'd ask the cats to pick their targets with care. And then I'd go into the riot area and do the same thing I did in Cleveland—I'd throw a few bricks."

What fewer whites have understood is the steady radicalization of increasing numbers of the Negro middle class in the North. It is customary to speak of the events of the '60's as the revolt of the black poor. But the poorest Negroes in fact are hard pressed merely to survive; their lives are too contingent to produce or to conform to proletarian ideologies. The revolutionary impulse has sprung instead from the relatively affluent, and particularly from their young. Martin Luther King came out of the Negro middle class. So did the sit-in kids and the Freedom Riders and Stokely Carmichael and Julian Bond. The Black Panther Party was born over cups of espresso around Oakland's Merrit College. The streets made Malcolm X but the black middle class made him a saint. For the rising voices of their own young had begun to stab the consciences of the relatively well off.* So had the riots and all that they revealed about the desperation and the rage of the ghetto *Lumpenproletariat*. And the very fact of their own progress was a goad. A poor man may riot; revolutions arise among people who have tasted something better than poverty but who feel that their progress has been brought into check by inimical outside forces—among people, that is, whose expectations are rising and are not being met.

The result was a drift into militancy that ran through the decade just past and now becomes its legacy to the decade just beginning:

---

* *All* such terms are relative in the black community. Middle class in the *Newsweek* Poll means anything more than $6,450 a year—barely the minimum U.S. government estimate of what a family of four needs to get by on.

THE BLACK MOOD II: THE MIDDLE CLASS

	1963	1966	1969
Believe whites want to keep Negroes down	19	39	47
Don't think whites have got better	25	34	47
Don't think whites will get better	9	18	32
Feel whites will budge only if blacks force them to	16	23	44
Think blacks must band together against whites	x	13	32
Approve the idea of black power	x	26	59
Feel the NAACP is doing an excellent job	79	58	20
Feel the Urban League is doing an excellent job	37	32	19
Think violence will be necessary	9	21	33
Believe the riots have helped	x	31	50
Would like a separate black nation	0	2	18
Don't think the U. S. is worth fighting for	7	8	20

Negroes with money thus have moved a far distance from the complacent, self-possessed "black bourgeoisie" described so acidly by the late sociologist E. Franklin Frazier. Today's black bourgeois as likely as not believes in black power, is chary of his white brothers, has little patience left for moderation and suspects that it will take black action, not black diplomacy, to get Negroes where they want to go.

He has, in a word, discovered his color—discovered that he, too, is black all day long and that much of his life is going to turn on that fact whether he Makes It or not. "Sometimes," said a black architect with a comfortable corporate job in Chicago, "I ask myself what am I doing making all this money? You know—you look at yourself and you say, 'I'm making it.' Big deal. Making *what?* If I've got some black pride, maybe I should be with black people that aren't making it." Whether or not he made that move was less important than his psychic leap from insulation to involvement—a process that was being repeated increasingly among blacks who were making it at work and on the campuses. Middle-class radicalism, as Daniel Patrick Moynihan once observed in conversation, is "perfectly normal, routine American stuff—it happens when you start educating a minority of a class." What was different about the blacks was their blackness. "The fact of race," said Moynihan, "is so powerful that these young militants can talk to that [lower] class. Race unites."

Race unites because of the condition of black people in America; it unites them because it has degraded and humiliated and imprisoned them so long. American liberalism failed them, and itself, by assuming that the question of color could some-how be skipped—that black people could be thought of as colored white people and be moved in ever-increasing numbers into that state of grace called brotherhood. The Movement itself accepted that premise in its early years; it sang about black and white together, and implicit in the songs was the presump-tion that love and commitment and common humanity could bring down the veil. It has not worked out that way. America has extended the privileges, if not all the immunities, of membership to a good many black people—more, probably, than anyone would have imagined possible when the 1960's began. Yet color remained an intractable and indissoluble fact, for those who made it and those who did not. White people, it developed, were not prepared to forget their color, and black people have not been permitted to forget theirs; and, with the discovery that this was so, color became steadily more rather than less important. "You don't catch hell because you're a Baptist or a Methodist," Malcolm X used to say, "you catch hell because you're black."

He was correct, of course, and now, in the 1970's, we have come into our inheritance: a climate in which incivility be-comes a style and abrasion a norm between the races; in which confrontation flourishes and communication fails; in which black people will insist on their difference as intransigently as whites have always done. One can hope that this will be a temporary condition—a painful time of transition between an insupportable old order and a happier new one. "All immigrant groups," said James Farmer, late of CORE and lately of the

Nixon Administration, "remain hyphenated Americans for one or two generations and get pushed around. They begin to lose the need for hyphenation when the oppression relaxes. I see the black man becoming an Afro-American to strengthen his identity—to discover the hyphen in order to lose it eventually. In the future, maybe we won't need that hyphen." But the history of past and present attempts to master the question of color is not necessarily heartening. Race has been not just an American but a human dilemma, and the failures to cope with it far outnumber the successes.

The hyphen, in any event, will still shadow relations between the races in America in the 1970's; black people are not yet finished with the process of discovering and exploring and celebrating their blackness. Blackness will dominate their politics. Negroes will become the majority in a half-dozen or more major cities in the 1970's; controlling them may or may not prove to be a prize worth having, but black people will insist upon it and demographic trends will deliver it to them. And blackness is likely to set the boundaries on what forms and what directions white beneficence will be able to take. "The language might be separatist but we still need Charlie," a black campus militant conceded. Yet Charlie, if he intends his programs to succeed, will have to permit blacks a meaningful voice in their formulation and their execution. "No matter how benevolent you are, you are still benevolent," said a Negro economist. "I'd rather make my own mistakes." To ignore this impulse, or to dismiss it as separatism, almost certainly will be self-defeating. Community control is a minority ideology in the ghettos, but events of the 1960's amply demonstrated that a minority so disposed can break a program—or burn a city.

And it was by no means assured that the cities have stopped burning. The fires got lower in the late 1960's but did not go out, and the threat of conflagration remains a very real one in the 1970's. There are, for one thing, the desperadoes of the ghetto—the revolutionaries who quite seriously believe that

whites are about to pack Negroes off to concentration camps or
even gas chambers and who therefore do not accept that they
have anything to lose by violence *including* their lives. And
there are the ordinary blacks for whom rioting has been so
painfully ambivalent an experience. Violence was never their
choice of weapons; black people have always preferred negotiation to war. But they suspect that rioting has helped their
cause—that it has, if nothing else, forced whites to see the
Invisible Man. And the record of inaction before the riots and
action afterward, however fitful or insubstantial or grudging,
can hardly be expected to dissuade them. "You get a new stop
sign after four accidents, a flood wall after three floods,"
Whitney Young remarked dolefully. "America historically re-
acted to tragedy and crisis. When the unemployment rate hit
twelve per cent or so, they didn't ask who's got skills—they put
a shovel in the poor man's hands because they were frightened."
The response to rioting has not been as dramatic as that. But
some shovels did get handed around, some dollars were allo-
cated, and a commission made up mostly of white people
isolated and announced an endemic disease called racism; and
that was more than had ever happened on West Madison
Street in Chicago or 116th Street in Harlem or 103rd Street in
Watts before the riots began.

So riots, in one sense, communicate; the tragedy of rioting is
that the communication comes out so wrong. What black
people are saying—and what white people ought never to lose
sight of—is that they want to be a part of America. They want
to come into that place with pride; that is why they find it so
necessary to rejoice in anything black and to reject anything
white. They want to come into that place with dignity; that is
why they talk about black power and insist on integration not as
an act of white philanthropy toward certain "qualified" Negroes
but as a commingling of equals. They want to come into that
place so badly that they feel they cannot wait any longer; that is
why cities burn. Black people want everything that is due them

as Americans. They will fight for their due because they hunger for it so much—and because they insist on believing that if only they fight hard enough they will win.

"We'll achieve brotherhood someday," said one militant writer who is not given to charitable judgments of white people. "America had to fight a civil war before it even became a nation." That view requires a great deal of faith. "I believe in little kids who come from the dirt and touch the sky," said Ferman Moore, who helped to pillage Watts in 1965 and now is trying to build it. That requires faith, too. Marlo Stewart and Elijah Brooks, growing up absurd on West Madison Street, are unlikely ever to touch the sky; it is probably too late for them. What America must now decide is how many more like them will be lost before it is too late for all of us.

APPENDIX A: A TECHNICAL NOTE BY THE GALLUP ORGANIZATION

The study had two major objectives:

1. To update the trends in the thinking of American Negroes established in prior *Newsweek* surveys conducted in 1963 and 1966 on political, social and economic issues. This involved the measurement of attitudes, hopes and aspirations in these areas for the future.

2. To measure Negro attitudes on issues and developments since the previous *Newsweek* studies, including the assassination of Martin Luther King, the Black Panther Party, the new African clothing and hair styles, Negro demonstrations in colleges and high schools, the meaning of "black is beautiful," "black power" and "soul."

The questionnaire was developed jointly by The Gallup Organization, Inc., and the *Newsweek* editorial staff. About two-thirds of the questions were asked in the previous studies; about one-third of them were developed by The Gallup Organization, Inc.

Every interview was conducted by a Negro interviewer and required an average of about seventy minutes. The interviewing was conducted between May 10 and June 1, 1969. A total of 977 interviews was obtained. Interviewing was conducted during the evening hours during the week, and all day on the weekend, times when people are most likely to be found at home.

To locate areas with Negro population, use was made of four independent nationwide samplings of the population 21 and older for the regular recurring Gallup national surveys between January 22 and the end of March 1969. About 320 sample locations were used for each of these surveys, from which the areas used in the survey were selected.

213

The 320 locations or areas were drawn using a sample design which can be described as that of a replicated probability sample down to the block level in the case of urban areas and to segments of townships in the case of rural areas.

The accumulated sample in each location was examined to determine the black-white ratio obtained. In 57 of the interviewing areas the proportion of Negroes in the sample was 10 per cent or more. These locations were selected as the sampling areas for the Negro sample. Such areas included about 92 per cent of all of the Negroes drawn into the four national samples. A density of 10 per cent or more was used as a criterion for selection because it included the vast majority of Negroes and provided an efficient sampling plan for the short time allowance available for the field work. These 57 areas provided the assigned interviewing locations for the Negro sample. To take into account the differing proportions of Negroes in the selected areas (the original selection of 320 areas was with probability of selection proportional to size of total population), a valuable sampling rate was used depending on the estimated proportion of Negroes in each area.

Interviewers were given maps of the area to which they were assigned, with two starting points indicated for each block area, and required to follow a specified direction. Interviewers, all of whom were Negroes themselves, were instructed to select a Negro respondent at each dwelling unit encountered occupied by Negroes by following a prescribed systematic method and by a male-female assignment, and not by individual judgment. This procedure was followed until the assigned number of interviews was completed.

The total of 977 interviews was obtained from 50 of the 57 areas selected.

In place of call-backs, a "times-at-home" weighting was applied to the sample of Negroes to compensate for those persons less frequently at home and thus underrepresented in the sample. This is a standard weighting procedure used in all Gallup polls. The sample was further balanced in terms of educational attainment, sex and regional distribution, using as a standard 1968 projections of the Census based upon the current Population Survey.

In interpreting survey results, it should be borne in mind that all sample surveys are subject to sampling error, that is, the extent to

COMPOSITION OF THE SAMPLE

	Number of Interviews	Balanced Sample Distribution*
ALL RESPONDENTS	977	100%
RESIDENCE		
Non-South	486	48%
South†	491	52%
TYPES OF COMMUNITY		
Central city	603	57%
Suburbs	76	6%
Small town and rural	298	37%
AGE		
18 to 29 years	295	25%
30 to 49 years	372	39%
50 years and over	280	34%
Undesignated	30	2%
HOUSEHOLD INCOME		
$6,450 or over	369	34%
$3,068 to $6,450	301	33%
Under $3,068	111	14%
Undesignated	196	19%

* See description of sample design for explanation of how the sample was balanced.
† South includes Alabama, Arkansas, Florida, Georgia, Kentucky, Louisiana, Mississippi, North Carolina, Oklahoma, South Carolina, Tennessee, Texas and Virginia.

which the results may differ from what would be obtained if the whole population surveyed had been interviewed. The size of such sampling errors depends largely on the number of interviews.

The following tables may be used in estimating the sampling error of any percentage in this report. The computed allowances have taken into account the effect of the sample design upon sampling error. They may be interpreted as indicating the range (plus or minus the figure shown) within which the results of repeated samplings in the same time period could be expected to vary, 95 per cent of the time, assuming the same sampling procedure, the same interviewers and the same questionnaire.

The first table shows how much allowance should be made for the sampling error of a percentage:

RECOMMENDED ALLOWANCE FOR SAMPLING ERROR OF A PERCENTAGE

In Percentage Points
(at 95 in 100 Confidence Level) *

Sample Size

	1,500	1,000	750	600	400	200	100
Percentages near 10	2	2	3	3	4	5	7
Percentages near 20	2	3	4	4	5	7	9
Percentages near 30	3	4	4	4	6	8	10
Percentages near 40	3	4	4	5	6	8	11
Percentages near 50	3	4	4	5	6	8	11
Percentages near 60	3	4	4	5	6	8	11
Percentages near 70	3	4	4	4	6	8	10
Percentages near 80	2	3	4	4	5	7	9
Percentages near 90	2	2	3	3	4	5	7

* The chances are 95 in 100 that the sampling error is not larger than the figures shown.

The table would be used in the following manner: Let us say a reported percentage is 33 for a group which includes 1,500 respondents. Then we go to row "percentages near 30" in the table and go across to the column headed "1,500." The number at this point is 3, which means that the 33 per cent obtained in the sample is subject to a sampling error of plus or minus 3 points. Another way of saying it is that very probably (95 chances out of 100) the average of repeated samplings would be somewhere between 30 and 36, with the most likely figure the 33 obtained.

In comparing survey results in two samples, such as, for example, men and women, the question arises as to how large must a difference between them be before one can be reasonably sure that it reflects a real difference. In the tables below, the number of points which must be allowed for in such comparisons is indicated.

Two tables are provided. One is for percentages near 20 or 80; the other for percentages near 50. For percentages in between, the error to be allowed for is between that shown in the two tables:

RECOMMENDED ALLOWANCE FOR SAMPLING ERROR OF THE DIFFERENCE

In Percentage Points
(at 95 in 100 Confidence Level) *

TABLE A *Percentage near 20 or percentages near 80*

Size of Sample	750	600	400	200
750	5			
600	5	6		
400	6	6	7	
200	8	8	8	10

TABLE B *Percentages near 50*

Size of Sample	750	600	400	200
750	6			
600	7	7		
400	7	8	8	
200	10	10	10	12

* The chances are 95 in 100 that the sampling error is not larger than the figures shown.

Here is an example of how the tables would be used: Let us say that 50 per cent of men respond a certain way and 40 per cent of women respond that way also, for a difference of 10 percentage points between them. Can we say with any assurance that the 10-point difference reflects a real difference between men and women on the question? The sample contains approximately 750 men and 750 women.

Since the percentages are near 50, we consult Table B, and since the two samples are about 750 persons each, we look for the number in the column headed "750" which is also in the row designated "750." We find the number 6 here. This means that the allowance for error should be 6 points, and that in concluding that the percentage among men is somewhere between 4 and 16 points higher than the percentage among women we should be wrong only about 5 per cent of the time. In other words, we can conclude with considerable confidence that a difference exists in the direction observed and that it amounts to at least 4 percentage points.

If, in another case, men's responses amount to 22 per cent, say, and women's 24 per cent, we consult Table A because these percentages are near 20. We look in the column headed "750" and see that the number is 5. Obviously, then, the 2-point difference is inconclusive.

APPENDIX B: THE QUESTIONNAIRE

SUGGESTED INTRODUCTION: I am from The Gallup Organization in Princeton, New Jersey. We are talking to people who live in this neighborhood and asking them for their opinion on some very important current topics. Here's the first question . . .

1. I want to ask about how you feel you and your family are personally doing compared to five years ago. As far as your (*ask for each item listed below*) goes, do you feel you are better off today than you were five years ago, worse off, or about the same as you were then?
   a. Your work situation?
   b. Your housing accommodations?
   c. Your pay?
   d. Being able to get your children a good education?
   e. Being able to live in any neighborhood you can afford?
2. Now, thinking ahead to five years from now, if you had to say right now, do you feel in your (*ask for each item listed above*) you will be better off, worse off, or about the same as you are right now?
3. All in all, compared with five years ago, do you think things for people such as yourself and your family are better, worse, or about the same?
4. As far as you personally are concerned, what do you feel are the two or three biggest problems facing Negro people that you feel something should be done about?
5. Do you feel that if you do the same work as a white man you will be paid the same as he will get for that work, or will you probably get paid less?
6. At work, would you rather work alongside mostly other Negroes,

or would you rather work with a mixed group of whites and Negroes?

7. In general, if you were to get a house, or apartment (flat), the same as a white person, do you feel you would pay more rent or the same as the white person would pay?

8. a. In living in a neighborhood, if you could find the housing you want and like, would you rather live in a neighborhood with Negro families, or in a neighborhood that had both whites and Negroes?

    b. Why do you feel this way? Anything else?

9. Do you feel that Negro children would do better or worse if they all went to a school along with white children today?

10. Would you like to see the children in your family go to school with white children, or not?

11. Of course, because of where they live today, many Negro children go to all-Negro schools and whites to all-white schools. Would you like to see children in your family be picked up in buses every day to go to school with white children in some other part of town, or not?

12. Do you think that Negro high school students whose grades aren't high enough to be admitted to college ought to be admitted anyway, or not?

13. a. All in all, do you feel your children (children in your family) are receiving as good an education as white children around here get, or are they getting not as good an education?

IF "INFERIOR EDUCATION," ASK b:

     b. What do you think should be done about this in this community?

On another topic . . .

14. Regardless of how you may vote, what do you usually consider yourself—a Republican, a Democrat, or what?

15. a. In politics, do you feel Negroes should work mainly together as a separate group outside the two political parties or as individuals within one or the other party?

     b. What's the main reason you feel that way?

16. Which party—the Republican or the Democratic—do you feel

will do more to help Negroes in the next few years, or do you think there isn't much difference between the two?

17. Do you feel Negro ministers and preachers have been outstanding in their work for rights for Negroes, pretty good, only fair, or poor?

18. Some people are saying that Negroes have tried to work out their problems with white people and there's been a lot of talk but not much action. Now, they say Negroes should give up working together with whites and just depend on their own people. Do you tend to agree or disagree with people who say this?

19. Some people feel that what Negroes should be asking for is the same chance as whites when it comes to such things as getting jobs and being admitted to college. Others say that to make up for past treatment, Negroes should get preference over whites in such things. What is your opinion?

20.   a. Have you heard or read about the Black Panther Party?

If "YES," ASK b & c:
        b. To the best of your understanding, what does the Black Panther Party stand for?
        c. On the whole, do you approve or disapprove of the Black Panther Party?

21. Have you stopped buying certain companies' products because you have heard they discriminate against Negroes?

22. For most things you buy, do you feel you pay more than white people do for the same thing, less, or the same as whites?

23.   a. In your opinion, do most Negroes have a special spirit or soul that most white people have not experienced?

If "YES," ASK b:
        b. How would you describe it in your own words?

24. Do you like the new natural hair styles many Negroes are wearing now, or not?

25.   a. As you know, some Negroes have begun to wear African clothing styles like the Dashiki and the Buba. Do you like these new styles, or not?

If "YES, LIKE," ASK b:
        b. Would you, yourself, wear these clothing styles?

26. In the cause of Negro rights, have you personally or has any member of your family: (*ask for each item listed below*)?
    a. Take(n) part in a sit-in
    b. March(ed) in a demonstration
    c. Picket(ed) a store
    d. Stop(ped) buying at a store
    e. Go(ne) to jail
27. If you were asked, would you: (*ask for each item listed above*)?
28. Do you think activities of these kinds have helped Negroes or hurt them in their effort to win their rights?
29. a. Some Negro leaders have said that Negroes can only succeed in winning rights if they use nonviolent means to demonstrate. Others disagree. Do you personally feel Negroes today can win their rights without resorting to violence, or do you think it will have to be an eye for an eye and a tooth for a tooth?
    b. Why do you believe this? Any other reason?
30. As far as all the things that have been going on lately with Negro rights, do you think things are moving about right these days, too fast, or too slow?
31. Do you think Negroes will get ahead better in this country by controlling their own schools, running their own businesses, and living together in their own neighborhoods, or do you think they will get ahead better through integration with the white people in schools, jobs, and neighborhoods?
32. In your opinion, are those Negroes who have taken part in the rioting and violence in certain cities mostly hoodlums and bad characters, or mostly good people driven to violence?
33. Regardless of who took part in them, do you think the riots have been justified, or not?
34. Do you think the riots that have taken place in large cities around the country have helped or hurt the cause of Negro rights, or don't you think it makes much difference?
35. Do you think there will be more riots in our cities in the months ahead, or not?
36. Would you join in something like that, or not?
37. What *other* kinds of violence, if any, do you think may take place in the months ahead?

Next are some questions about education . . .
38.   a. Have you heard or read about recent disruptions in high
           schools in which Negro students were involved?

IF "YES," ASK b:
        b. Do you think the actions of the Negro high school stu-
           dents who were involved were justified, or not?
39. Have you heard or read about recent demonstrations on col-
    lege campuses by Negro college students?
40. In your opinion, are Negro college students who get involved
    in these demonstrations helping or hurting the Negro cause?
41. Some Negro college students have carried guns during these
    demonstrations on college campuses. Do you approve or dis-
    approve of that?
42. Some people have urged Negroes generally to arm themselves.
    Do you think this is a good idea or a poor idea?

On the next topic . . .
43. Do you think the day will ever come or not when Negroes
    will have their own separate nation somewhere in the U.S.?
44. Would you, yourself, like to see the day when there is one,
    or not?
45. If the United States got into a big world war today, would
    you personally feel this country was worth fighting for, or not?
46. Do you think the present draft laws are fair or unfair to
    Negroes?
47. Now where do you think a young Negro just starting out will
    have a better chance to get a break—in the armed forces or
    in civilian life?
48.   a. Do you think that Negroes are sending a higher per-
           centage (number) of young men to Vietnam than any
           other group in the population, about the same, or less?

IF "HIGHER," ASK b:
        b. Do you think this is fair or unfair?
49. I want to read you some statements about the war in Vietnam.
    Tell me for each if you tend to agree or disagree:
        a. Money spent in Vietnam means less money for civil
           rights and poverty programs here at home.

b. Negroes should be against the war in Vietnam because they have less freedom to fight for.

c. When Negroes fight in Vietnam, they prove they are as good as any other people.

d. Negroes make better soldiers in combat than whites.

50. Do you think a Negro who gets to college and is qualified can get as good a job, a better job, or not as good a job as a white man with the same qualifications?

51. Do you think a Negro high school student with good grades has as good a chance, not as good a chance, or a better chance of getting into a top college than a white student with the same grades?

52. All in all, do you think the opportunities for Negroes to get ahead in the professions have improved a lot in the past five years, gotten worse, or remain about what they were then?

53. Now I want to read off to you a list of people—some living and some dead—and groups prominent in the fight for Negro rights in the past few years. For each, I wish you would tell me how you would rate the job that person or group has done— excellent, pretty good, only fair, or poor?

    a. NAACP?

    b. CORE?

    c. Richard Hatcher?

    d. Martin Luther King?

    e. Stokely Carmichael?

    f. Urban League?

    g. Malcolm X?

    h. Julian Bond?

    i. Elijah Muhammad?

    j. SNCC?

    k. Ralph Abernathy?

    l. Black Panther Party ?

    m. Bayard Rustin?

    n. Carl Stokes?

    o. Black Muslims?

    p. Whitney Young?

54. Do you think the methods the civil rights leaders use, like marches, picketing, and demonstrations, are helping or hurting the cause?

55. Do you think the leaders of the civil rights movement have gotten involved too much in the Vietnam war question, too little, or about the right amount?
56. Now I would like to ask you a question about Martin Luther King. In your opinion, since his assassination have his ideas about nonviolence been gaining support or losing support?
57. Do you think his assassination was the result of a conspiracy or that it was the act of one man only?
58. Are you pretty much satisfied that a full and honest investigation was made to find out who killed Martin Luther King?
59. Now I want to give you a list of different people and groups that are run by white people. Do you think (*ask for each item listed below*) have been more helpful or more harmful to Negro rights?
    a. White churches?
    b. Local police?
    c. Labor unions?
    d. White businesses?
    e. Catholic priests?
    f. Jews?
    g. Real estate companies?
    h. The Federal government under Nixon?
    i. Congress?
    j. U.S. Supreme Court?
    k. State government?
    l. The Federal anti-poverty program?
    m. White college students?
60. Now I'm going to ask you about the various ways people obtain news and information. Would you tell me how good a job you think each is doing when it comes to reporting news about the Negro community truthfully and fairly—excellent, pretty good, only fair, or poor?
    a. Most TV stations?
    b. Most newspapers?
    c. Most radio stations?
    d. Most news magazines?
    e. Motion pictures?
61. Do you think the police in this area do a good job or not so good a job of preventing crime in this neighborhood?

62. In some places in the nation there have been charges of police brutality. Do you think there is any police brutality in this area, or not?

63. On a number of occasions there have been shooting incidents between some black militants and some police. Who do you think is more to blame for this trouble—the black militants or the police who were involved?

64. On the whole, do you think most white people want to see Negroes get a better break, or do they want to keep Negroes down, or do you think they don't care one way or the other?

65. Again just your impression, do you think most Jews want to see Negroes get a better break or do they want to keep Negroes down, or do you think they don't care one way or the other?

66. Just your impression, do you think white people in the North care more about giving Negroes a better break than do white people in the South, or don't you think there is much difference?

67. Compared to five years ago, do you think white people have changed their attitude about Negro rights for the better, for the worse, or has there not been much change?

68.   a. In the next five years, do you think the attitude of white people about Negro rights will get better, worse, or stay about the same?
    b. Why do you think it will go that way?

69. In the end, do you think white people will take a better attitude toward Negroes mainly because they will be forced to by Negro action, or mainly because they can be persuaded that this is the only right thing to do?

70. In both the South and North, there are some whites who want to see Negroes get a better break. But they also think that progress on Negro rights will not be as fast as Negro groups want. They are known as white moderates. On the whole, do you think they are more helpful or more harmful to Negro rights?

Next, some more general questions . . .

71. Do you think birth control information should be available to anyone who wants it, or not?

72. If welfare payments were the same in all parts of the country,

do you think people on welfare would still want to live in the big cities, or not?

73. Do you think that the welfare system, as it now exists, tends to *help* Negroes in the long run, or tends to *hurt* them in the long run?

74.   a. How would you rate the job Richard M. Nixon has done as President—excellent, pretty good, only fair, or poor?

   b. What are the two or three main reasons you feel this way? Any other reasons?

On the next topic . . .

75. What does the phrase "black power" mean to you?

76. Do you favor the idea of black power, or not?

77. Many Negro leaders are saying that "black is beautiful." Do you think that most Negroes agree that "black is beautiful"?

78.   a. Do you agree or disagree that Negroes can get what they want only by banding together as black people against the whites, because the whites will never help Negroes?

   b. Why do you feel that way?

79. Do you think Negroes have more to gain or more to lose by resorting to violence?

80.   a. Which term do you like *most*—colored people, Negroes, blacks, or Afro-Americans?

   b. Which term do you like *least*?

Now for a few final questions about yourself and your family. . . .

1. How long have you lived in this state?

2. In what part of the country were you born and raised—the East, the South, the Midwest, or the West?

3. How many persons 18 years and over are there living in this household, including yourself? Include lodgers or any relatives living in this household.

4. Are there any children 13 to 17 years of age now living in this household? How many?

5. And are there any children 12 years of age or younger living in this household? How many?

6. What was the last grade or class you *completed* in school?

7. And what was the last grade or class your father *completed* in school?

8. When you were in your teens, did you have any friends who were white?

9. Could you tell me the kind of business or industry the chief wage earner (head of household) in your immediate family works in, and the kind of work he does there?

10.   a. Are you the chief wage earner in this family?

IF "NO," ASK b:

      b. Could you tell me the kind of business or industry you work in and the kind of work you do there?

11. Altogether, how much do the people in your family who live here earn a week?

12. (IF HEAD OF HOUSEHOLD EMPLOYED) How much does the head of the household earn a week?

13. Do you receive any welfare or relief money?

14. Here is a question we always ask to find out when people are at home to watch TV: As you think back over the last previous three Saturdays (INTERVIEWER: *Or Sunday, if this is the day of the interview*), how many of these days were you, yourself, at home at about this same hour? (INTERVIEWER: *If interview is on a weekday, ask about the three weekdays immediately prior to the day of the interview—not including Saturdays and Sundays.*)

15. Have you bought anything on the installment or credit plan in the last year?

16. Do you own or rent your home?

17. How many rooms do you have?

18. And may I have your age?

19. *Record whether* male or female.

20. *Record whether* private house, housing project or other apartment house.

So that my office can check my work in this interview if it wants to, may I have your name, address, and telephone number, please?

APPENDIX C THE TABLES

The pages that follow contain detailed tables for most (though not all) of the questions in the *Newsweek* Poll. The tables appear here in approximately the order in which they are discussed in the text. The tables include the responses of the total national samples in the 1963 and 1966 polls. Readers who are interested in more detailed comparative figures—in, say, the response of Northern low-income Negroes to a specific question in 1963 or 1966—may consult William Brink and Louis Harris, *Black and White: A Study of U.S. Racial Attitudes Today*, New York, 1967. The figures have been rounded to the nearest whole number; some columns of percentages as a result do not add up exactly to 100. A dash in the tables means less than 1 per cent.

CHAPTER 1

3. All in all, compared with five years ago, do you think things for people such as yourself and your family are better, worse, or about the same?

	TOTAL SAMPLE	1963 %	1966 %	1969 %
Better		x	67	70
Worse		x	5	5
About the same		x	23	19
Not sure		x	5	6

NORTH	Total %	Under 30 %	30–49 %	50 and Older %	Low Income %	Low Middle Income %	Middle Income %
Better	60	64	62	55	62	70	60
Worse	7	5	3	16	8	8	6
About the same	24	26	27	17	21	17	27
Not sure	9	5	8	12	10	5	6

SOUTH	Total %	Under 30 %	30–49 %	50 and Older %	Low Income %	Low Middle Income %	Middle Income %
Better	80	86	76	81	74	80	88
Worse	3	2	–	5	9	1	–
About the same	15	9	22	12	15	17	9
Not sure	3	4	3	3	2	3	3

49a. I want to read you some statements about the war in Vietnam. Tell me for each if you tend to agree or disagree: Money spent in Vietnam means less money for civil rights and poverty programs here at home.

TOTAL SAMPLE	1963 %	1966 %	1969 %
Agree	x	44	77
Disagree	x	27	11
Not sure	x	29	12

NORTH	Total %	Under 30 %	30–49 %	50 and Older %	Low Income %	Low Middle Income %	Middle Income %
Agree	80	80	81	76	76	87	78
Disagree	9	11	9	8	14	7	10
Not sure	12	10	10	17	10	7	12
SOUTH							
Agree	75	71	81	70	68	82	73
Disagree	13	16	8	16	18	9	17
Not sure	12	13	10	14	14	9	10

49b. Negroes should be against the war in Vietnam because they have less freedom to fight for.

TOTAL SAMPLE	1963 %	1966 %	1969 %
Agree	x	35	56
Disagree	x	44	31
Not sure	x	21	13

NORTH	Total %	Under 30 %	30–49 %	50 and Older %	Low Income %	Low Middle Income %	Middle Income %
Agree	52	60	47	48	60	52	53
Disagree	35	29	40	38	34	36	34
Not sure	13	11	13	15	7	12	13

SOUTH	Total %	Under 30 %	30–49 %	50 and Older %	Low Income %	Low Middle Income %	Middle Income %
Agree	60	64	64	54	64	66	49
Disagree	27	21	25	32	22	23	42
Not sure	13	15	11	14	14	11	9

47. Now where do you think a young Negro just starting out will have a better chance to get a break—in the armed forces or in civilian life?

TOTAL SAMPLE	1963 %	1966 %	1969 %
Armed forces	x	47	36
Civilian life	x	26	37
Not sure	x	27	27

NORTH	Total %	Under 30 %	30–49 %	50 and Older %	Low Income %	Low Middle Income %	Middle Income %
Armed forces	24	19	30	24	33	25	23
Civilian life	44	50	41	43	34	42	50
Not sure	32	31	29	33	34	32	27
SOUTH							
Armed forces	46	45	41	52	64	52	29
Civilian life	32	28	37	28	16	27	48
Not sure	22	28	22	20	20	21	24

30. As far as all the things that have been going on lately with Negro rights, do you think things are moving about right these days, too fast, or too slow?

TOTAL SAMPLE	1963 %	1966 %	1969 %
About right	31	35	22
Too fast	3	4	7
Too slow	51	43	59
Not sure	15	18	12

NORTH	Total %	Under 30 %	30–49 %	50 and Older %	Low Income %	Low Middle Income %	Middle Income %
About right	20	16	24	20	9	29	19
Too fast	6	5	5	9	11	8	2
Too slow	62	70	62	54	65	56	66
Not sure	12	10	10	17	15	8	13

SOUTH	Total %	Under 30 %	30–49 %	50 and Older %	Low Income %	Low Middle %	Middle Income %
About right	24	24	22	27	27	24	25
Too fast	7	6	8	8	4	6	7
Too slow	56	59	61	50	58	57	58
Not sure	12	12	10	16	11	14	10

CHAPTER 2

53. Now I want to read off to you a list of people—some living and some dead—and groups prominent in the fight for Negro rights in the past few years. For each, I wish you would tell me how you would rate the job that person or group has done—excellent, pretty good, only fair, or poor?

a. NAACP?

TOTAL SAMPLE	1963 %	1966 %	1969 %
Excellent	75	58	37
Pretty good	16	23	39
Only fair	3	6	13
Poor	0	1	4
Not sure	6	12	6

NORTH	Total %	Under 30 %	30–49 %	50 and Older %	Low Income %	Low Middle %	Middle Income %
Excellent	27	21	24	38	38	35	20
Pretty good	44	46	50	35	36	42	48
Only fair	19	18	20	16	20	14	22
Poor	6	9	5	5	0	5	7
Not sure	4	5	2	6	7	4	2
SOUTH							
Excellent	47	36	43	59	63	51	39
Pretty good	35	45	36	27	26	28	41
Only fair	8	11	10	4	5	8	12
Poor	2	2	4	0	0	4	1
Not sure	8	7	7	10	7	9	7

b. CORE?

	TOTAL SAMPLE	1963 %	1966 %	1969 %
Excellent		38	34	16
Pretty good		21	26	30
Only fair		7	9	16
Poor		1	2	5
Not sure		33	29	33

NORTH	Total %	Under 30 %	30–49 %	50 and Older %	Low Income %	Low Middle Income %	Middle Income %
Excellent	12	13	10	12	16	14	12
Pretty good	34	35	39	29	19	33	40
Only fair	19	23	16	18	13	17	22
Poor	7	3	8	11	0	6	6
Not sure	29	26	29	30	52	29	21
SOUTH							
Excellent	21	15	19	26	37	21	15
Pretty good	26	29	30	22	28	24	27
Only fair	14	12	16	13	9	13	19
Poor	3	3	2	4	4	2	3
Not sure	36	42	33	36	22	40	36

c. Richard Hatcher?

	TOTAL SAMPLE	1963 %	1966 %	1969 %
Excellent		x	x	7
Pretty good		x	x	17
Only fair		x	x	9
Poor		x	x	1
Not sure		x	x	67

NORTH	Total %	Under 30 %	30–49 %	50 and Older %	Low Income %	Low Middle Income %	Middle Income %
Excellent	6	5	6	7	3	3	7
Pretty good	20	24	22	15	7	19	27
Only fair	8	11	7	6	1	10	8
Poor	1	1	1	2	0	1	2
Not sure	65	59	65	70	90	67	56

SOUTH	Total %	Under 30 %	30–49 %	50 and Older %	Low Income %	Low Middle Income %	Middle Income %
Excellent	9	10	7	9	7	10	10
Pretty good	14	12	18	11	10	10	20
Only fair	9	4	11	10	6	7	7
Poor	1	–	0	2	5	–	0
Not sure	68	74	64	67	71	72	63

d. Martin Luther King?

TOTAL SAMPLE	1963 %	1966 %	1969 %
Excellent	78	75	83
Pretty good	10	13	12
Only fair	3	2	2
Poor	1	1	1
Not sure	8	9	3

NORTH	Total %	Under 30 %	30–49 %	50 and Older %	Low Income %	Low Middle Income %	Middle Income %
Excellent	80	71	89	83	76	85	79
Pretty good	15	23	10	12	13	12	16
Only fair	2	4	–	2	4	2	2
Poor	1	2	0	2	8	0	1
Not sure	2	0	1	1	0	2	2
SOUTH							
Excellent	85	81	82	90	78	86	88
Pretty good	8	13	10	4	12	5	10
Only fair	1	0	2	1	1	2	1
Poor	1	4	0	–	0	3	0
Not sure	5	2	6	5	8	4	2

e. Stokely Carmichael?

TOTAL SAMPLE	1963 %	1966 %	1969 %
Excellent	x	7	12
Pretty good	x	12	19
Only fair	x	8	18
Poor	x	5	28
Not sure	x	68	24

NORTH	Total %	Under 30 %	30–49 %	50 and Older %	Low Income %	Low Middle Income %	Middle Income %
Excellent	13	19	13	5	12	12	16
Pretty good	18	23	13	18	19	17	19
Only fair	19	19	20	19	9	19	19
Poor	30	23	35	31	27	26	35
Not sure	21	17	19	27	33	26	13
SOUTH							
Excellent	11	17	11	7	14	7	11
Pretty good	19	19	16	23	14	23	15
Only fair	17	16	24	11	15	17	18
Poor	26	28	22	29	22	25	36
Not sure	27	20	28	30	35	28	20

f. Urban League?

TOTAL SAMPLE	1963 %	1966 %	1969 %
Excellent	27	25	15
Pretty good	27	25	31
Only fair	9	8	18
Poor	1	1	5
Not sure	36	41	31

NORTH	Total %	Under 30 %	30–49 %	50 and Older %	Low Income %	Low Middle Income %	Middle Income %
Excellent	15	12	17	15	11	11	19
Pretty good	38	34	40	37	38	44	38
Only fair	21	23	23	16	23	19	25
Poor	7	9	2	10	1	7	6
Not sure	21	21	18	22	26	20	13
SOUTH							
Excellent	16	20	13	16	21	12	16
Pretty good	26	22	34	19	21	24	35
Only fair	15	10	16	17	5	12	25
Poor	3	3	2	3	4	3	1
Not sure	41	45	36	45	51	50	24

g. Malcolm X?

TOTAL SAMPLE	1963 %	1966 %	1969 %
Excellent	x	x	13
Pretty good	x	x	14
Only fair	x	x	14
Poor	x	x	21
Not sure	x	x	39

NORTH	Total %	Under 30 %	30–49 %	50 and Older %	Low Income %	Low Middle %	Middle Income %
Excellent	18	27	19	8	6	12	25
Pretty good	17	25	16	10	22	17	17
Only fair	15	14	15	17	8	20	16
Poor	22	12	27	29	29	23	21
Not sure	27	22	23	36	35	27	21
SOUTH							
Excellent	7	9	9	4	2	6	11
Pretty good	11	16	14	4	8	11	13
Only fair	13	12	16	11	9	13	13
Poor	20	19	19	21	21	15	31
Not sure	49	44	42	60	60	56	32

h. Julian Bond?

TOTAL SAMPLE	1963 %	1966 %	1969 %
Excellent	x	14	25
Pretty good	x	17	23
Only fair	x	10	10
Poor	x	2	2
Not sure	x	57	40

NORTH	Total %	Under 30 %	30–49 %	50 and Older %	Low Income %	Low Middle %	Middle Income %
Excellent	24	25	26	24	17	24	28
Pretty good	23	23	23	19	21	25	26
Only fair	9	12	4	11	6	11	8
Poor	3	1	4	3	1	1	4
Not sure	42	39	43	43	56	39	34

SOUTH	Total %	Under 30 %	30–49 %	50 and Older %	Low Income %	Low Middle %	Middle Income %
Excellent	26	22	30	25	15	26	32
Pretty good	24	22	23	26	21	24	26
Only fair	12	13	13	9	19	11	12
Poor	1	1	1	1	1	–	3
Not sure	38	42	34	40	44	39	28

i. Elijah Muhammad?

TOTAL SAMPLE	1963 %	1966 %	1969 %
Excellent	5	4	9
Pretty good	10	8	13
Only fair	6	7	16
Poor	29	36	24
Not sure	50	45	38

NORTH	Total %	Under 30 %	30–49 %	50 and Older %	Low Income %	Low Middle %	Middle Income %
Excellent	5	8	5	1	0	4	7
Pretty good	14	14	17	9	7	17	12
Only fair	19	20	15	19	23	23	16
Poor	30	21	37	32	13	28	35
Not sure	33	37	26	38	57	28	31
SOUTH							
Excellent	12	10	12	14	21	10	5
Pretty good	13	12	16	11	11	15	12
Only fair	13	20	11	12	14	15	14
Poor	19	19	23	15	9	19	29
Not sure	43	39	38	49	46	41	41

k. SNCC?

TOTAL SAMPLE	1963 %	1966 %	1969 %
Excellent	10	23	11
Pretty good	8	21	21
Only fair	3	10	13
Poor	1	4	7
Not sure	78	42	48

	Total	Under 30	30–49	50 and Older	Low Income	Low Middle	Middle Income
NORTH	%	%	%	%	%	%	%
Excellent	11	13	13	8	5	4	18
Pretty good	23	26	26	19	17	26	22
Only fair	16	12	17	15	10	17	16
Poor	7	8	5	9	0	5	9
Not sure	43	41	39	49	68	48	35
SOUTH							
Excellent	12	11	13	9	16	9	12
Pretty good	19	16	21	18	14	16	21
Only fair	10	9	13	9	3	13	13
Poor	7	10	7	7	6	7	10
Not sure	53	54	47	58	61	55	44

1. Ralph Abernathy?

TOTAL SAMPLE	1963 %	1966 %	1969 %
Excellent	x	x	26
Pretty good	x	x	38
Only fair	x	x	18
Poor	x	x	6
Not sure	x	x	12

	Total	Under 30	30–49	50 and Older	Low Income	Low Middle	Middle Income
NORTH	%	%	%	%	%	%	%
Excellent	21	15	28	17	22	22	22
Pretty good	41	46	40	39	45	45	42
Only fair	19	22	17	19	19	21	18
Poor	7	9	6	6	4	3	11
Not sure	12	8	9	19	10	10	8
SOUTH							
Excellent	31	27	31	33	28	30	26
Pretty good	36	35	39	33	40	35	39
Only fair	17	21	15	16	17	22	16
Poor	6	7	5	6	2	6	10
Not sure	11	10	10	13	12	8	10

m. Black Panther Party?

	TOTAL SAMPLE	1963 %	1966 %	1969 %
Excellent		x	x	5
Pretty good		x	x	10
Only fair		x	x	10
Poor		x	x	22
Not sure		x	x	53

NORTH	Total %	Under 30 %	30–49 %	50 and Older %	Low Income %	Low Middle Income %	Middle Income %
Excellent	7	14	7	2	1	5	11
Pretty good	10	18	9	5	6	10	12
Only fair	12	13	11	11	3	7	16
Poor	26	20	27	32	43	26	23
Not sure	45	35	46	51	48	52	38
SOUTH							
Excellent	3	3	5	1	4	2	3
Pretty good	10	18	11	4	11	11	9
Only fair	7	9	6	8	7	7	9
Poor	19	22	20	17	10	18	30
Not sure	61	49	59	70	68	63	49

n. Bayard Rustin?

	TOTAL SAMPLE	1963 %	1966 %	1969 %
Excellent		x	10	3
Pretty good		x	12	12
Only fair		x	8	8
Poor		x	2	3
Not sure		x	68	74

NORTH	Total %	Under 30 %	30–49 %	50 and Older %	Low Income %	Low Middle Income %	Middle Income %
Excellent	5	4	8	3	1	3	9
Pretty good	14	17	11	11	13	14	13
Only fair	8	13	6	7	0	8	12
Poor	4	5	3	4	0	4	5
Not sure	70	62	73	74	86	72	62

SOUTH	Total %	Under 30 %	30–49 %	50 and Older %	Low Income %	Low Middle Income %	Middle Income %
Excellent	2	2	2	1	0	1	3
Pretty good	10	5	12	10	5	6	16
Only fair	7	7	9	4	2	5	10
Poor	3	5	2	3	6	2	3
Not sure	79	80	75	82	86	86	68

o. Carl Stokes?

TOTAL SAMPLE	1963 %	1966 %	1969 %
Excellent	x	x	21
Pretty good	x	x	24
Only fair	x	x	10
Poor	x	x	4
Not sure	x	x	41

NORTH	Total %	Under 30 %	30–49 %	50 and Older %	Low Income %	Low Middle Income %	Middle Income %
Excellent	24	19	29	24	27	27	22
Pretty good	27	32	25	24	31	31	28
Only fair	14	20	11	12	2	10	18
Poor	5	3	10	1	4	4	4
Not sure	31	26	25	40	36	28	29
SOUTH							
Excellent	19	18	18	20	14	16	26
Pretty good	22	21	25	18	7	22	31
Only fair	7	9	5	8	7	6	9
Poor	3	2	4	2	2	4	2
Not sure	50	51	49	52	70	53	32

p. Black Muslims?

TOTAL SAMPLE	1963 %	1966 %	1969 %
Excellent	4	4	4
Pretty good	7	5	9
Only fair	6	6	14
Poor	38	43	34
Not sure	45	42	39

NORTH	Total %	Under 30 %	30–49 %	50 and Older %	Low Income %	Low Middle Income %	Middle Income %
Excellent	6	12	6	1	0	4	9
Pretty good	7	14	7	1	5	9	7
Only fair	17	18	15	17	23	12	20
Poor	42	31	46	52	45	44	41
Not sure	28	26	26	29	27	31	22
SOUTH							
Excellent	2	3	1	1	0	2	3
Pretty good	11	19	13	4	12	11	12
Only fair	11	12	14	7	10	10	13
Poor	27	27	28	27	24	24	38
Not sure	50	39	45	60	55	54	34

q. Whitney Young?

TOTAL SAMPLE	1963 %	1966 %	1969 %
Excellent	x	16	19
Pretty good	x	17	23
Only fair	x	7	13
Poor	x	1	3
Not sure	x	59	42

NORTH	Total %	Under 30 %	30–49 %	50 and Older %	Low Income %	Low Middle Income %	Middle Income %
Excellent	17	8	20	22	9	17	19
Pretty good	27	29	27	25	30	24	30
Only fair	16	20	14	14	8	19	16
Poor	4	9	4	0	0	4	5
Not sure	36	34	34	39	53	36	30
SOUTH							
Excellent	22	13	24	25	27	20	19
Pretty good	18	20	23	12	6	18	28
Only fair	10	13	8	9	7	10	11
Poor	2	3	1	3	4	1	2
Not sure	48	50	44	51	56	51	40

56. Now I would like to ask you a question about Martin Luther King. In your opinion, since his assassination, have his ideas about nonviolence been gaining support or losing support?

TOTAL SAMPLE		1963 %	1966 %	1969 %
Gaining		x	x	30
Losing		x	x	52
About the same		x	x	10
Not sure		x	x	8

NORTH	Total %	Under 30 %	30–49 %	50 and Older %	Low Income %	Low Middle Income %	Middle Income %
Gaining	24	28	23	22	24	30	13
Losing	59	59	61	55	51	56	70
About the same	8	7	8	9	8	7	10
Not sure	9	6	8	15	17	7	7
SOUTH							
Gaining	36	28	37	41	42	38	28
Losing	45	58	41	42	36	46	57
About the same	12	12	12	11	16	9	11
Not sure	7	3	10	6	6	6	4

CHAPTER 3

27. If you were asked, would you:

TOTAL SAMPLE	1963 %	1966 %	1969 %
Take part in a sit-in	49	52	40
March in a demonstration	51	54	44
Picket a store	46	49	41
Stop buying at a store	62	69	57
Go to jail	47	45	33

NORTH	Total %	Under 30 %	30–49 %	50 and Older %	Low Income %	Low Middle Income %	Middle Income %
Take part in a sit-in	43	57	47	27	25	45	53
March in a demonstration	49	63	51	36	28	51	62
Picket a store	43	59	47	25	29	46	55
Stop buying at a store	56	67	56	44	44	57	66
Go to jail	32	45	35	19	16	31	43

	Total %	Under 30 %	30–49 %	50 and Older %	Low Income %	Low Middle Income %	Middle Income %
SOUTH							
Take part in a sit-in	37	47	41	28	36	34	46
March in a demonstration	40	54	45	27	35	37	50
Picket a store	38	51	42	28	34	36	51
Stop buying at a store	58	71	61	49	55	61	67
Go to jail	33	39	37	25	32	30	36

28. Do you think activities of these kinds have helped Negroes or hurt them in their effort to win their rights?

TOTAL SAMPLE	1963 %	1966 %	1969 %
Helped	x	x	68
Hurt	x	x	13
Not sure	x	x	18

	Total %	Under 30 %	30–49 %	50 and Older %	Low Income %	Low Middle Income %	Middle Income %
NORTH							
Helped	67	73	69	59	73	64	75
Hurt	15	11	17	19	24	16	13
Not sure	17	16	15	23	3	21	12
SOUTH							
Helped	70	73	72	65	64	72	70
Hurt	12	6	10	16	21	10	8
Not sure	19	20	18	19	15	18	22

14. Regardless of how you may vote, what do you usually consider yourself—a Republican, a Democrat, or what?

TOTAL SAMPLE	1963 %	1966 %	1969 %
Republican	11	9	7
Democrat	74	70	76
Independent	9	7	8
Other	1	2	1
Not sure	5	12	7

NORTH	Total %	Under 30 %	30–49 %	50 and Older %	Low Income %	Low Middle %	Middle Income %
Republican	6	3	5	11	10	6	6
Democrat	71	62	73	77	79	73	68
Independent	11	17	9	8	5	8	14
Other	2	2	4	0	0	2	4
Not sure	9	17	9	3	7	11	9
SOUTH							
Republican	7	7	7	7	3	8	7
Democrat	81	74	81	86	89	80	81
Independent	6	8	7	4	4	6	8
Other	1	—	1	—	0	1	1
Not sure	5	11	4	4	4	5	3

15a. In politics, do you feel Negroes should work mainly together as a separate group outside the two political parties or as individuals within one or the other party?

TOTAL SAMPLE	1963 %	1966 %	1969 %
Mainly as a separate group	9	7	10
Mainly within parties	67	74	68
Both	8	6	10
Not sure	16	13	13

NORTH	Total %	Under 30 %	30–49 %	50 and Older %	Low Income %	Low Middle %	Middle Income %
Mainly as a separate group	13	20	12	7	5	10	17
Mainly within parties	64	50	77	64	52	70	65
Both	7	9	4	8	16	5	7
Not sure	16	21	8	21	27	15	11
SOUTH							
Mainly as a separate group	7	5	10	6	1	10	8
Mainly within parties	72	72	69	74	75	66	79
Both	11	15	11	10	12	14	8
Not sure	10	8	11	9	12	10	5

16. Which party—the Republican or the Democratic—do you feel
will do more to help Negroes in the next few years, or do you think
there isn't much difference between the two?

TOTAL SAMPLE	1963 %	1966 %	1969 %
Republican	4	3	4
Democratic	63	69	62
Other	0	—	—
No difference	18	14	24
Not sure	15	14	11

NORTH	Total %	Under 30 %	30–49 %	50 and Older %	Low Income %	Low Middle Income %	Middle Income %
Republican	3	4	3	3	7	4	3
Democratic	57	51	55	65	86	49	53
Other	—	—	0	0	0	—	0
No difference	27	33	29	19	3	30	33
Not sure	13	12	13	14	5	16	11
SOUTH							
Republican	4	3	5	3	3	4	4
Democratic	67	70	64	66	73	65	67
Other	—	0	0	—	0	0	0
No difference	21	16	22	24	19	24	24
Not sure	8	10	8	7	6	8	5

69. In the end, do you think white people will take a better attitude toward Negroes mainly because they will be forced to by Negro
action, or mainly because they can be persuaded that this is the
only right thing to do?

TOTAL SAMPLE	1963 %	1966 %	1969 %
Mainly force of action	28	24	34
Mainly per- suasion	52	51	46
Not sure	20	25	20

	Total %	Under 30 %	30–49 %	50 and Older %	Low Income %	Low Middle %	Middle Income %
NORTH							
Mainly force of action	37	46	34	30	31	31	44
Mainly persuasion	46	45	48	49	43	52	43
Not sure	17	9	19	21	26	17	13
SOUTH							
Mainly force of action	32	39	25	34	37	32	27
Mainly persuasion	46	35	54	44	46	43	52
Not sure	23	26	21	23	17	25	21

CHAPTER 4

29a. Some Negro leaders have said that Negroes can only succeed in winning rights if they use nonviolent means to demonstrate. Others disagree. Do you personally feel Negroes today can win their rights without resorting to violence, or do you think it will have to be an eye for an eye and a tooth for a tooth?

TOTAL SAMPLE	1963 %	1966 %	1969 %
Can win without violence	63	59	63
Will have to use violence	22	21	21
Not sure	15	20	16

	Total %	Under 30 %	30–49 %	50 and Older %	Low Income %	Low Middle %	Middle Income %
NORTH							
Can win without violence	58	49	55	73	72	57	52
Will have to use violence	25	36	26	12	7	22	33
Not sure	17	15	20	15	22	21	16
SOUTH							
Can win without violence	68	55	71	71	71	67	70
Will have to use violence	18	29	18	10	15	14	21
Not sure	15	16	11	19	15	19	9

79. Do you think Negroes have more to gain or more to lose by resorting to violence?

	TOTAL SAMPLE	1963 %	1966 %	1969 %
More to gain		x	15	18
More to lose		x	67	65
Not sure		x	18	17

NORTH	Total %	Under 30 %	30–49 %	50 and Older %	Low Income %	Low Middle Middle %	Middle Income %
More to gain	18	28	16	12	16	16	22
More to lose	62	52	65	71	68	69	57
Not sure	20	20	19	17	16	15	21
SOUTH							
More to gain	18	22	19	13	21	15	13
More to lose	67	58	67	74	71	66	74
Not sure	15	20	14	13	8	19	13

32. In your opinion, are those Negroes who have taken part in the rioting and violence in certain cities mostly hoodlums and bad characters, or mostly good people driven to violence?

	TOTAL SAMPLE	1963 %	1966 %	1969 %
Mostly hoodlums		x	x	24
Mostly good people		x	x	25
Both kinds		x	x	41
Not sure		x	x	11

NORTH	Total %	Under 30 %	30–49 %	50 and Older %	Low Income %	Low Middle Middle %	Middle Income %
Mostly hoodlums	27	18	31	30	31	31	23
Mostly good people	25	34	21	23	10	22	29
Both kinds	37	40	37	33	48	37	39
Not sure	11	8	10	14	11	10	8
SOUTH							
Mostly hoodlums	20	22	16	24	14	18	33
Mostly good people	25	26	30	20	26	18	31
Both kinds	44	42	44	45	52	56	26
Not sure	11	10	10	11	8	8	10

33. Regardless of who took part in them, do you think the riots have been justified, or not?

TOTAL SAMPLE	1963 %	1966 %	1969 %
Justified	x	x	31
Not justified	x	x	48
Not sure	x	x	21

NORTH	Total %	Under 30 %	30–49 %	50 and Older %	Low Income %	Low Middle %	Middle Income %
Justified	36	47	33	26	40	32	42
Not justified	44	32	49	51	41	47	38
Not sure	20	21	18	23	19	22	20
SOUTH							
Justified	27	25	28	26	21	31	28
Not justified	51	50	54	50	61	50	48
Not sure	22	25	18	25	19	19	24

34. Do you think the riots that have taken place in large cities around the country have helped or hurt the cause of Negro rights, or don't you think it makes much difference?

TOTAL SAMPLE	1963 %	1966 %	1969 %
Helped	x	34	40
Hurt	x	20	29
Not much difference	x	17	16
Not sure	x	29	15

NORTH	Total %	Under 30 %	30–49 %	50 and Older %	Low Income %	Low Middle %	Middle Income %
Helped	38	50	35	28	21	33	50
Hurt	34	20	36	44	42	37	24
Not much difference	15	20	17	9	16	13	17
Not sure	13	10	12	19	22	17	9

SOUTH	Total %	Under 30 %	30–49 %	50 and Older %	Low Income %	Low Middle %	Middle Income %
Helped	42	43	42	42	36	45	39
Hurt	26	18	25	31	43	19	24
Not much difference	17	25	14	15	7	21	19
Not sure	16	15	19	12	14	15	18

36. Would you join in something like that, or not?

TOTAL SAMPLE	1963 %	1966 %	1969 %
Would join a riot	x	15	11
Would not join	x	61	68
Not sure	x	24	22

NORTH	Total %	Under 30 %	30–49 %	50 and Older %	Low Income %	Low Middle %	Middle Income %
Would join a riot	10	16	9	3	2	8	14
Would not join	66	56	64	82	79	64	62
Not sure	24	28	27	15	19	29	24
SOUTH							
Would join a riot	11	17	12	7	11	12	8
Would not join	70	64	73	70	72	64	80
Not sure	19	19	15	23	17	24	12

42. Some people have urged Negroes generally to arm themselves. Do you think this is a good idea or a poor idea?

TOTAL SAMPLE	1963 %	1966 %	1969 %
A good idea	x	x	25
A poor idea	x	x	59
Not sure	x	x	16

NORTH	Total %	Under 30 %	30–49 %	50 and Older %	Low Income %	Low Middle %	Middle Income %
A good idea	23	32	20	17	17	25	25
A poor idea	59	53	61	64	75	62	58
Not sure	18	15	19	19	8	14	18

SOUTH	Total %	Under 30 %	30–49 %	50 and Older %	Low Income %	Low Middle %	Middle Income %
A good idea	27	29	31	22	25	31	18
A poor idea	59	59	53	66	55	54	70
Not sure	14	12	16	12	21	15	12

CHAPTER 5

64. On the whole, do you think most white people want to see Negroes get a better break, or do they want to keep Negroes down, or do you think they don't care one way or the other?

TOTAL SAMPLE	1963 %	1966 %	1969 %
Better break	25	27	20
Keep Negroes down	41	38	43
Don't care either way	17	16	26
Not sure	17	19	10

NORTH	Total %	Under 30 %	30–49 %	50 and Older %	Low Income %	Low Middle %	Middle Income %
Better break	18	10	23	22	31	21	16
Keep Negroes down	44	51	46	34	26	48	48
Don't care either way	28	30	24	31	32	26	26
Not sure	10	9	8	13	11	6	11
SOUTH							
Better break	22	14	17	33	28	25	15
Keep Negroes down	43	47	47	37	43	45	38
Don't care either way	24	31	25	20	17	22	34
Not sure	10	9	11	10	12	8	13

66. Just your impression, do you think white people in the North care more about giving Negroes a better break than do white people in the South, or don't you think there is much difference?

TOTAL SAMPLE	1963 %	1966 %	1969 %
Northerners care more	38	37	36
Not much difference	47	41	53
Not sure	15	22	11

NORTH	Total %	Under 30 %	30–49 %	50 and Older %	Low Income %	Low Middle Income %	Middle Income %
Northerners care more	30	30	27	36	28	29	29
Not much difference	60	66	65	46	55	63	65
Not sure	11	5	8	19	17	8	6
SOUTH							
Northerners care more	43	42	43	44	48	35	43
Not much difference	45	46	48	42	33	54	48
Not sure	12	13	10	14	19	11	9

70. In both the South and North, there are some whites who want to see Negroes get a better break. But they also think that progress on Negro rights will not be as fast as Negro groups want. They are known as white moderates. On the whole, do you think they are more helpful or more harmful to Negro rights?

TOTAL SAMPLE	1963 %	1966 %	1969 %
More helpful	29	30	41
More harmful	31	26	31
Not sure	40	44	28

NORTH	Total %	Under 30 %	30–49 %	50 and Older %	Low Income %	Low Middle Income %	Middle Income %
More helpful	33	29	37	32	26	35	37
More harmful	38	39	41	33	26	36	40
Not sure	29	31	22	35	48	29	23
SOUTH							
More helpful	49	33	54	54	49	57	39
More harmful	24	32	22	22	22	21	28
Not sure	27	35	25	24	29	22	33

67. Compared to five years ago, do you think white people have changed their attitude about Negro rights for the better, for the worse, or has there not been much change?

TOTAL SAMPLE	1963 %	1966 %	1969 %
Better	52	56	54
Worse	2	2	4
Not much change	32	29	36
Not sure	14	13	6

NORTH	Total %	Under 30 %	30–49 %	50 and Older %	Low Income %	Low Middle Income %	Middle Income %
Better	48	38	49	60	49	48	50
Worse	7	8	6	6	0	8	9
Not much change	39	49	43	24	36	39	39
Not sure	6	6	2	11	15	5	3
SOUTH							
Better	60	53	55	70	68	62	60
Worse	2	2	1	2	6	1	–
Not much change	33	36	41	23	21	31	37
Not sure	6	9	4	5	6	6	3

68a. In the next five years, do you think the attitude of white people about Negro rights will get better, worse, or stay about the same?

TOTAL SAMPLE	1963 %	1966 %	1969 %
Better	73	69	61
Worse	2	2	6
About the same	11	13	22
Not sure	14	16	12

NORTH	Total %	Under 30 %	30–49 %	50 and Older %	Low Income %	Low Middle Income %	Middle Income %
Better	55	54	53	61	53	53	56
Worse	9	12	9	5	3	11	9
About the same	25	26	25	20	32	26	23
Not sure	12	8	14	14	12	10	12

	Total %	Under 30 %	30–49 %	50 and Older %	Low Income %	Low Middle %	Middle Income %
SOUTH							
Better	66	63	68	67	71	62	71
Worse	3	–	5	4	5	4	3
About the same	19	22	19	18	12	22	19
Not sure	12	15	8	12	12	12	7

59a. Now I want to give you a list of different people and groups that are run by white people. Do you think white churches have been more helpful or more harmful to Negro rights?

TOTAL SAMPLE	1963 %	1966 %	1969 %
Helpful	23	30	39
Harmful	23	16	20
Not sure	54	54	41

	Total %	Under 30 %	30–49 %	50 and Older %	Low Income %	Low Middle %	Middle Income %
NORTH							
Helpful	40	29	47	43	26	47	38
Harmful	22	35	14	20	14	17	29
Not sure	39	36	39	37	60	37	33
SOUTH							
Helpful	38	19	43	44	54	35	32
Harmful	19	24	16	19	17	16	20
Not sure	43	57	42	36	29	49	48

b. Local police?

TOTAL SAMPLE	1963 %	1966 %	1969 %
Helpful	x	26	25
Harmful	x	33	46
Not sure	x	41	29

	Total %	Under 30 %	30–49 %	50 and Older %	Low Income %	Low Middle %	Middle Income %
NORTH							
Helpful	18	12	15	30	31	15	14
Harmful	57	70	60	38	33	59	68
Not sure	25	18	25	32	36	26	19

	Total %	Under 30 %	30–49 %	50 and Older %	Low Income %	Low Middle %	Middle Income %
SOUTH							
Helpful	32	21	33	39	42	34	24
Harmful	35	48	36	26	21	35	44
Not sure	33	31	32	35	37	31	32

c. Labor unions?

TOTAL SAMPLE	1963 %	1966 %	1969 %
Helpful	38	43	45
Harmful	25	13	20
Not sure	37	44	35

	Total %	Under 30 %	30–49 %	50 and Older %	Low Income %	Low Middle %	Middle Income %
NORTH							
Helpful	40	39	35	52	40	40	38
Harmful	30	30	34	27	18	24	40
Not sure	30	31	31	22	42	37	22
SOUTH							
Helpful	50	46	53	48	46	53	50
Harmful	12	11	14	10	6	9	16
Not sure	39	44	33	42	49	38	34

d. White businesses?

TOTAL SAMPLE	1963 %	1966 %	1969 %
Helpful	18	31	39
Harmful	38	19	25
Not sure	44	50	37

	Total %	Under 30 %	30–49 %	50 and Older %	Low Income %	Low Middle %	Middle Income %
NORTH							
Helpful	39	32	43	42	32	41	39
Harmful	29	39	31	19	14	29	35
Not sure	33	29	27	39	54	31	26
SOUTH							
Helpful	39	29	37	46	41	40	37
Harmful	21	24	23	17	18	14	29
Not sure	41	47	40	37	41	46	35

e. Catholic priests?

TOTAL SAMPLE	1963 %	1966 %	1969 %
Helpful	55	53	52
Harmful	5	3	9
Not sure	40	44	39

NORTH	Total %	Under 30 %	30–49 %	50 and Older %	Low Income %	Low Middle %	Middle Income %
Helpful	53	42	59	61	48	52	54
Harmful	14	28	8	9	9	13	17
Not sure	33	30	33	30	43	34	29
SOUTH							
Helpful	51	42	54	55	52	50	52
Harmful	4	5	5	2	3	2	5
Not sure	45	54	42	43	45	48	44

f. Jews?

TOTAL SAMPLE	1963 %	1966 %	1969 %
Helpful	42	33	34
Harmful	9	5	16
Not sure	49	62	49

NORTH	Total %	Under 30 %	30–49 %	50 and Older %	Low Income %	Low Middle %	Middle Income %
Helpful	31	24	33	37	33	25	33
Harmful	22	34	18	14	4	28	24
Not sure	48	42	49	49	64	47	43
SOUTH							
Helpful	38	30	42	40	36	44	37
Harmful	11	15	10	9	7	8	12
Not sure	51	56	48	51	57	48	51

g. Real estate companies?

TOTAL SAMPLE	1963 %	1966 %	1969 %
Helpful	15	22	22
Harmful	44	29	43
Not sure	41	49	35

NORTH	Total %	Under 30 %	30–49 %	50 and Older %	Low Income %	Low Middle %	Middle Income %
Helpful	17	15	21	14	15	21	15
Harmful	52	59	52	50	43	51	60
Not sure	31	27	27	36	42	28	24
SOUTH							
Helpful	27	18	30	30	36	24	18
Harmful	34	43	36	25	20	35	50
Not sure	40	40	34	45	45	41	33

h. The Federal government under Nixon?*

TOTAL SAMPLE	1963 %	1966 %	1969 %
Helpful	83	74	25
Harmful	2	2	30
Not sure	15	24	45

NORTH	Total %	Under 30 %	30–49 %	50 and Older %	Low Income %	Low Middle %	Middle Income %
Helpful	16	14	20	15	14	14	18
Harmful	39	50	32	36	32	39	44
Not sure	45	36	48	48	54	46	38
SOUTH							
Helpful	33	24	29	43	50	30	23
Harmful	22	28	22	17	17	23	25
Not sure	46	48	49	40	33	47	52

* The 1963 figures represent ratings of "the Federal government under Kennedy." The 1966 figures rate "the Federal government under Johnson."

i. Congress?

TOTAL SAMPLE	1963 %	1966 %	1969 %
Helpful	54	60	52
Harmful	9	3	16
Not sure	37	37	32

NORTH	Total %	Under 30 %	30–49 %	50 and Older %	Low Income %	Low Middle %	Middle Income %
Helpful	42	39	48	40	36	48	38
Harmful	25	31	24	19	19	22	31
Not sure	33	30	28	41	46	30	31
SOUTH							
Helpful	62	51	66	65	71	61	60
Harmful	7	13	7	4	1	5	13
Not sure	31	36	27	32	28	34	28

j. U.S. Supreme Court?

TOTAL SAMPLE	1963 %	1966 %	1969 %
Helpful	80	65	64
Harmful	2	3	8
Not sure	18	32	28

NORTH	Total %	Under 30 %	30–49 %	50 and Older %	Low Income %	Low Middle %	Middle Income %
Helpful	58	53	63	62	51	64	56
Harmful	12	23	11	4	2	16	13
Not sure	30	25	27	34	48	20	31
SOUTH							
Helpful	70	57	77	71	84	67	68
Harmful	5	11	3	3	1	3	8
Not sure	25	33	21	25	15	30	24

k. State government?

TOTAL SAMPLE	1963 %	1966 %	1969 %
Helpful	33	42	36
Harmful	35	16	28
Not sure	32	42	36

NORTH	Total %	Under 30 %	30–49 %	50 and Older %	Low Income %	Low Middle %	Middle Income %
Helpful	35	35	37	36	26	39	35
Harmful	31	40	30	19	25	32	36
Not sure	34	25	33	44	49	29	29

	Total %	Under 30 %	30–49 %	50 and Older %	Low Income %	Low Middle %	Middle Income %
SOUTH							
Helpful	37	30	33	45	46	34	30
Harmful	25	29	29	20	22	25	35
Not sure	38	42	38	35	32	41	36

l. The Federal anti-poverty program?

TOTAL SAMPLE	1963 %	1966 %	1969 %
Helpful	x	66	68
Harmful	x	3	9
Not sure	x	31	23

	Total %	Under 30 %	30–49 %	50 and Older %	Low Income %	Low Middle %	Middle Income %
NORTH							
Helpful	63	50	70	68	68	72	58
Harmful	14	24	11	9	0	16	16
Not sure	24	26	19	24	32	13	27
SOUTH							
Helpful	73	66	74	77	77	70	79
Harmful	4	5	5	3	0	7	6
Not sure	23	29	21	20	23	23	16

m. White college students?

TOTAL SAMPLE	1963 %	1966 %	1969 %
Helpful	x	47	42
Harmful	x	5	15
Not sure	x	48	43

	Total %	Under 30 %	30–49 %	50 and Older %	Low Income %	Low Middle %	Middle Income %
NORTH							
Helpful	50	41	58	52	30	54	53
Harmful	14	23	11	10	8	12	17
Not sure	36	36	31	38	62	34	30
SOUTH							
Helpful	35	27	39	35	32	37	36
Harmful	17	19	20	12	14	11	21
Not sure	49	54	42	53	54	52	43

65. Again just your impression, do you think most Jews want to see Negroes get a better break or do they want to keep Negroes down, or do you think they don't care one way or the other?

	TOTAL SAMPLE	1963 %	1966 %	1969 %
Better break		x	x	28
Keep Negroes down		x	x	19
Don't care either way		x	x	32
Not sure		x	x	21

NORTH	Total %	Under 30 %	30–49 %	50 and Older %	Low Income %	Low Middle Income %	Middle Income %
Better break	24	15	23	35	33	20	22
Keep Negroes down	27	38	27	17	10	29	33
Don't care either way	32	34	34	29	24	32	31
Not sure	18	14	17	19	33	19	14
SOUTH							
Better break	33	26	31	40	27	33	37
Keep Negroes down	11	11	12	11	10	9	13
Don't care either way	32	41	36	23	25	35	34
Not sure	24	23	21	27	39	23	16

61. Do you think the police in this area do a good job or not so good a job of preventing crime in this neighborhood?

	TOTAL SAMPLE	1963 %	1966 %	1969 %
Good job		x	x	36
Not so good		x	x	45
Not sure		x	x	19

NORTH	Total %	Under 30 %	30–49 %	50 and Older %	Low Income %	Low Middle Income %	Middle Income %
Good job	34	25	35	44	38	39	30
Not so good	56	68	54	42	52	52	61
Not sure	10	7	11	14	9	9	9

SOUTH	Total %	Under 30 %	30–49 %	50 and Older %	Low Income %	Low Middle %	Middle Income %
Good job	37	28	39	40	43	33	40
Not so good	35	47	35	28	24	35	41
Not sure	28	25	26	32	34	32	18

62. In some places in the nation there have been charges of police brutality. Do you think there is any police brutality in this area, or not?

TOTAL SAMPLE	1963 %	1966 %	1969 %
Yes	x	x	39
No	x	x	37
Not sure	x	x	23

NORTH	Total %	Under 30 %	30–49 %	50 and Older %	Low Income %	Low Middle %	Middle Income %
Yes	50	58	52	36	33	42	62
No	34	27	33	47	53	39	23
Not sure	16	16	15	18	14	18	15
SOUTH							
Yes	30	36	31	24	17	33	35
No	40	32	44	41	46	34	41
Not sure	30	31	25	35	37	34	24

78a. Do you agree or disagree that Negroes can get what they want only by banding together as black people against the whites, because the whites will never help Negroes?

TOTAL SAMPLE	1963 %	1966 %	1969 %
Agree	x	25	27
Disagree	x	64	59
Not sure	x	11	14

NORTH	Total %	Under 30 %	30–49 %	50 and Older %	Low Income %	Low Middle %	Middle Income %
Agree	30	45	26	25	22	34	32
Disagree	54	43	57	61	47	56	53
Not sure	16	13	17	14	32	10	15

SOUTH	Total %	Under 30 %	30–49 %	50 and Older %	Low Income %	Low Middle %	Middle Income %
Agree	24	31	29	16	20	24	25
Disagree	64	58	62	71	70	62	66
Not sure	12	12	10	13	10	14	10

23a. In your opinion, do most Negroes have a special spirit or soul that most white people have not experienced?

TOTAL SAMPLE	1963 %	1966 %	1969 %
Yes	x	x	54
No	x	x	22
Not sure	x	x	24

NORTH	Total %	Under 30 %	30–49 %	50 and Older %	Low Income %	Low Middle %	Middle Income %
Yes	60	79	62	39	38	62	67
No	20	8	19	32	27	25	13
Not sure	20	13	19	29	35	14	20
SOUTH							
Yes	48	59	50	39	33	49	56
No	24	22	25	24	22	27	26
Not sure	29	20	25	37	45	24	18

80a. Which term do you like *most*—colored people, Negroes, blacks, or Afro-Americans?

TOTAL SAMPLE	1963 %	1966 %	1969 %
Colored people	x	x	20
Negroes	x	x	38
Blacks	x	x	19
Afro-Americans	x	x	10
Don't care	x	x	6
Not sure	x	x	7

NORTH	Total %	Under 30 %	30–49 %	50 and Older %	Low Income %	Low Middle %	Middle Income %
Colored people	14	3	15	25	28	17	9
Negroes	32	29	38	26	32	36	31
Blacks	27	40	26	18	17	22	34
Afro-Americans	14	16	14	13	19	18	13
Don't care	4	3	1	10	5	3	3
Not sure	8	9	5	9	0	4	10
SOUTH							
Colored people	25	19	22	31	28	21	18
Negroes	43	45	44	42	52	44	43
Blacks	10	15	10	7	6	8	17
Afro-Americans	7	11	5	5	4	8	8
Don't care	8	3	9	11	5	12	8
Not sure	7	7	9	4	6	8	6

80b. Which term do you like *least?*

TOTAL SAMPLE	1963 %	1966 %	1969 %
Colored people	x	x	31
Negroes	x	x	11
Blacks	x	x	25
Afro-Americans	x	x	11
Don't care	x	x	6
Not sure	x	x	15

NORTH	Total %	Under 30 %	30–49 %	50 and Older %	Low Income %	Low Middle %	Middle Income %
Colored people	35	46	35	20	25	33	39
Negroes	13	15	13	11	20	10	16
Blacks	20	15	16	30	22	22	15
Afro-Americans	12	8	15	14	10	12	13
Don't care	4	3	1	10	5	3	3
Not sure	16	13	20	16	19	21	14
SOUTH							
Colored people	28	36	23	27	31	26	32
Negroes	9	5	10	11	6	8	13
Blacks	30	35	31	26	30	34	25
Afro-Americans	10	6	8	15	11	8	9
Don't care	8	3	9	11	5	12	8
Not sure	15	15	18	11	19	12	13

24. Do you like the new natural hair styles many Negroes are wearing now, or not?

	TOTAL SAMPLE		1963 %	1966 %	1969 %		
	Yes		x	x	45		
	No		x	x	48		
	Not sure		x	x	7		

NORTH	Total %	Under 30 %	30–49 %	50 and Older %	Low Income %	Low Middle Income %	Middle Income %
Yes	50	76	44	28	42	49	58
No	41	19	46	59	49	43	35
Not sure	10	5	10	14	9	8	7
SOUTH							
Yes	40	57	43	26	26	41	50
No	55	38	54	67	68	54	45
Not sure	5	6	3	7	7	4	5

25a. As you know, some Negroes have begun to wear African clothing styles like the Dashiki and the Buba. Do you like these new styles, or not?

	TOTAL SAMPLE		1963 %	1966 %	1969 %		
	Yes		x	x	35		
	No		x	x	54		
	Never heard of them		x	x	5		
	Not sure		x	x	7		

NORTH	Total %	Under 30 %	30–49 %	50 and Older %	Low Income %	Low Middle Income %	Middle Income %
Yes	43	65	43	16	34	44	50
No	46	28	43	71	56	42	42
Never heard of them	3	2	3	4	6	6	1
Not sure	9	6	11	9	5	9	7
SOUTH							
Yes	28	38	31	17	18	29	33
No	61	55	58	69	67	63	56
Never heard of them	6	2	5	10	11	6	3
Not sure	5	6	6	4	4	3	8

77. Many Negro leaders are saying that "black is beautiful." Do you think that most Negroes agree that "black is beautiful"?

	TOTAL SAMPLE	1963 %	1966 %	1969 %
Yes		x	x	74
No		x	x	16
Not sure		x	x	9

NORTH	Total %	Under 30 %	30–49 %	50 and Older %	Low Income %	Low Middle %	Middle Income %
Yes	75	86	71	69	78	74	77
No	15	6	20	18	18	17	14
Not sure	10	8	9	13	5	9	9
SOUTH							
Yes	74	71	78	72	81	72	71
No	17	19	14	20	14	22	21
Not sure	9	10	9	8	5	7	8

76. Do you favor the idea of black power, or not?

	TOTAL SAMPLE	1963 %	1966 %	1969 %
Favor		x	25	42
Don't favor		x	37	31
Not sure		x	38	27

NORTH	Total %	Under 30 %	30–49 %	50 and Older %	Low Income %	Low Middle %	Middle Income %
Favor	50	68	47	38	31	46	59
Don't favor	28	16	30	40	39	27	27
Not sure	22	16	24	22	30	27	14
SOUTH							
Favor	34	49	42	17	19	30	52
Don't favor	34	21	31	45	52	33	24
Not sure	32	30	27	38	29	37	24

CHAPTER 6

45. If the United States got into a big world war today, would you personally feel this country was worth fighting for, or not?

TOTAL SAMPLE	1963 %	1966 %	1969 %
Worth fighting for	81	87	79
Not worth fighting for	9	6	14
Not sure	10	7	7

NORTH	Total %	Under 30 %	30–49 %	50 and Older %	Low Income %	Low Middle Income %	Middle Income %
Worth fighting for	76	60	83	84	86	81	73
Not worth fighting for	17	31	11	10	5	12	20
Not sure	7	8	6	6	9	7	8
SOUTH							
Worth fighting for	81	70	82	87	88	79	78
Not worth fighting for	11	19	13	5	3	11	20
Not sure	8	12	5	8	10	10	3

43. Do you think the day will ever come or not when Negroes will have their own separate nation somewhere in the U.S.?

TOTAL SAMPLE	1963 %	1966 %	1969 %
Yes	x	x	12
No	x	x	75
Not sure	x	x	14

NORTH	Total %	Under 30 %	30–49 %	50 and Older %	Low Income %	Low Middle Income %	Middle Income %
Yes	13	17	5	20	12	8	12
No	71	75	75	59	70	70	78
Not sure	16	8	20	21	18	22	11
SOUTH							
Yes	11	12	12	8	12	11	9
No	78	78	77	79	78	76	86
Not sure	11	10	11	13	10	14	5

44. Would you, yourself, like to see the day when there is one [a separate Negro nation], or not?*

	TOTAL SAMPLE	1963 %	1966 %	1969 %
Yes		4	4	21
No		87	89	69
Not sure		9	7	10

NORTH	Total %	Under 30 %	30–49 %	50 and Older %	Low Income %	Low Middle Income %	Middle Income %
Yes	20	27	13	24	16	19	18
No	69	66	73	62	78	65	74
Not sure	12	7	15	14	7	16	8
SOUTH							
Yes	22	23	24	20	18	27	12
No	70	71	66	74	77	64	78
Not sure	8	6	10	7	5	8	10

* The comparable question in 1963 and 1966 was "Some Negro leaders have proposed that whites and Negroes won't live well together so the only solution is to set up a separate Negro state or states in this country or in Africa. Do you favor or oppose this idea?"

6. At work, would you rather work alongside mostly other Negroes, or would you rather work with a mixed group of whites and Negroes?

	TOTAL SAMPLE	1963 %	1966 %	1969 %
Mostly other Negroes		11	10	11
Mixed group		76	80	82
Not sure		13	10	7

NORTH	Total %	Under 30 %	30–49 %	50 and Older %	Low Income %	Low Middle Income %	Middle Income %
Mostly other Negroes	9	16	8	3	5	11	10
Mixed group	86	78	90	90	94	81	86
Not sure	5	6	3	7	1	8	4

SOUTH	Total %	Under 30 %	30–49 %	50 and Older %	Low Income %	Low Middle %	Middle Income %
Mostly other Negroes	14	12	14	15	15	11	12
Mixed group	78	83	74	79	77	80	79
Not sure	8	6	12	6	9	8	9

10. Would you like to see the children in your family go to school with white children or not?

TOTAL SAMPLE	1963 %	1966 %	1969 %
Go with whites	70	70	78
Not go with whites	10	11	9
Not sure	20	19	14

NORTH	Total %	Under 30 %	30–49 %	50 and Older %	Low Income %	Low Middle %	Middle Income %
Go with whites	81	73	83	88	69	79	82
Not go with whites	7	13	6	3	9	8	6
Not sure	12	14	11	9	22	12	12
SOUTH							
Go with whites	75	82	68	78	64	77	80
Not go with whites	10	10	13	7	13	11	8
Not sure	15	8	19	15	23	12	12

9. Do you feel that Negro children would do better or worse if they all went to a school along with white children today?

TOTAL SAMPLE	1963 %	1966 %	1969 %
Better	65	69	70
Worse	3	2	5
About the same	19	18	14
Not sure	13	11	10

	Total	Under 30	30–49	50 and Older	Low Income	Low Middle	Middle Income
NORTH	%	%	%	%	%	%	%
Better	69	64	74	69	63	69	73
Worse	6	11	4	4	6	10	4
About the same	16	17	15	14	13	14	16
Not sure	10	8	6	13	19	8	7
SOUTH							
Better	72	73	69	74	70	75	69
Worse	5	6	5	4	1	4	6
About the same	13	15	13	12	11	11	18
Not sure	11	7	13	11	19	11	7

11. Of course, because of where they live today, many Negro children go to all-Negro schools and whites to all-white schools. Would you like to see children in your family be picked up in buses every day to go to school with white children in some other part of town, or not?

TOTAL SAMPLE	1963 %	1966 %	1969 %
Yes	50	49	45
No	30	35	36
Not sure	20	16	19

	Total	Under 30	30–49	50 and Older	Low Income	Low Middle	Middle Income
NORTH	%	%	%	%	%	%	%
Yes	38	32	38	47	45	44	36
No	40	48	42	31	27	40	45
Not sure	22	20	21	22	28	16	19
SOUTH							
Yes	52	54	47	57	54	54	48
No	32	33	36	26	31	29	39
Not sure	16	13	17	17	16	17	13

8a. In living in a neighborhood, if you could find the housing you want and like, would you rather live in a neighborhood with Negro families, or in a neighborhood that had both whites and Negroes?

	TOTAL SAMPLE	1963 %	1966 %	1969 %			
	Negroes	20	17	16			
	Whites and Negroes	64	68	74			
	Not sure	16	15	10			

NORTH	Total %	Under 30 %	30–49 %	50 and Older %	Low Income %	Low Middle %	Middle Income %
Negroes	11	17	8	9	10	9	11
Whites and Negroes	80	77	84	82	76	84	81
Not sure	9	6	8	9	14	7	8
SOUTH							
Negroes	21	18	22	22	24	20	23
Whites and Negroes	67	75	63	67	63	69	69
Not sure	11	7	15	11	14	11	8

18. Some people are saying that Negroes have tried to work out their problems with white people and there's been a lot of talk but not much action. Now, they say Negroes should give up working together with whites and just depend on their own people. Do you tend to agree or disagree with people who say this?

	TOTAL SAMPLE	1963 %	1966 %	1969 %			
	Agree	x	11	16			
	Disagree	x	81	72			
	Not sure	x	8	12			

NORTH	Total %	Under 30 %	30–49 %	50 and Older %	Low Income %	Low Middle %	Middle Income %
Agree	14	23	11	11	7	15	13
Disagree	72	64	79	73	76	74	76
Not sure	14	12	11	17	18	11	11
SOUTH							
Agree	18	20	19	15	14	18	16
Disagree	72	73	70	74	80	70	76
Not sure	10	7	11	11	6	12	9

31. Do you think Negroes will get ahead better in this country by controlling their own schools, running their own businesses, and living together in their own neighborhoods, or do you think they will get ahead better through integration with the white people in schools, jobs, and neighborhoods?

	TOTAL SAMPLE	1963 %	1966 %	1969 %
Community control		x	x	13
Integration		x	x	78
Not sure		x	x	10

NORTH	Total %	Under 30 %	30–49 %	50 and Older %	Low Income %	Low Middle %	Middle Income %
Community control	16	30	8	10	22	12	17
Integration	74	59	87	75	68	76	76
Not sure	10	11	6	15	9	12	7
SOUTH							
Community control	10	11	11	8	8	10	13
Integration	81	80	79	83	86	80	79
Not sure	10	9	10	9	7	10	9

Index

271